A crash course in

FORTRAN 77

Donald M Monro

Imperial College of Science, Technology and Medicine

University of London

Edward Arnold

A division of Hodder & Stoughton

LONDON MELBOURNE AUCKLAND

First published in Great Britain 1989
Reprinted 1991

To Don and Norine Afflecu

British Library Cataloguing in Publication Data

Monroe, Donald M. (Donald Martin)
   A crash course in Fortran.
   1. Computer languages. Programming
   languages. Fortran 77 language
   I. Title
   005.13′3

   ISBN 0–7131–3582–4

The text and illustrations were prepared by the author using the
typesetting facilities of the University of London Computer Centre

Printed and bound in Great Britain for Edward Arnold, a division of
Hodder and Stoughton Limited, Mill Road, Dunton Green,
Sevenoaks, Kent TN13 2YA by J. W. Arrowsmith Ltd, Bristol

Preface

This book is intended to accomplish two objectives: first to help you learn to use the FORTRAN language quickly but effectively, and second to highlight some current ideas about computer programming and how to express them in FORTRAN 77. Following the heartwarming success of my *Crash Course in Pascal*, I use a similar approach here, and also make numerous comparisons with Pascal. Many people will want to know more than one language, so I hope this is helpful to those who will learn both FORTRAN 77 and Pascal, in any order.

FORTRAN is now a very large language. This is partly because it has evolved through several generations and continues to support some obsolete features. Very few people need to know all of it, and in this book I have tried to isolate the parts that we must know from the bits that are either specialized or old fashioned.

Chapters 1 to 8 are the vital fundamentals. In Chapter 9, I preach about good programming, and Chapters 10 to 13 complete the essentials. Many would feel that Chapter 16, on multidimensional arrays, is also essential.

Chapters 14 and 15 demonstrate how it is possible to attack some important issues in modern programming that might at first seem impossible in FORTRAN 77. You will see there how to implement recursion and abstract data structures using pointers, with the advantage that they are both efficient, if awkward to program. Chapters 17 to 20 deal with specialist topics.

Originally I had intended to leave out a lot of the bad bits of FORTRAN. As it turned out, nothing is omitted, although many obsolete features are dealt with briefly, with suitable health warnings. To be specific, multiple entries and alternate returns from subprograms are crimes that are sentenced to the Appendix, as are some particularly horrid control statements.

On the subject of the Appendix, It was a tremendous effort to summarize all of FORTRAN 77 in so few pages, and I really do hope that you will find it useful.

Soon we will know the precise shape of the next FORTRAN, FORTRAN 8X. It will be several years before it becomes widely available, but perhaps FORTRAN will become more important than ever before. I have emphasized the features of FORTRAN that will persist, and helped you to avoid the parts that will eventually be eliminated. This way, I hope to provide a preparation for the new FORTRAN, as well as an introduction to the one we have now.

As usual, these things take much longer than they should, in this case nearly three years of Saturdays. To a boring drudge like me this is no great loss, but the real victims are my family. Sorry.

D M Monro
London
January 1989

Contents

Eleven Subroutines 83

Twelve Arrays 93

Thirteen Arrays as arguments 103

Fourteen Recursion is possible 115

Fifteen About data structures 123

Sixteen Multidimensional arrays 133

Seventeen Sharing variables 145

Eighteen About characters 155

Nineteen Types and typing 165

Twenty Records and files 179

Appendix A summary of FORTRAN 77 195

Index 211

One

Introduction

1 Computers, programming and people

When you program a computer, you give it instructions about how to manipulate data. You might wish to say:

'Take the number A and add to it the number B and call the result C.'

This is a program, expressed in the natural language English. It could be a computer program, but we would not wish to express such a simple instruction in so many words. It is more sensible to write:

LET C=A+B (as you would in the language BASIC)

or just

C=A+B (in FORTRAN)

or possibly

c:=a+b; (in Pascal)

Computers can obey a range of commands, and computer programming languages are used to give the orders. A computer normally makes no errors, but also exercises no independent critical judgement - it does not understand what it is being told, at least not yet. You will soon find that much of the effort in computer programming is devoted to finding errors, not just in the grammar of FORTRAN (or any other language), but most importantly in the instructions that you give, and in the order that you give them.

Do not blame the computer for errors. In your first few hours as a programmer, you will lose count of your own errors. Occasionally you will find errors in the way the computer system has been programmed by other people. But in a lifetime you may never encounter a mistake made by the machine itself.

2 The evergreen FORTRAN

FORTRAN, designed by John Backus, was one of the earliest 'high-level' computer languages used, appearing in 1954. The name means 'FORmula TRANslation'. After revision in 1958, and standardization in 1966 as FORTRAN IV, it became the most widely used vehicle for data processing and numerical computation in Science and Engineering. FORTRAN has always closely expressed the way that a real computer functions. It can be startlingly efficient in both its speed and in its use of the memory of a computer. This continues to be one valid reason for using it in large computations. In FORTRAN IV, however, the statements of the language eventually began to look ugly in relation to developing ideas of well-structured programs. The FORTRAN 77 version has gone some way towards correcting these difficulties. More work is presently being done to develop FORTRAN 8X, which will probably not be widely available until the 1990s. It is intended that FORTRAN 77 programs will work in FORTRAN 8X, and so the language will continue its remarkable endurance.

One reason for this endurance is the 'portability' of FORTRAN programs. Other languages which offer similarly wide facilities (like, for example 'C') are not standardized, and you cannot rely on their availability on all computers. Some, like Pascal, have their standards so narrowly drawn that real programming requires the use of nonstandard extensions, locking programs into the system on which they were developed.

So FORTRAN 77 is a language that many people need to use. We must concentrate on learning to use its facilities effectively. Effective programming features efficiency, readability and clear structure. FORTRAN by its nature lends itself to efficiency in competent hands. However we have to be especially careful to achieve readability and clear structure, which are important if programs are to be easily maintained and transported. You will find all these aspects of programming emphasized in this course.

3 Programs and interaction

The days when people learning to write computer programs had to present programs on punched cards and wait for results to be returned on paper are nearly gone. Now we expect to use our own computer, workstation or terminal. Programs are created and edited on interactive screens. When we want to try a program, we expect it to happen at once, at least for small programs. You will find that the layout of a FORTRAN program still reflects the original use of punched cards. Despite this, FORTRAN can be as interactive as any other language.

A number of steps are carried out in developing computer programs. A systematic programmer will design, implement, test, apply and document a program. First, programs are designed away from the computer, by thinking carefully about the problem to be solved, and specifying the steps that a program will have to carry out. This is not done in a computer language, but in something resembling ordinary English, perhaps assisted by diagrams and fragments of programs.

Next, in the implementation phase, the program is written in FORTRAN or some other language using the design as a guide. Only then do you bring the program to the computer to test and apply it.

When you use the computer interactively, you carry out two basic processes. In one you are defining your program, either when you first create it or later when you may alter it. Most people call this editing. When you want to try the program, you ask the computer to 'execute' it and sit back to watch the fun (unless you are expected to respond to the program).

This 'define' and 'execute' cycle (or edit and run) is repeated as often as is necessary to make the program acceptable as correct FORTRAN. Then you must test it, by trying to anticipate situations it will encounter in use. Probably you will have to alter it some more as you find unexpected errors. When you are satisfied with a program, at last you can use it, but it is still of no use to anyone else. This is why you should take the trouble to document your program as the final step.

The scale of documentation depends on the circumstances. If this is a little program for your own use, the only documentation you need is probably a copy of it. If it is a large one to be used by others, you will have to write quite detailed descriptions of its design, and most important, a manual for using it. Documentation is a weak point in almost every development effort. We must try to do better.

The life of a real program does not end there-it may only be beginning. A program may be rewritten, enhanced, corrected, moved to other computers or even translated into other languages. These are all good reasons for making the documentation effort in the first place. If you return to a program after months or years and find you cannot understand it any more, then you too will be grateful for your own documentation.

4 A crash course

This book, as the title would imply, is for people who want to learn some FORTRAN quickly. This will include people who know some BASIC or Pascal before coming to FORTRAN and need a brief introduction. The full FORTRAN language is very large as you will find if you try to learn it all. The pressure of time in many courses will dictate that only fundamentals can be covered, and I have tried to choose a subset of FORTRAN to satisfy that need, as well as giving pointers to additional features.

As a conversion course, you should be able to master the basics in a few days, assuming unlimited access to a suitable computer. As an introduction, how long it takes depends on how far and how intensively it is studied. Before you start, line up your friendly adviser and a computer to use. If you are a beginner you will have far more trouble with the computer system than with the FORTRAN. Start at the beginning and take only as much as you want or need. Wherever you choose to stop, you have had a crash course in a subset of FORTRAN 77 which grows as you progress through further chapters.

You should spend at least twice as much time in practice as in study. The text is rich with examples, many of them small, to give you lots of models of programming. There are many small exercises in the text. Try as many as you can on the way through. At the end of most chapters there are some problems, generally in increasing order of difficulty. Do some of these too. When solving exercises or problems, work them out first on paper before approaching the computer-it is harder to think at the keyboard and the results are never as good.

Finally, if you are in doubt about something, do not hesitate to try it out on your computer. That is the joy of interactive computing. Have a nice day!

Two

Simple Programs

1 This is a program

FORTRAN uses easily recognized English words, some required punctuation, and some expressions using numbers. You can see all of these in this actual program:

```
PRINT*,2.Ø+2.Ø
END
```

Here we can see some features of any FORTRAN program. Each line is a statement; you can have only one statement on a line. We will see later that one statement can use several lines.

The PRINT statement instructs the computer to add together the real constants 2.0 and 2.0 and display the result somewhere. The word PRINT is historical. If you use FORTRAN interactively the result will usually be displayed in front of your very eyes. The star in the PRINT statement allows the computer to make up its own mind about the style of presentation of the result —how many decimal places and so on. When you get further into FORTRAN, you will be able to control the layout with some extra effort. But for now we hitch our wagon to a star.

The END statement indicates the end of the program, and when it is reached the computer knows it has finished the job. All programs end with END.

The order of statements tells you what is going to happen. In this one, first the sum 2.0+2.0 is printed and then the program ends. So far, so good.

Exercise Deduce the meaning of these little programs:

| (i) | `PRINT*,4.Ø-2.0`
`END` | (ii) | `PRINT*,SQRT(2.Ø)`
`END` |

Exercise Tax is charged at 15% on goods purchased in shops. How would you compute the total price of an article which costs $5.00 before tax? What is the price before tax of an article that costs $1.00 with tax? (No, it is not $0.85!) How would you compute that?

2 The layout of FORTRAN programs

FORTRAN began on punched cards. Although most people do not use them any more, the way FORTRAN is written down and presented to a computer still reflects this origin. Soon the layout of FORTRAN will be relaxed—a very grand committee is working on it now—but in the meantime we have to follow the convention. Each statement of FORTRAN belongs on its own line. The actual statement starts in column 7 and can only go as far as column 72. Even if your computer allows some less strict layout, you should get in the habit of starting a statement in column 7. The chances are that the TAB key on a computer terminal will do this for you.

The first six columns have special uses. If you put the letter C or a star in column 1, then the rest of that line can contain any comment you want. You can also put comments after column

72 in any line. These are the only ways of including comments in a FORTRAN program. Later, we will see that some FORTRAN statements need to be labelled, and the label is always a number put anywhere in columns 1 to 5. So what about column six? That is a bit special. It is used when a statement of FORTRAN gets too long for one line. When this happens, you leave the first five columns blank in the next line, and put any symbol except zero or blank in column six. You can then use columns 7 to 72 as a continuation. You can keep on adding to your statement up to a maximum of 20 lines in all (19 continuations). Comment lines in between are not counted.

SUMMARY:

Column 1	C or * to begin a comment line.
otherwise	Columns 7 to 72 are a FORTRAN statement, or part of one.

Columns 1 to 5 may contain a label
        unless 6 has a continuation symbol, not Ø or blank.
Columns 73 and onwards are comments.

Example This program is very silly, but has all these features. You can identify Column 1 from the C in the comment lines:

```
C THIS LINE IS A COMMENT. THE NEXT LINE
C HAS A LABEL JUST TO SHOW YOU ONE
   10 PRINT*,
C THIS STATEMENT IS BROKEN INTO TWO LINES
C NOTICE THE FIRST + IS THE CONTINUATION SYMBOL
     +2.Ø+2.Ø
      END
```

3 Type it in

Right from the start, we should know how to create a program. This is different in every computer. You will have to put a program into your computer as some kind of text file, and if you are lucky this is done using a screen editor, which shows your program as you enter it, and allows you to correct it.

FORTRAN uses a limited set of characters, again for historical reasons. Officially FORTRAN 77 knows only the capital letters A to Z, the digits 0 to 9 and 13 special symbols. Often you will see the number 0 crossed to distinguish it from the letter O. I do this in all my examples.

Here is a list of the special characters with their official names. Official names always have more syllables:

	Blank	(	Left parenthesis ('left bracket')
=	Equals	)	Right parenthesis ('right bracket')
+	Plus	,	Comma
−	Minus	'	Apostrophe ('quote')
*	Asterisk ('star')	:	Colon
/	Slash	$	Currency symbol ('dollar sign')
.	Decimal Point ('period' or 'full stop')		

The restriction you are most likely to notice is that you must use capital letters. Some computers will happily let you type in lower case letters, and then reject your FORTRAN, so watch it. Some computers will accept lower case. It is best to follow the FORTRAN convention.

Exercise Find out how to enter a FORTRAN program into your computer. Find out how to have a look at it once it is in there. On my computer, I can do this either with the editor, or with a command. Enter this tiny program carefully. If you make a mess of it, find out how to fix it up, and do so. Don't run it yet, I want you to read the next section first:

```
PRINT*,2.0+2.0
END
```

4 Try it out

The other thing you may want to know about right away is the PROGRAM statement. If you have one, it is the very first statement of a program (you can have comments before it). It is optional, so if you leave it out of most programs it does not matter. If you put it in, its exact form varies from computer to computer, although most computers will accept

```
PROGRAM name
```

where name is a name you make up. The rules about names are covered a bit later. For now, use up to six capital letters. If you get sick of being told that your program has no PROGRAM statement, just put one in.

Exercise Run the little program that you entered in the previous section. Is your computer fussing about a PROGRAM statement? So add one:

```
PROGRAM SIMPLE
PRINT*,2.0+2.0
END
```

5 Get it right

Now we are ready to start real FORTRAN programming. Be sure that you can create a program and run it. Be sure that you know how to alter a program. When a program does not work, you will have to find out why, and correct it. Do not go on until you have polished these basic skills.

Three

Some real calculations

1 These are real numbers

Most numbers in FORTRAN are either integer numbers or real numbers. Integers are introduced in the next chapter. A real number in FORTRAN is simply a number which has decimal places. When you write a number with a decimal point in FORTRAN, you are using a basic real constant.

Example These are basic real constants

2.Ø	2.71828	-1
23.ØØ67	Ø.ØØ324	+.254

A basic real constant always has a decimal point, and may have a sign. You can write 5.0 as 5. but not as 5 with no decimal point. If you leave out the decimal point you are making an integer, which could be a serious mistake. You can write 0.01 as .01. I think it is clearer with the extra zero, and so I always write it that way.

Real numbers can use scientific notation when they become very large or small. When you intend 2.4×10^{-23}, you would probably not want to write

Ø.ØØØ ØØØ ØØØ ØØØ ØØØ ØØØ ØØØ Ø24

Instead you write 2.4E-23 to get the same value. Scientific notation is defined as

value **E** *exponent*

The *value* is any number (including what looks like an integer) and the *exponent* is an integer. Either the *value* or *exponent* can be signed. You are completely free to put in spaces to make the number look better. (In FORTRAN you are permitted to put spaces nearly anywhere, or leave them out.) A PRINT* statement might decide to use scientific notation, for example this one is certain to print an exponent:

PRINT*,Ø.ØØØØØØØØØØØØØØØ622

Exercise Write these out as ordinary basic real constants:

3 E+10	(The speed of light-what units?)
6.625 E-27	(Planck's constant.)
6.025 E23	(Avogadro's number — number of molecules in a mole.)

Now find these and write them in scientific notation:

The mass of an electron.
The energy $e=mc^2$ in a gram of any substance.

2 Some arithmetic

In FORTRAN values are combined into expressions using arithmetic operators, and brackets for clarity. The available operations are:

addition   `3.0+4.0` result 7.0   division   `3.0/4.0`   result 0.75

subtraction   `3.0-4.0` result -1.0   exponent   `3.0**4.0`   result 81.0

multiplying   `3.0*4.0`   result 12.0   (raise to a power)

(i) Addition and subtraction

The + or - symbols indicate addition and subtraction, but may also be used as a sign:

      `14.3 + 7.6 + 9.2`   or   `+8.Ø - 1.Ø`

(ii) Multiplication

To multiply we use a star (the standard says 'asterisk'— why do people like polysyllables when simple words will do?)

      `5.Ø*4.Ø`   or   `-19.2*11.Ø`

Unlike in algebra, multiplication in FORTRAN is never implied. You always have to write the star.

     Wrong: Right

     `6.Ø(7.Ø)`   `6.Ø* (7.Ø)`

                        although the brackets are not necessary.

(iii) Division

The operator for division is the slash. With real numbers a computer does division as precisely as it can. If you try to divide a value by zero (or by a very small number which the computer cannot handle) it will be detected and your program will probably fail.

      `1.Ø/8.Ø`   or   `-42.7/3.21`

(iv) Exponentiation

Two stars, `**`, make one operator which raises the value on its left to the power on its right. This operator is missing from Pascal:

      `3.Ø**2.Ø`   (result 9.0)

A real number raised to an integer power gives a real result. This is the only situation in this chapter where an integer value should be used:

      `9.Ø**2`   (result 81.0)

There are two restrictions. The value zero can only be raised to a positive nonzero power, and a negative number can only be raised to an integer power. Both are fundamental properties of numbers, and violation of either will cause a program to fail.

In FORTRAN you cannot use more than one operator between two values, so brackets are often necessary:

     Wrong: Right

     `19.Ø + -3.Ø`   `9.ØØ + (-3.Ø)`

     `Ø.Ø7*-9.Ø`   `Ø.Ø7* (-9.Ø)`   or   `-9.Ø*Ø.Ø7`

     `2.19**-7`   `2.19** (-7)`

3 Get your priorities right

So what does this mean:

        3.Ø**4.Ø**5.Ø

or indeed this:

        3.Ø + 4.Ø / 5.Ø

We need some rules to help us with these. There are two basic rules:

First rule: Some operations have higher priority than others. The higher priority operations are done first. This is the priority:

(things in brackets)	Highest
**	
* or /	
+ or −	Lowest

Second rule: Operations of the same priority are evaluated from left to right. Unfortunately, exponentiation is an exception to this rule.

Example Consider the expression 3.0+5.0*2.0**4. The order of working this out is:

(i) 2.0**4 is calculated, result 16.0.
(ii) This is multiplied by 5.0, result 80.0
(iii) 3.0 is added, result 83.0.

The same expression is clearer if it is written this way:

        3.Ø+(5.Ø*(2.Ø)**4)

By arranging brackets in pairs, an expression is clarified. Brackets can also alter the order of evaluation because items in brackets are given high priority.

People often make mistakes about the priority of operations in expressions. Be sure you understand these:

        3.Ø+4.Ø/5.Ø   means 3.Ø+(4.Ø/5.Ø)   not   (3.Ø+4.Ø)/5.Ø
        4.Ø/2.Ø+6.Ø   means 4.Ø/2.Ø)+6.Ø   not   (4.Ø/(2.Ø+6.Ø)

Every programmer gets a division like the last one wrong sometimes. Strong typing won't help you here! I call this the slash trap. Watch for it.

Because it is a rule exception (only Mr FORTRAN knows why), the expression

        2.Ø**3.Ø**4.Ø means 2.Ø**(3.Ø**4.Ø) not (2.Ø**3.Ø)**4.Ø

Exercise It is important to get practice in writing expressions. Check out each of the operations and the truth of what I have said about them, by writing simple programs like:

        PRINT*,2.Ø**3.Ø**4
        END

Exercise What is the value of each of the folowing expressions:

3.0+1.0/2.0	3.0+(1.0/2.0)	3.0+1.0)/2.0	1.0+2.0*3.0
(1.0+2.0)*3.0	1.0+(2.0*3.0)	1.0/2.0+3.0	1.0/(2.0+3.0)
(1.0/2.0)+3.0	1.0+2.0**3.0	(1.0+2.0)**3.0	1.0+(2.0**3.0)

4 Give a value a name

It is very useful to give a name to a value so it can be remembered and used again, so variables are used just as in algebra. In FORTRAN, names can have up to 6 symbols. This makes it difficult to give meaningful names, but we can try. A name must begin with a letter, and the remaining symbols can be letters or numbers. Recall that we must use only capital letters.

These are correct FORTRAN names (but not necessarily the names of real values):

Z	ZILCH	DALEKS
THETA	IMPULS	RPRIME

These are wrong:

3XY	(begins with a number)	**IMPULSIVE** (too many symbols)
A$	(contains illegal $)	**Fred3** (has lower case letters)

The most basic types of variables in FORTRAN are the REAL and INTEGER types, and FORTRAN has a spelling convention to imply them. Integer names start with I, J, K, L, M, or N. Real names start with anything else.

These are real names in FORTRAN:

OCTAL	DUMMY	WIPE
FASTER	X	R2D2

Earlier I warned you about assuming the multiplication operation. In algebra you might write xy when you mean x times y. In FORTRAN, XY is the name of a real variable. To multiply X by Y you must write **X*Y**.

EXERCISE Identify the real constants and variables in this list:

58.3	E1Ø	METOO	B58	A/B	154
7.E	3Z	WRONG	3E1Ø	X1.1	L5A

5 Give a name a value

Now that we have variables, we can compute with them. When a program begins, the values of all variables are undefined, and it is an error to try to use them in an expression. One way to give a value to a variable is to use an assignment statement. All traditional computing languages can assign the result of an expression to a variable. In FORTRAN you write

variable name = expression

for example

        X=Y+46.Ø

In obeying this statement, the computer evaluates Y+46.0, and the real result is assigned to X. Clearly, Y must have a value before this is done, otherwise it is undefined, and your program will crash. It does not matter whether X already had a value.

Example We can use assignment statements to find the functions sin, cos and tan in a right angled triangle such as in Fig. 3.1. From the diagram,

$$\cos B = \frac{a}{(a^2 + b^2)^{1/2}} \qquad \sin B = \frac{b}{(a^2 + b^2)^{1/2}} \qquad \tan B = \frac{b}{a}$$

The values of a and b can be set up in assignment statements. Then the hypotenuse can be computed, and finally the trig things worked out and printed. The program could be:

```
A=1.Ø
B=1.Ø
HYP=(A*A+B*B)**Ø.5
COST=A/HYP
SINT=B/HYP
TANT=B/A
PRINT*,COST,SINT,TANT
END
```

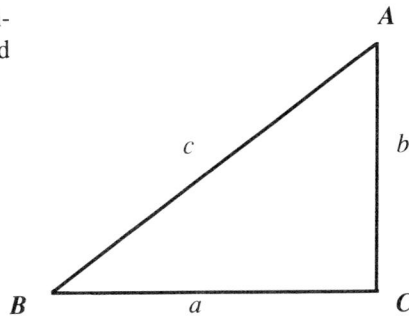

Fig.3.1. A triangle with sides *a*, *b*, *c*.

Notice the list of items in the PRINT statement, separated by commas. We know that the statements of a program are obeyed in sequence, and therefore we can organize the program to compute each value before it is needed, using values that are already known.

Exercise Write a program to find the period of a pendulum given its length (which you set in an assignment statement). At the surface of the earth, if the length is in metres, the period in seconds for a small amplitude of swing is

$$period = 2\,\pi\,\sqrt{length/9.81)}$$

Notice how the square root was done in the triangle example. What is the period of a 1 metre pendulum? Well then, what is the length of a one second pendulum? Use another program and they can check each other. Thinking caps!

6 Print a result

A page full of numbers is boring and baffling. The results from a FORTRAN program are improved by adding captions. This is done easily. A message can be added to the list of things in a PRINT statement:

```
PRINT*,'YOUR GRANDMOTHER WEARS ARMY BOOTS'
END
```

The dreadful insult will be printed when the program is run. A series of legal FORTRAN symbols between apostrophes (single quotes) is called a character string constant. To include the apostrophe itself in a message, write two of them. Is this true:

```
PRINT*,'THIS DOESN''T WORK'
END
```

We can improve our little triangle program, and understand its output better, with a few string constants:

```
A=1.Ø
B=1.Ø
PRINT*,'GIVEN SIDES ARE ',A,B
HYP=(A*A+B*B)**Ø.5
PRINT*,'HYPOTENUSE = ',HYP
COST=A/HYP
```

```
SINT=B/HYP
TANT=B/A
PRINT*,'COS = ',COST
PRINT*,'SIN = ',SINT
PRINT*,'TAN = ',TANT
END
```

The five PRINT statements produce five lines of output, each PRINT beginning a new line. This always happens in FORTRAN. The output is

```
GIVEN SIDES ARE      1.000      1.000
HYPOTENUSE =   1.414
COS =   0.707
SIN =   0.707
TAN =   1.000
```

although your computer might render the numbers differently.

This is a useful place to pause and consider the PRINT statement. With a star after the keyword PRINT, we call it a list-directed PRINT. Its form is

> **PRINT*** [, *list*]

The square bracket is a forbidden symbol in a FORTRAN program — I use it to indicate an optional item when I explain the grammar of a statement. In the PRINT statement, the *list* is an optional list of items separated by commas. You can print variables, constants, expressions formed from them, or character string constants.

Every new PRINT statement starts a new line of output. If you put PRINT with no list, you get a blank line. With a list-directed PRINT, indicated by the star, the computer is free to arrange layout. If there is a lot of printing to do, it may use additional lines.

Exercise Improve your pendulum programs using captions.

7 Some functions

Fortran has a rich variety of functions built into it which provide lots of standard operations, many of them mathematical. For example in this program, the SQRT function gives you the square root of 2:

```
PRINT*,'EVERYONE KNOWS, ROOT 2 = ',SQRT(2.Ø)
END
```

The expression in brackets after SQRT is called its argument. If you put 2 instead of 2.0, it won't work, because SQRT is not available for integers, as you could see from the table of integer functions in Chapter 4. Table 3.1 is a list of functions which take a real argument and produce a real result. You can include functions freely in any arithmetic expression, giving values to the arguments. The arguments can also be expressions, containing more functions if required, including a further reference to the function itself.

Example The precision of computers varies, so the author of a program to be used on several machines may not know how many digits to use in giving constants like π. This program shows you how to compute π, and should also give an indication of the precision of your computer:

```
PRINT*,'PIE IS ',4.Ø*ATAN(1.Ø)
END
```

Table 3.1 Real functions of real arguments in FORTRAN 77. Despite some integer looking names, all give a real result if their arguments are real. They may not be available for integers, see Chapter 4. All trigonometric functions work in radians.

Name	Meaning
ABS(X)	The absolute value of X.
ACOS(X)	Arccos, an angle whose cos is X.
INT(X)	Integer part of X, i.e. decimal places removed.
ANINT(X)	X rounded to the nearest whole number.
ASIN(X)	Arcsin, an angle $-\pi/2 \leq$ angle $\leq \pi/2$ whose sin is X.
ATAN(X)	Arctan, an angle $-\pi/2 \leq$ angle $\leq \pi/2$ whose tan is X.
ATAN2(Y,X)	Arctan, an angle $-\pi/2 \leq$ angle $\leq \pi/2$ with tan angle=Y/X.
COS(X)	Cosine of X, X in radians.
COSH(X)	Hyperbolic cosine, (EXP(X)+EXP(−X))/2.0.
DIM(X,Y)	Positive difference, X−MIN1(X,Y).
EXP(X)	Exponential function e^X, e is base of natural logs.
LOG(X)	Natural logarithm (base e) of X.
LOG10(X)	Logarithm of X to base 10.
MAX(X,Y,...)	Maximum value of X,Y,...
MIN(X,Y,...)	Minimum value of X,Y,...
MOD(X,Y)	The remainder of X/Y, i.e. X−AINT(X/Y)*Y
SIGN(X,Y)	Transfer the sign of Y to X.
SIN(X)	Sine of X, X in radians.
SQRT(X)	Square root of X. Fails if X negative.
SINH(X)	Hyperbolic sine, (EXP(X)−EXP(−X))/2.0.
TAN(X)	Tan of X ,X in radians, fails if X a multiple of π.
TANH(X)	Hyperbolic tangent, SINH(X)/COSH(X).

Exercise Find the value of e, the base of natural logarithms, using a function from Table 3.1. How accurate is the value you get? Subtle question: do you blame the computer or the function?

8 Problems

Problem 3.1 There is no official world record for the marathon because the courses vary so much, even though the distance is supposed to be 26 miles and 385 yards. There is, however, a fastest time both for men and women. Find out what they are this week. Use FORTRAN 77 to work out the speed in miles per hour that this represents. Then do kilometres per hour. How many minutes and seconds per mile are the runners taking on average? What is the time per kilometre? Now do it all for your best time. You haven't! Why not?

Problem 3.2 The cosine law gives the cosine of an angle from the sides of any triangle. Using the same notation as Fig. 3.1,

$$cos\ A = (b^2 + c^2 - a^2)\ /2ab$$

This is true for any of the angles, and for any triangle. Write a program which computes all three angles in degrees, given all three sides.

Problem 3.3 If you invest d dollars for n time periods at an interest rate of $r\%$ per period, the yield y is

$$y = d \, (1 + r/100)^n$$

You can turn the formula around in various ways.

(i) The payments on your new car add up to $24000 over two years. The cash price would be $20000 now. Nice car! What is the annual interest rate? (Answer 9.54%)

(ii) You want to put away some money now, to get $1000 in 16 years. How much must you invest at 6%, 8%, 10% per annum? (Answer $393.65 at 6%) (iii) How many full years does it take to at least double an investment at 6%, 8%, 10%? (Answer 12 years at 6%)

(iv) How much must you pay per month to repay a loan of $10000 in 10 years at 10% per annum? This is tricky.

Problem 3.4 In a thin rotating ring or flywheel, the circumferential stress which tries to pull the rim apart is

$$\sigma = \rho \, r^2 \, \omega^2$$

where ρ is the density in kilograms/metre^3, r the radius in metres and ω the rate of spin in radians/second.

Write a program to calculate the maximum speed given the maximum safe stress for the material used to make the rim. From the information you can find, identify the material that you can safely spin the fastest. Also find the material that will store the most energy in a flywheel when it spins at its maximum speed.

Problem 3.5 One method of computing the value of e^x uses the continued fraction:

$$e^x = 1 + \cfrac{x}{1 - \cfrac{x}{2 + \cfrac{x}{3 - \cfrac{x}{2 + \cfrac{x}{5 - \cfrac{x}{2 + \cfrac{x}{7 - \cfrac{x}{2 + \text{etc.....}}}}}}}}}$$

This has to be programmed from the bottom up. Investigate the use of this formula as a means of finding e^x.

Four

Introducing integers

1 Constants and variables

Real numbers, which are generally approximate, are the workhorses of numerical calculation in FORTRAN. Integers, on the other hand, are exact whole number values and have some special uses.

An integer constant is a number without a decimal point. The maximum size of integers varies between computers, as we will discuss in the next chapter. These are integer constants:

5   −53   +1Ø24   36ØØØØ

The name of an integer variable follows the same rules as any name in FORTRAN—up to six letters or digits with the first symbol a letter. You can tell an integer from a real by the first letter of its name. Integer names begin with I, J, K, L, M or N. This is implicit typing, a characteristic of FORTRAN which has its advantages and its disadvantages. These are the names of integer variables:

NUTS   L   KPRIME   I73   JOHN

The misuse of reals and integers for each other can cause you trouble in any computer language. That is why we look at them separately before mixing them together in the next chapter.

Exercise Classify these as *integer* or *real* and as *variable* or *constant*. For example 5 is an *integer constant*.

```
154     B52     PRIME   E1Ø     57.3    1.
MEETOO  3.E1Ø   3Z      C3PO    X3.3    R2D2
```

2 Arithmetic and integers

An integer expression follows the same rules as we saw for reals in the previous chapter. If all the numbers involved in an expression are integers, then the result is an integer. (If you sneak a real in anywhere, you will get a real result, which we do not want just yet.)

```
14+27   is   41          39−49   is   −1Ø
−6*9    is   −54          3**3    is   27
```

When an integer division is done, the result could be exact, as

```
81/9    is   9           −26/13   is −2
```

but if the result is not exact, it is chopped off to give the correct sign, but the next lowest absolute value:

```
41/5    is   8       −65/7   is −9      5/7   is   Ø
```

If you are used to Pascal, notice that it is the type of the terms divided that determines if the result is integer. There is no special operator for integer division.

An assignment statement can evaluate an integer expression and assign the result to an integer variable in an assignment statement:

variable=expression

for example in

```
IRESLT=ITOP/IBOT
```

We do not want to convert results from real to integer or the other way around just yet.

3 The bit left over

When we divide two integers, we get a truncated result. Often we are interested in the bit left over after division, which is the integer remainder. In FORTRAN this is not obtained using an operator, but it can easily be worked out. Suppose we divide an integer dividend (numerator) ITOP by an integer divisor IBOT. The result IRESLT is

```
IRESLT=ITOP/IBOT
```

We can easily get the remainder, IREM:

```
        IREM=ITOP-IRESLT*IBOT
or      IREM=ITOP-(ITOP/IBOT)*IBOT
```

The expression (ITOP/IBOT)*IBOT is not equal to ITOP unless the division happens to be exact. There is also a function for this as we will see.

Example If you are going to send 31 tons of antiques from Europe to America by container ship, you will have to send them in 4 ton containers. This bit of FORTRAN tells you how many full containers are needed:

```
C PROGRAM DEMONSTRATES INTEGER QUOTIENT AND REMAINDER
        NANTIQ=31
        NFILLS=4
        PRINT*,'TO PACK UP ',NANTIQ,' TONS OF ANTIQUES,'
C QUOTIENT, TRUNCATED
        NFULL=NANTIQ/NFILLS
        PRINT*,'YOU NEED ',NFULL,' FULL CONTAINERS.'
```

This carries on to tell you how much is left over. Can you see how it works?

```
C REMAINDER
        KOVER=NANTIQ-NFULL*NFILLS
        PRINT*,'YOU WILL HAVE ',KOVER,' WORMY TONS LEFT OVER.'
```

If you are considering paying for a partly empty container, then you can also compute how many containers you need to send all the antiques:

```
C QUOTIENT MOVED UP
        NOTFUL=(NANTIQ+NFILLS-1)/NFILLS
        PRINT*,'THEY WOULD ALL FIT IN ',NOTFUL,' CONTAINERS.'
        END
```

4 Read something in

We cannot go on forever restricting computing to data values defined by constants. We need to enter data to a program when it is running. A simple form of the READ statement allows us to do it:

READ ★ [, *list*]

This is called a *list-directed* READ. It refers to the obvious input unit (your terminal if you are running interactively) for the values to be given in the correct order and of the correct type. In response you would usually give the values on one line, separated by blanks and/or a comma. If several variables are named in the list, the computer will keep reading lines of input until it has been given enough information.

Exercise Try this program, which asks for two integers. Notice that it prompts you for the values, which is always a good thing to do:

```
PRINT*,'PLEASE ENTER TWO INTEGERS ..'
      READ*,I,J
      PRINT*,'THANK YOU, YOU GAVE ME ',I,' AND ',J
      END
```

The first time you run it, enter both values on one line. Next time just enter the first number, and push RETURN (or ENTER or whatever that key is called on your keyboard). Push it again. The computer persists? So give it the second value. Now try giving it a number which has a decimal place. Ouch.

Now rewrite the program so that it asks for two reals. What happens if you give an integer for one of them. Oh! Does it accept values with an exponent? Ah.

A real can be given in any of the forms of a basic real constant. A number which looks like an integer is also accepted as input to a request for a real—the decimal place is assumed to be at the end. A real, however, is not acceptable as input in place of an integer. Remember this.

5 Do it again

Here is a program that never stops. Do not run it, at least not yet:

```
C WARNING - THIS PROGRAM WASTES RESOURCES
      PRINT*,'BET YOU CAN''T '
   10 PRINT*,'STOP ME .. '
      GO TO 10
      END
```

Normally a computer program is obeyed in sequence, each statement taken in the order that the program is written. However there are control statements in all languages which change this. The GO TO statement alters the sequence in which FORTRAN statements are obeyed. In this case, the program returns to the statement with the label 10 on it, over and over and over . . .

The GO TO statement is written

GO TO *label*

where exactly one statement with that *label* must exist in the same program unit. You may recall that the *label* is a number of up to five digits which go somewhere in columns 1 to 5 of the line of FORTRAN.

GO TO is an unpopular statement, because it allows people to write horrible programs. There is nothing horrible about the structure of the program above, although one of the faults of GO TO is evident—it doesn't give us any glimmer of why it is there. Pascal people would certainly prefer:

```
program tedious;
   {Warning - this program wastes resources}
   const eternity=false;
   begin
     writeln(' Bet you can''t ');
     repeat
       writeln('stop me .. ')
   until eternity
 end.
```

FORTRAN persons (who often call themselves Real Programmers) would counter that even such a simple program reveals the absurdity of Pascal. It is not our purpose to get involved in any such controversy here. Just for fun, however, show Mr or Ms Pascal this program and ask sweetly why there are semicolons in some places and not others.

Exercise I would like you to run the deadly program with GO TO in it, but first you must find out how you are going to stop it. One day you will put yourself in a similar situation by accident, sooner rather than later. Find out, run it, and halt it.

Exercise Here is a program that gives the wrong answer. It is intended to find the average of two numbers. I want you to find out how to stop a program that is waiting for input. Find out how to stop this program, run it, and correct it:

```
C FIND THE AVERAGE OF TWO NUMBERS
   10  PRINT*,'ENTER TWO REAL NUMBERS TO AVERAGE'
       READ*,XONE,XTWO
       AVG=XONE+XTWO/2.0
       PRINT*,'THE AVERAGE = ',AVG
       PRINT*
       GO TO 10
       END
```

6 Counting and stopping-introducing IF

Integers are ideal for counting because they are exact whole numbers. This little program starts at 1 and counts forever:

```
C EINE KLEINE KOUNTINGPROGRAM
       ICOUNT=1
   10 PRINT*,'NEXT IS ',ICOUNT
       ICOUNT=ICOUNT+1
       GO TO 10
       END
```

Notice how it is done. First the integer variable ICOUNT is given an initial value. Later it has 1 added to it by the statement

```
ICOUNT=ICOUNT+1
```

Remember that this is an assignment statement. It causes the computer first to work out the expression on the right hand side, and then to assign this to the variable on the left hand side. Here count is replaced by itself plus 1.

Ideally we want a program to be able to stop automatically. It is very easy. This program counts like the previous one, but stops at 10. It does this by making a decision about the GO TO that causes it to repeat:

```
C COUNT TO TEN MARK I
      ICOUNT=1
   10 PRINT*,'NEXT IS ',ICOUNT
      ICOUNT=ICOUNT+1
      IF(ICOUNT.LE.10) GO TO 10
      END
```

The key to this is the IF statement that we use to make a decision. It consists of

IF *(logical expression)* *executable statement*

The *logical expression* makes a decision, whose result is TRUE or FALSE. If it is TRUE, then the *executable statement* is obeyed. In the little example, the *executable statement* was a GO TO. Others are possible.

The simplest *logical expression* compares two values. We will see more complicated ones in Chapter 7. For now, we consider a simple comparison only, which is officially called a *relational expression:*

arithmetic   relational   arithmetic
expression   operator   expression

All this jargon means simply that two values are compared, for example, in this statement:

IF(ICOUNT.LE.10) GO TO 10

which says 'if icount is less than or equal to 10, go to label 10.'

The types of the values compared could be different, and there are further rules about that as we will see. For the moment, we are working only with integers. These are the the operators that FORTRAN will recognize for making comparisons:

.GT.	greater than	.GE.	greater or equal
.LT.	less than	.LE.	less or equal
.EQ.	equal to	.NE.	not equal

All possible combinations are covered, and used in an IF statement; this gives us many opportunities for structuring programs. We have to learn to structure them well.

Examples There are other ways to count to 10:

```
C COUNT TO TEN MARK II
      ICOUNT=0
   10 ICOUNT=ICOUNT+1
      PRINT*,'NEXT IS ',ICOUNT
      IF(ICOUNT.LT.10) GO TO 10
      END
```

```
C COUNT TO TEN MARK III
      ICOUNT=1
   10 IF (ICOUNT.GT.10) GO TO 20
      PRINT*,'NEXT IS ',ICOUNT
      ICOUNT=ICOUNT+1
      GO TO 10
   20 END
```

The third version may seem strange to you, but it is different in an important way. The stopping condition is tested at the beginning rather than at the end of the repeated section. We will see in Chapter 8 that this is an important structure, although using GO TO it does not look so nice.

7 Even smarter—Euclid's algorithm and the IF block

We can do more with the IF statement than just count. In FORTRAN, IF is the usual way of making any kind of decision. Suppose we have two integers called *mini* and *maxi*. We want to be sure that *mini* is not greater than *maxi*. Using the basic IF statement, we could write:

```
IF(MAXI.GE.MINI) GO TO 20
      ITEMP=MAXI
      MAXI=MINI
      MINI=ITEMP
   20 PRINT*,'MAXI = ',MAXI,' MINI = ',MINI
```

The IF statement decides whether *maxi* is greater than *mini*. If not, they have to be switched. Notice that the switching takes three statements, and so I have used an IF with GO TO. This is not a pretty sight. The need to use a block of statements when a decision is made arises often, and so there is a better form of IF which expresses this more naturally. You see it in this alternative version of the same statements:

```
IF(MAXI.LT.MINI) THEN
      ITEMP=MAXI
      MAXI=MINI
      MINI=ITEMP
   END IF
   PRINT*,'MAXI = ',MAXI,' MINI = ',MINI
```

The block IF is covered in more detail later. For now write the word THEN in the IF statement, and then close the IF block with the END IF line:

> **IF** (*logical expression*) **THEN**
> *statement*
> *statement*
>   :
> **END IF**

Example 'Algorithm' is the name given to a recipe for calculating a result from some data. A very old one (much older than computers) is Euclid's algorithm for finding the greatest common factor (GCF) of two numbers. If you have two integers, for example *mini* and *maxi*, then the greatest common factor is the largest integer which will exactly divide into each of them. Suppose this is n. Then we are looking for the largest value of n for which the remainders of *mini/n* and *maxi/n* are 0.

It is very easy if you know how, because if *maxi* > *mini*, then

maxi/*n* – *mini*/*n* = (*maxi*-*mini*)/*n*   (for integers this is only true if the division is exact)

Therefore the GCF of *maxi* and *mini* is the same as the GCF of *maxi*–*mini* and *mini*. We can keep subtracting *mini* from *maxi*, switching them if necessary to keep *maxi* > *mini*. Eventually *maxi* will be the same as *mini*, and we have the answer. We can see this using some actual numbers. If *maxi* = 77 and *mini* = 28, then

First	*maxi* = 77 and *mini* = 28,	*maxi* – *mini* = 49
Second	*maxi* = 49 and *mini* = 28,	*maxi* – *mini* = 21
Third	*maxi* = 28 and *mini* = 21,	*maxi* – *mini* = 7 (here we switch)
Fourth	*maxi* = 21 and *mini* = 7,	*maxi* – *mini* = 14
Fifth	*maxi* =14 and *mini* = 7,	*maxi* – *mini* = 7 (here we have the answer 7)

This is not quite Euclid's algorithm, because we have to notice that subtracting *maxi* from *mini* over and over is wasteful. It is shortened using remainders:

First	*maxi* = 77 and *mini* = 28,	remainder of *maxi*/*mini*=21
Second	*maxi* = 28 and *mini* = 21,	remainder of 28/21=7
Third	*maxi* = 21 and *mini* = 7,	remainder of 21/7 is 0 and *mini* is the result

Here is a little program to do this. The first IF is our block from a few pages back for keeping *maxi* greater than or equal to *mini*. The second IF keeps repeating the process until the answer is obtained. (What's that you say? No I'm sorry, there is no REPEAT . . . UNTIL structure in FORTRAN 77.)

```
PRINT*,'PROGRAM TO FIND GREATEST COMMON FACTOR'
      PRINT*,'ENTER TWO INTEGERS'
      READ*,MAXI,MINI
C IF NECESSARY SWITCH THE NUMBERS SO THAT MAXIMINI
   1Ø IF(MAXI.LT.MINI) THEN
         ITEMP=MAXI
         MAXI=MINI
         MINI=ITEMP
      END IF
      PRINT*,'MAXI = ',MAXI,' MINI = ',MINI
C COMPUTE THE REMAINDER OF MAXI/MINI
      MAXI=MAXI-(MAXI/MINI)*MINI
      PRINT*,'REMAINDER OF MAXI/MINI = ',MAXI
C GO BACK AND DO IT AGAIN IF NOT FINISHED YET
      IF(MAXI.GT.Ø) GO TO 1Ø
      PRINT*,'THE GREATEST COMMON FACTOR IS ',MINI
      END
```

Exercise Now you do some work. Make a terrific program for converting a decimal number to any other base.

8 Some functions

There are only a few functions in FORTRAN which give integer results with integer arguments, as in Table 4.1. Notice particularly the MOD function. We have calculated the remainder after integer division several times before, and MOD is a function that makes it easier.

MOD(MAXI,MINI) is the same as **MAXI-(MAXI/MINI)*MINI**

Table 4.1 Integer functions of integer arguments in FORTRAN 77. All give an integer result for integer arguments. All but MOD also give a real result for real arguments.

Name	Meaning
ABS(I)	Absolute value of I.
DIM(I,J)	Positive difference, I-MIN(I,J)
MAX(I,J,...)	Maximum value of I, J, ...
MIN(I,J,...)	Minimum value of I, J, ...
MOD(I,J)	Remainder of I/J, i.e. I-(I/J)*J
SIGN(I,J)	Transfer of sign; sign of J times ABS(I)

Example We can do lots of complicated little integer calculations to do with calendars. Suppose we have a date given as three integers, IDAY, IMONTH and IYEAR, for example IDAY=4, IMONTH=7 and IYEAR=1776 (the beginning of civilization as we know it). The number of days in a month varies, so how can we work out the number of days since the beginning of the year? There is a formula to help us, known as Zeller's congruence. The leap year problem can be avoided by counting from March 1. We define a fake month number which counts March as the first month, and call this MFAKE. This is

MFAKE=MOD(IMONTH+9,12)+1

Can you see how that works? Now the number of days since last March 1 is

NDAYS=IDAY+28*(MFAKE-1)+(13*MFAKE-1)/5-2

This calculation assumes that all months have 28 days, and does the mysterious correction,

(13*MFAKE-1)/5-2

thanks to the great Zeller. This is all we need, except that January and February have been treated as part of next year. We have to subtract 365 if the month is one of those, and add 1 if we have a leap year. Assuming we are not dealing with an exact century, we can compute an integer LEAP which is 1 for a leap year, 0 otherwise. We can also get an integer JANORF which is 1 in January or February, 0 otherwise:

JANORF=MFAKE/11
      LEAP=1-MIN(1,MOD(IYEAR,4))

Finally, we correct the day number:

NDAYS=NDAYS+59-365*JANORF+LEAP*(1-JANORF)

Here is a program. If you follow all the steps, then you have a pretty good grasp of integer arithmetic. So can you do Problems 4.4 and 4.6?

```
PRINT*,'PROGRAM TO COMPUTE NUMBER OF DAYS THIS YEAR'
      PRINT*,'ENTER INTEGERS - DAY MONTH YEAR'
      READ*,IDAY,IMONTH,IYEAR
C MAKE THE MONTHS START AT MARCH
      MFAKE=MOD(IMONTH+9,12)+1
C NUMBER OF DAYS COUNTED FROM LAST MARCH 1
      NDAYS=IDAY+28*(MFAKE-1)+(13*MFAKE-1)/5-2
C CORRECT FOR JAN OR FEB AND LEAP YEAR
      JANORF=MFAKE/11
```

```
LEAP=1-MIN(1,MOD(IYEAR,4))
NDAYS=NDAYS+59-365*JANORF+LEAP*(1-JANORF)
PRINT*,'THE GIVEN DATE IS DAY NUMBER ',NDAYS
END
```

9 Problems

Problem 4.1 The calendar calculation could have been done using a few IF statements instead of all that integer trickery. So try it.

Problem 4.2 Develop a program to find the least common multiple (LCM) of two integers. The product of the numbers is a multiple of course, but it may not be the least.

Problem 4.3 Prime integers have no factors except 1. The first few are 1, 2, 3, 5, 7, 11, 13, 17. To find if a number is prime, try dividing it by 2 and also all odd integers less than its square root. Do this. You may find something unpleasant about the square root function. Sorry.

Problem 4.4 1 March 1600 was a Wednesday. Write a program to find the number of days between any two dates since then. To do this you will have to know that years which divide exactly by 4 are leap years. However exact centuries are not leap years unless they can be divided exactly by 400. There has been only one of these centurial leap years since the Gregorian reformation of the calendar in 1582. There is another coming soon. I wonder how many forests will be wasted printing incorrect diaries and calendars?

Problem 4.5 Fermat's last theorem stated that there were no integer solutions other than zero to

$$x^n + y^n = z^n$$

for $n > 2$. So don't waste your computer time trying to find them. Instead find all the solutions of the right angled triangle

$$x^2 + y^2 = z^2$$

which are integers with $z < 100$. For example the solution

$$3^2 + 4^2 = 5^2$$

has been used to make square corners since ancient times.

Problem 4.6 Write a program which finds the date of Easter according to the rule expressed by the Council of Nicea in AD 325. It should be on the Sunday following the first full moon which occurs on or after March 21. First work out the moon's phase at 00:00 on 21 March, move forward to the next full moon, and then move forward to the next Sunday. Recently, Easter was held on the wrong day according to this definition. When?

Data: The moon was full on Friday, 5 October 1979 at 35.32 minutes past 19:00 Greenwich Mean Time, and the mean period for the moon's phases can be taken as 29.53059 days.

Although the data is in Greenwich Mean Time, the events on which Easter is based took place some distance to the east. You will find that the time zone used to define midnight is critical, and the Council of Nicea gave no guidance on this point because they did not know about the earth's rotation. In fact the date is not worked out this way, because the same meeting adopted an approximate algorithm which is still used.

Five

FORTRAN is for computation

1 Types and typing

This section is mainly aimed at programmers familiar with Pascal or other languages which have what is called strong typing. However anyone new to FORTRAN would be well advised to read it, and to look at it again some other time if they don't understand it at first.

It is a characteristic of FORTRAN that the types of real and integer names are implied by their spelling; we can call this implicit typing. This is an historical feature but reflects the nature of the language, which is strongly identified with the kinds of numerical calculations commonly done in Science and Engineering. In these calculations, the most important types are reals and integers, and arrays of each.

Implicit typing has advantages and disadvantages. To those used to it, the advantage is that names do not have to be declared. You simply write a variable name where you need it, and one is created. In addition fewer programs are rejected by the computer compared to a language such as Pascal, where a program will not be permitted to execute until every variable is accounted for by a declaration of its type. Pascal programmers tolerate a high level of rejection in favour of greater (but not absolute) security when a program is finally allowed to run.

The disadvantage of implicit typing also relates to spelling mistakes. If a name is spelled incorrectly in an expression, for example on the right hand side of an assignment, usually the program will fail when it runs. This is because the rogue variable you have unintentionally created is probably a new one and its value will be undefined. If by bad luck your mistake is the name of another variable, then you quietly get an incorrect result. Again a Pascal program is protected as long as the spelling mistake does not happen to be the name of another suitable item.

So in FORTRAN you get away with a bit less programming effort, but you have to live with a feeling of insecurity. Every FORTRAN program is susceptible to spelling mistakes which may pass unnoticed until the unpleasant day when someone else points out that your results are wrong. Always take great care in testing FORTRAN for correct results. Of course this is good advice in any language.

You can do explicit typing in FORTRAN if you want to. For data types other than real or integer, it is necessary. For reals and integers there is no point. It will not save you from your spelling mistakes, and it can cause confusion if you cross the implicit typing convention.

2 More about variables

Every variable in FORTRAN has a *name*, a *type* and a *value*. The *name* can be up to six symbols long. The first symbol must be a letter, and the rest are letters or digits.

Most FORTRAN programs use the predominant types real and integer. The type of a variable is implied by its spelling. Names beginning with I, J, K, L, M or N are integer. All others are real. Stick with this.

The value of a variable is undefined when a program begins, unless you have taken special steps to define it in advance. (This is done with the DATA statement described in Chapter 12.) You must give it an actual value before you try to use it in any way that requires its value. A variable can become defined in various ways. We have seen two ways so far. One is in an assignment statement:

variable = expression

The other is by using a READ statement, which so far we know only in list-directed form:

READ* [, *list*]

3 Conversions

In the previous chapters, I asked you not to mix up your real and integer calculations. Now we will see how to do this. FORTRAN will convert between reals and integers in one of three ways. You can use a special function, it can be done by an assignment statement or it can sneak up on you in the evaluation of an expression. We will look at these possibilities in turn.

Table 3.1 was a list of all the FORTRAN 77 generic functions that give a real function of a real argument. Table 4.1 was the same for integers. Three functions which convert between real and integer values, are given in Table 5.1, and they complete the list of functions available for reals and/or integers. There are other functions for the types character, complex and double precision, found in Chapters 18 and 19.

Table 5.1 Generic functions for conversions between real and integer values. X is a real argument, I is an integer argument.

Name	Meaning
INT(X)	Convert real X to integer by truncation. INT(5.2)=5; INT(–3.5)=–3.
NINT(X)	Convert X to nearest integer, i.e. round it.
	Same as INT(X+SIGN(0.5,X)), if you follow that.
REAL(I)	Convert integer I to a real value.

You may have noticed that most of the functions in Table 4.1 also appeared in Table 3.1. These are ABS, DIM, MAX, MIN and SIGN. Full FORTRAN 77 interprets these functions according to the type of the argument.

ABS(X) is a real function of the real variable X.
ABS(I) is an integer function of the integer variable I.

Unfortunately, the real functions which do not appear in Table 4.1—there are lots of them—cannot be used with integer arguments. For example a trap that I have fallen into several times is to write something like SQRT(2), which is rejected. If you want the square root of 2, you have to write SQRT(2.0) or SQRT(REAL(2)). This suggests that when an argument is an expression, it is important to know what type it will be. This is dealt with shortly.

There is another typing trap with these functions. You cannot mix the types of arguments in any generic function which has several arguments. You might get caught by something like MOD(X,2) because 2 is an integer.

Type changing is also done in assignment statements. Whenever you assign a value in the statement

variable = expression

the result of the *expression* is converted for you if necessary. This is friendly (much friendlier than being scorned for writing SQRT(2)).

Therefore J=X has exactly the same effect as J=INT(X)

Example If we want to convert a distance given in kilometres to miles, yards, feet and inches, we have to use truncation of a real value to chop away its decimal places several times along the way. There are 1.60934 kilometres in a mile. Given the kilometres, RKILOS, we can find the real distance in miles RMILES, complete with as many decimal places as the computer can manage:

          RMILES=RKILOS/1.60934

We really want the whole miles which we call HMILES, and the fragment of a mile left over called FRAG. Notice that we have a disaster on our hands if we try to call the kilometre distance anything beginning with K!

          HMILES=INT(XMILES)
          FRAG=RMILES-HMILES

Would you agree that we could have said

          FRAG=MOD(RMILES,1.0)

Now the FRAG can be made into whole yards and a new FRAG in yards

          RYARDS=FRAG*1769.0
          HYARDS=INT(RYARDS)
          FRAG=RYARDS-HYARDS

and we can proceed to get feet and inches as well.

Exercise Write the complete program to convert kilometres to miles, yards, feet and inches. In the inches, how many decimal places are appropriate? Can you think of a way of making the program round inches to that precision?

4 Expressions

So far we have steered clear of expressions which mix up reals and integers. The result of an expression has a type, just as does a variable or a constant. So how do we know what it is? The two rules are quite clear.

Rule 1 You get an integer result if every term of the expression is of type integer.

Examples These are integer expressions:

      I-(I/J)*J   (Not the same as in Pascal)   4*I+MOD(I2,7)

    ABS(MAX(I,0)-MIN(I,J))   (With an integer argument, ABS gives an integer result)

Rule 2 If any term of an expression is real, you get a real result. Two special kinds of terms are also real. Raising a real number to an integer exponent is real, as is raising an integer to a real power.

Examples These are real expressions which involve only real terms:

```
B*B-4.Ø*A*C        Y+SQRT(Z)  X**7       I**SQRT(2.Ø)

X**2 + Y**2        LOG(X)-LOG(Y)
```

These expressions are real because they contain at least one real term:

```
X+4    -    4-SQRT(16-4*A*C)/(2*A)       4+MOD(X,Y)+MOD(I,J)
```

Although an expression containing a real term will always give a real result, it is possible that during its evaluation some integer arithmetic may occur. This could cause a great deal of trouble if you blunder into integer division by mistake. Therefore it is useful to know how expressions are evaluated.

Before you come to evaluate an expression, every variable used by it should be defined. If not, you will probably get a silly result, and may well be rejected by the computer. You will also be rejected for impossible operations, such as dividing by zero, raising zero to a zero or negative power, or raising a negative number to a real power. If it happens, it is your fault.

Expressions are worked out according to the priority rules described earlier, although the computer is allowed to change the order of operations if the result is mathematically equivalent.

In evaluating an expression, an integer is converted to a real when it is about to be involved in an operation with a real value. If you know the priority rules, it is easy to work out when this will happen.

Example This simple looking expression has hidden depths:

```
Y+INDEX/7
```

The term INDEX/7 is an integer division which gives an integer result, not a real one. This integer result is then converted to real before Y is added to it.

A sloppy programmer might have intended:

```
Y+INDEX/7.Ø
```

in which case there is trouble-the result is different unless the value of INDEX is a multiple of 7. We hope it didn't mean this:

```
(Y+INDEX)/7.Ø
```

because if it did, we have a double disaster.

5 Range

Although you write computer programs in a language like FORTRAN which is supposed to be standard from one computer to another, there are often important differences between the numbers in different machines which can cause the same program to give different results, perhaps in an important way!

A computer has a limited number of digits available to it. Because an integer value is exact, when the computer runs out of digits, it will not try to be approximate about an integer. This is why the range of integers is always less than the range of reals.

Example We can try to find the integer range of a machine by starting with the integer value 1 and doubling it until something nasty happens. In this program, the value ITEST is doubled to give us JTEST, and then checked to see if division by two gets us back to ITEST again:

```
      PRINT*,'DOUBLING TO FIND LIMIT OF INTEGER RANGE'
      JTEST=1
 10   ITEST=JTEST
      PRINT*,'TESTING ',ITEST
      JTEST=ITEST*2
      IF(ITEST.EQ.JTEST/2) GO TO 10
      PRINT*,'SORRY, ',ITEST,' DOUBLED WAS ',JTEST
      END
```

When you run this program you will receive no error message when the integer becomes too large. This condition is called overflow, and you are never warned about it, at least not on any computer I have ever used. This is one reason why a program may work on one machine and not on another. On many mini- or microcomputers, this will work:

```
PRINT*,180*180
```

but this will not:

```
PRINT*,181*181
```

Exercise When our test programs above have failed, we still do not know the range of integers precisely, only a big number which is right and an even bigger one that is wrong. Find exactly the largest positive integer, and the most negative one as well—their magnitudes may be different. What is the largest integer that can be squared safely? One day you will be glad that you know about this problem. It happens in Pascal too.

Exercise The real range is much larger. Find it, but since it will take a long time by doubling, start with 2.0 and try squaring. When that fails, double from the largest safe number that you found by squaring. The range is so large that there is no need to find it any more precisely than you can by doubling. Unless of course you want to.

6 Precision

Integers are exact, but reals are approximations. How approximate are they? The answer varies from about six decimal digits to thirty or more between different computers. Not surprisingly, the most precise are usually the most expensive. We can find the limits of precision on a particular machine in a similar way to finding the integer range. Here I compare the real number 1.0 with 1.0 + DELTA in an IF statement. DELTA is halved each time around. Eventually the computer cannot tell the difference. This tells us the value of DELTA, which is so tiny that the computer cannot distinguish 1.0 from 1.0 + DELTA. It will also not be able to tell the difference between 10.0 + DELTA*10.0 and 10.0, or indeed between X + DELTA*X and X for any value of X. It sounds important, doesn't it?

```
      PRINT*,'SEARCHING FOR THE LIMITS OF REAL PRECISION'
      DELTA=1.0
 10   DELTA=DELTA/2.0
      PRINT*,'TESTING DELTA = ',DELTA
      IF(1.0.NE.1.0+DELTA) GO TO 10
      PRINT*,'SORRY, CANNOT TELL 1.0 FROM 1.0 + ',DELTA
      END
```

Exercise Find DELTA more precisely. Can you understand why it is unsafe to compare two real values for equality?

7 Problems

Problem 5.1 At the conclusion of the Indianapolis 500 mile motor race, the average speed of the winning car is announced. Write a program to work out the elapsed time. Check that for 180 miles per hour you get 2 hours 46 minutes and 40 seconds.

Problem 5.2 Write an arithmetic assignment statement that converts a real number to the next lowest integer. This is trickier than it seems. Of course you need a program to test it.

Problem 5.3 In the old British currency system there were 4 farthings in a penny, 12 pennies in a shilling and 20 shillings to the pound. Now the currency is decimalized, and the pound is a piece of chocolate wrapped in gold foil. There are 100 new pence to the pound, so that 4.27 pounds is 4 pounds and 27 new pence. Write programs to:
(i) Convert old currency to new, rounding down. (The customer always loses.)
(ii) Convert new currency to old, rounding up. (Guess who always loses.)

Problem 5.4 The earth has a period of revolution about the sun of 3155150 seconds. What is this in days, hours, minutes and seconds? How many years will it take for the Gregorian calendar, described in Chapter 4, to drift 7 days out of synchronization with the seasons? No, not on your calculator, write a computer program. Is the given data accurate enough to tell you this, and how precisely?

Problem 5.5 This is a problem about the range of numbers. The factorial of a positive integer n is the product of all the integers from 1 to n, written

$$n! = n\,(n{-}1)\,(n{-}2)\ldots(2)\,(1)$$

Write a program to find the factorial of an integer. The factorials of quite modest integers are large. Find out the largest value of n for which your computer will give you the correct answer. Do this by detecting an incorrect answer. Then do the same with reals.

Problem 5.6 This one presents problems of precision. In the triangle *ABC* in Fig. 5.1 we can use the cosine law to find cos *A*:

$$\cos A = (\,b^2 + c^2{-}a^2\,)\,/\,(\,2bc\,)$$

This looks innocent enough, but it is loaded with precision problems. In a skinny triangle, we will not be able to tell the difference between cos *A* when vertex *A* is at (K,2) from cos *A* when *A* is at (K+1,2) for some distressingly modest value of K. Write a program and see. Can you predict it theoretically from DELTA?

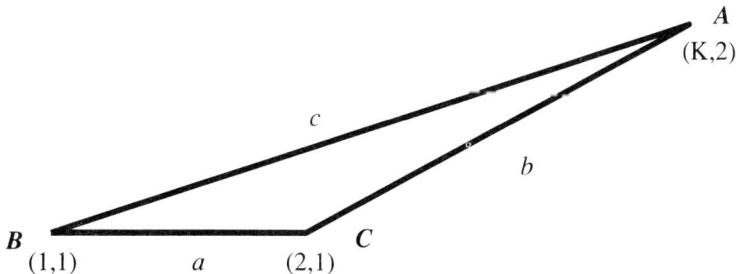

Fig.5.1 Computing cos A could present numerical difficulties.

Six

FORMAT revealed

1 Who decides?

In previous chapters, we have allowed the computer to decide about the layout of printed results. We had some control because we knew that every PRINT statement began a new line of output. Apart from that, we left it up to the computer. Although all my examples should work on any computer, I do not know exactly what the results will look like, because each computer system will have its own ideas about arranging output—how many decimal places to show, when to print signs, when to use scientific notation, how many spaces to use between items and so on. The list-directed PRINT always leaves these things up to the computer:

> PRINT* [, *list*]

The star in this statement tells the computer to make up its own mind about layout. All we can be sure of is that a new line will begin, and all the items in the list will be printed. If the list is large, more than one line might be used. The PRINT list consists of a mixture of items separated by commas.

2 You decide—the FORMAT specification

In the list-directed PRINT, the star is actually a FORMAT identifier. In its place we can put our own specification telling the computer how we want the results laid out. We are then using FORMAT-directed printing.

Example This program should produce the same layout on every computer. (The computer is still given the option to print plus signs or not in front of positive numbers):

```
C PRINT THE SINE OF 45 DEGREES.  (TAN 45 DEGREES IS 1.Ø)
C
C GET THE ANGLE IN RADIANS FROM THE ATAN FUNCTION
      RADS=ATAN(1.Ø)
      PRINT'(''SINE 45 DEGREES, OR '',F8.6,'' RADIANS IS '',F8.6)',
     +RADS,SIN(RADS)
      END
```

The output will be:

```
SINE 45 DEGREES, OR .785398 RADIANS IS .707107
```

This is achieved by the FORMAT specification, given in this case as a character string constant in the PRINT statement itself. Notice the brackets enclosing it which are always required, and the double quotation marks because they are inside a character string constant.

We could alternatively put the FORMAT specification in a separate labelled FORMAT statement. The FORMAT statement can go nearly anywhere in the program, although many programmers group them together either near the beginning or the end. Any number of PRINT, READ or WRITE statements can use the same FORMAT statement. In this program it is tidier to use a FORMAT statement:

```
C PRINT THE SINE OF 45 DEGREES.  (TAN 45 DEGREES IS 1.Ø)
C
C DEFINE A FORMAT STATEMENT TO CONTROL THE OUTPUT
C
   1Ø FORMAT('SINE 45 DEGREES, OR ',F8.6,' RADIANS IS ',F8.6)
C
C GET THE ANGLE IN RADIANS FROM THE ATAN FUNCTION
        RADS=ATAN(1.Ø)
        PRINT 1Ø, RADS, SIN(RADS)
        END
```

The syntax of PRINT is:

> **PRINT** *FORMAT identifier* [, *list*]

where the *FORMAT identifier* can be a star specifying list-directed output, an explicit character string constant giving the FORMAT specification, or the label of a FORMAT statement. The *list* is a list of items that are to be printed separated by commas. You can include the names of variables or constants, expressions and character strings. We will see in Chapter 12 that array items or implied DO-loops can also be used.

If you decide to control the layout, then you have to give a correct FORMAT specification which matches up with the list of items to be printed. For every type of data there are one or more possible FORMAT specifiers. The specifier F8.6 used above asks for a real number to be printed in a field eight spaces wide with six decimal places. We will see in the next section a number of FORMAT specifiers. A FORMAT specification is a list of these specifiers, separated by commas. For every item in the list there has to be a matching FORMAT specifier-of the correct type and in the correct order. There are lots of examples of this to come.

3 Some FORMAT specifiers for integers and reals

When you ask for items to be printed in a PRINT statement, a new line of output is begun which contains a number of fields, one for each item printed. If you are asking for a lot of output, additional new lines might also occur along the way. With list-directed output, you leave this to the computer. If you want to control the layout yourself, you must provide a list of FORMAT specifiers for the fields of output. They have to match up exactly with the list of items you are trying to PRINT.

(i) Integer fields—I editing

The one and only specifier for an integer field is the I specifier:

[*number*] **I** *width* [. *digits*]

In its simplest form, **I** *width* specifies that one integer is to be right justified in a field of *width* spaces.

Example This

```
C DEMONSTRATE INTEGER EDITING IN FORMAT
C
C USE FORMAT STATEMENTS IN THIS VERSION
C
   1Ø FORMAT('SOME POWERS OF TWO')
   2Ø FORMAT(I4,I5,I6)
C
C DO IT
C
      PRINT 1Ø
      PRINT 2Ø,2**8,2**1Ø,2**14
      END
```

will print this:

```
   256 1Ø24 16384
. . . . . . . . . . . . . .
```

The dots shown here would not be printed by a computer, they are there to enable you to count the spaces on this page.

Exercise Run the program just given. Are there any spaces unaccounted for? If so ask an expert, or read on. What does a list-directed PRINT give you in place of the FORMAT specification (**I4,I5,I6**) above?

In the more complex form:

[*number*] **I** *width* [.*digits*]

the optional positive nonzero integer constant *number* specifies that a number of integer fields is to occur in sequence. If no *number* is given, the specifier behaves as if *number* were 1. Instead of writing **I5,I5,I5** in a FORMAT specification, it is usual to write **3I5** .

The optional zero or positive integer constant *digits* specification specifies that a minimum of *digits* digits is to be written. This will produce leading zeros. For example, if the specification is **I5.3**, any number less than 100 will have leading zeros. If digits is 0, the number zero would not be printed. Without *digits* given, therefore, the I specification behaves as if *digits* were 1.

The specifier **I** *width* is the same as **1I** *width*.**1**.

(ii) Real fields—F editing

The F specification is used to print real numbers with decimal places. F is short for *floating point*, which is what the representation of real numbers inside computers is often called. History again! It is

[*number*] **F** *width*.*digits*

Number, *width* and *digits* are integer constants. Note that for reals, *digits* is compulsory in the F specifier. It means that *number* real numbers are to be printed in a field which is *width* spaces wide, and *digits* decimal digits are to be printed. If *number* is not given, it is taken as 1. The computer might print a sign, and it must print a decimal point. Because you probably want a space between numbers so you can read them, it is silly to make *width* less than *digits*+3. If the computer cannot obey your F specification, it will print *width* stars instead, and you will have to try again to see your results.

Example Let us discover if sin(π/4) is really 1/√2. It is, of course, but knowing what we do about the precision of computers, the computer may not think so. So this program lets you check out the accuracy of the SIN and SQRT functions:

```
C LOOK AT SOME ACCURACY, PRINTING LOTS OF DIGITS
   1Ø FORMAT(F25.2Ø)
C FIRST SIN(PIE/4)
      PIEBY4=ATAN(1.Ø)
      THESIN=SIN(PIEBY4)
      PRINT*,'THIS IS SIN(PIE/4)'
      PRINT 1Ø, THESIN
C MATHEMATICALLY, 1/SQRT(2) IS THE SAME
      THESQR=1.Ø/SQRT(2.Ø)
      PRINT*,'THIS IS 1.Ø/SQRT(2.Ø)'
      PRINT 1Ø, THESQR
C SO WHAT DOES FORTRAN SAY
      IF(THESQR.NE.THESIN) THEN
         PRINT*,'BOO, HISS, THEY ARE NOT THE SAME'
      ELSE
         PRINT*,'HURRAY, THEY ARE THE SAME'
      END IF
C HOW BIG IS THE DIFFERENCE
      PRINT*,'THIS IS THE DIFFERENCE',ABS(THESIN-THESQR)
      END
```

Exercise Run the above test on your computer. You may have to reduce the *digits* in the F specifier. So which is wrong, and by how much? If they are exactly the same, you have some pretty good library functions there! In the previous chapter we discovered DELTA, the smallest real number for which the machine can distinguish DELTA from 1.0 + DELTA. What else does this tell you about ATAN, SIN and SQRT on your computer?

4 Spaces, captions and new lines

(i) Spaces-X editing

The X description asks for a series of blanks to appear in the printed line:

number **X**

If there is any danger that your output is going to appear on a lineprinter, then always begin a new line of FORMAT-directed output with at least one space. This is because the first character in a line of output is usually interpreted as a carriage control character by a lineprinter. Terrible things can happen to you if anything other than a blank appears there, such as an abrupt decline in your popularity when you make the printer jump to a zillion new pages. They would have to cut down a forest just to run your program. List-directed printing provides any necessary space automatically.

(ii) Captions in FORMAT

Clear presentation of the results of a calculation always requires titles and other captions. We know how to include messages in list-directed output:

```
        PRINT*,'HELLO SAILOR'   or          PRINT 75
        END                            75 FORMAT(1X,'HELLO SAILOR')
                                          END
```

The specification **1X**, which is necessary if the output is to appear on a lineprinter, could have been incorporated into the message:

```
        PRINT 75
    75 FORMAT(' HELLO SAILOR')
        END
```

This is wrong:

```
        PRINT 26,' QUOTIENT = ',ITOP/IBOT
    26 FORMAT(1X,I5)
```

Why? The FORMAT specification makes no provision for the characters **' QUOTIENT = '** to be printed. A program with this in it would fail when it tried to match the list of PRINT items with the FORMAT. It can be done by character editing as we will see in Chapter 18, but even then it is not ideal. It is better to follow this advice (not a rule):

In FORMAT-directed output, put your messages in the FORMAT specification.

In list-directed output, include messages in the list.

(iii) New lines-the slash

Every PRINT starts a new line. List-directed output might or might not begin further new lines of its own accord. In FORMAT-directed output, you are in trouble if you run out of room in a line. By putting the / character in a FORMAT specification, you force a new line to begin at that point. The slash does not need a comma to separate it from other FORMAT specifiers. A new line will also begin if your list of items to be printed runs off the end of your FORMAT. If this happens, the computer starts using your FORMAT again, in a slightly complicated way as we will soon see. We get new lines from:

(i) Every PRINT (or READ or WRITE), even those with no list of items to read or write.
(ii) A FORMAT that has run out of specifications while the list of items to read or write has not been finished.
(iii) A slash, '/', in the FORMAT.

Example This prints three lines, as we would expect.

```
C PRINT SOME POWERS OF TWO ON SEPARATE LINES
        PRINT*,'HERE ARE SOME POWERS OF TWO'
        PRINT*,2**8
        PRINT*,2**12
        PRINT*,2**14
        END
```

This also produces three lines using slashes in the FORMAT specification:

```
C PRINT SOME POWERS OF TWO ON SEPARATE LINES
        PRINT*,'HERE ARE SOME POWERS OF TWO'
        PRINT'(1X,I4/I5/I6)', 2**8, 2**12, 2**14
        END
```

So does this by using the FORMAT over until the list is satisfied:

```
C PRINT SOME POWERS OF TWO ON SEPARATE LINES
   1Ø FORMAT(1X,I6)
      PRINT*,'HERE ARE SOME POWERS OF TWO'
      PRINT 1Ø, 2**8, 2**12, 2**14
      END
```

Exercise The *yield* on one unit of currency invested so that it earns *i*% in each of *n* accounting periods is:

$$yield = (\, 1 + i \,)^n$$

Write a program to print a table of yields for various interest rates over a few different accounting periods. Label the columns and make it pretty.

5 Reading in values

We have discussed FORMAT using the PRINT statement for output. There is also a WRITE statement which will be described in Chapter 20 which is used for more general files, and which has the same FORMAT facilities.

The READ statement comes in several forms. The list-directed READ is familiar already:

> READ* [, *list*]

To turn this into FORMAT-directed form, just give a FORMAT specification such as

> READ '(2I1Ø)',INT1,INT2   or   READ 1Ø,INT1,INT2
> 1Ø FORMAT(2I1Ø)

It is unlikely that an interactive program will use FORMAT-directed input, because of the unnatural constraints this places on the input line. While it is often good presentation to PRINT in a rigid layout, it would usually not be a convenient way of entering information at a keyboard. Therefore with READ you are probably not going to use FORMAT very often.

The syntax of READ is:

> **READ** *FORMAT identifier* [, *list*]

where the FORMAT identifier can be

(i) ★ to indicate list-directed formatting
(ii) a character string giving the FORMAT
(iii) the label of a FORMAT statement.

We will see a form of READ for use with more general files in Chapter 20.

The list of items for input is more restricted than for output, for obvious reasons. An input list item must be something that can be given a value. Therefore it cannot be a caption or an expression. Of the objects that we have seen so far, only the names of variables can appear in an input list.

As with PRINT, the FORMAT specification must match up exactly with the list of items. An integer variable must be matched to an I field. A real variable name must match with either the F specification that we know already, or with an E or G field as we will soon see. The FORMAT specification can include slashes or X fields. A FORMAT specification used for input cannot contain a character string constant.

Each READ statement begins a new line of input. Further new lines may occur while the statement is being processed, either by a / in the specification, or when the specification is exhausted. The input line is divided into fields, whose width is given by the specifiers in the FORMAT. When you give the input, each item must lie within the bounds of its field, and be of the correct type. With integers, this makes the layout rigid, but there is some flexibility with reals.

In reading integers, the layout is strict. You must give exactly what the program asks for.

Example The statements

```
     READ 20  ,JOLLY,JELLY
  20 FORMAT(2I5)
```

require the input data to occur in two fields of five spaces each.

Real numbers can use the F specification.

> [number] **F** *width.digits*

In the input, you can leave out the decimal point and it will automatically be inserted just before the last *digits* digits of the number. Otherwise, you can enter a decimal point yourself and put it anywhere you want. Whatever you do, the number has to stay entirely inside the field.

Example We want to enter the integer 69 and the real 1.4. We could write

```
     READ '(I5,F5.1)',INDEX,VALUE
```

and then enter

```
      69    14
 . . . . . . . . . .
```

to have the decimal placed for us. It is also correct to enter

```
      69 1.4
 . . . . . . . . . .
```

in which we have moved the number and its decimal point.

6 Cover the range—E and G editing

The range of real numbers is so wide that it is not convenient to represent all their digits for very large or very small values. This is why we use the exponential form of real constants, encountered in Chapter 3. Similarly, for input or output of real numbers, the E specification is available:

> [*number*] **E** *width.digits*

Here, *number* is a repetition factor, meaning that the specification is to apply to *number* fields of input or output. The *width* is the total field width, and this applies strictly to either input or output just as in other forms of editing. The value of *digits* specifies the number of decimal places to be used.

The output produced when a real value is matched to an E specification has two parts. First is a real number called the mantissa, which is always scaled so that its first decimal place is significant. Then an exponent is printed with it to specify the power of 10 used for scaling. Most often this will be

*s∅.dd ... ddd **E**sdd*

where *s* is a sign and *d* is a digit. There are so many symbols in this representation that *width* has to be much larger than *digits*. I recommend that

width > digits + 7

although you may have to make it as large as digits + 10 on some computers.

Examples Using a specification E15.5, the following numbers could be printed as shown:

3 x 10^{10} `. . . . 0.30000E+11`   −7.32 x 10^{24} `. . . . -0.73200E+25`

16.35 x 10^{-4} `. . . . 0.16350E-02`   −4.28 x 10^{-15} `. . . . -0.42800E-14`

When input is requested using the E field, you are allowed considerable latitude in the input data, provided it always falls inside the field width, which is rigid. If you give the decimal point and the exponent you can place the number anywhere in the field. To read in 3 x 10**10 with a field specification E15.5, you can provide any of these (and others):

`. . . . Ø.3ØØØØE+11`   `. . . . 3.Ø E +1Ø`   `. . . . 3.E+1Ø`

You can leave out E and indicate only the sign:

`. . . . 3.Ø+1Ø . . . .`

If the decimal point is left out, it is placed before the final *digits* digits of the mantissa:

`. . . . 3ØØØØE+11`   *or*   `. . . . 3ØØØØ+11 . . . .`

You do not need the exponent or decimal point at all. Any value acceptable to an F field can be given as input to an E specifier. Furthermore, any value acceptable to E can be given to F!

The G specification is also used for real data. This has the ability to switch its presentation of output data according to the size of the value. If the value is small enough, a printed number in F form is used. If it is too large for that, the E form comes out. The specification is:

[*number*] **G** width . digits [**E** exponent]

    number is the number of fields of this type

    width is the total width of this field

    digits is the number of significant digits

    exponent, if given, is the number of digits in the exponent. If not given it is 2.

The field width has to be much greater than the number of digits requested. If the exponent size is not given, make

width > digits + 7

If the exponent size is given, use

width > digits + exponent + 5

The G field does nothing special for you on input. All forms of input acceptable to E or F editing can be given as input to a G field. In fact all forms of real input are interchangeable.

7 To satisfy or not to satisfy

These are the questions:

What happens when the data list of PRINT, READ or WRITE runs out of FORMAT? When this occurs we say the data list is *unsatisfied*.

What happens when the data list of PRINT, READ or WRITE is satisfied, but there is more FORMAT?

As you might have guessed, I have the answers. When the data list is unsatisfied, printing or reading must continue, and so the FORMAT specification is used again. However the rule about it is complicated:

A simple FORMAT, with no embedded repetitions is started again from the beginning, over and over again as many times as are necessary to satisfy the data list. For each repetition, you get a new line.

Example You probably do not mean this:

```
      I=1
      K=-53
      J=1Ø24
      WRITE(*,44)I,K,J
   44 FORMAT(1X,'HERE ARE THREE NUMBERS',I5)
      END
```

because it gives you this:

```
HERE ARE THREE NUMBERS     1
HERE ARE THREE NUMBERS   -53
HERE ARE THREE NUMBERS  1024
```

Example Surely you do not mean this? What does it do?

```
      PRINT 42,42
   42 FORMAT('THE MEANING OF LIFE, THE UNIVERSE ETC. IS ')
      END
```

To help you here, the FORMAT specification can include repeated groups of specifiers. If you enclose any series of specifications in brackets, you can make them repeat on the same line.

Example This is a pretty and useful row of stars:

```
      PRINT'(1X,5Ø(''*''))'
      END
```

All of this means that a FORMAT or part of it can be repeated in three ways:

(i) Editing descriptions for data fields are repeatable, such as 3I3.

(ii) Groups of fields can be repeated if they are placed in brackets:

   number (group)

(iii) Running out of FORMAT with more data to come will cause a FORMAT to be repeated. But from where?

When a FORMAT is repeated with an unsatisfied data list, the computer looks back from the end of the FORMAT for a right bracket. If there is one, the repetition starts with that group.

Otherwise the whole FORMAT is repeated. Notice that it is the final embedded group that is repeated. So this gives us what we wanted previously:

```
    I=1
    K=-53
    J=1Ø24
    WRITE(*,44)I,K,J
 44 FORMAT(1X,'HERE ARE THREE NUMBERS'/(I5))
    END
```

Finally, when a data list is satisfied, a FORMAT specification will continue to be used until a field is encountered that needs a data item. This way you can splice new lines, or messages onto the end of the output.

Example

```
    I=99
    PRINT 69,I
 69 FORMAT(' THE FIRST'/I4//1X,' SHALL BE LAST'/' ...EH?')
    END
```

8 When to use FORMAT

Because of the convenience of list-directed input and output, it is easy for a programmer never to use FORMAT-directed forms. But good program design is not always for the convenience of the programmer alone.

Use FORMAT:

(i) When attractive layout of results is required.
(ii) When the arrangements for input are to be standardized, for example for processing large amounts of data from external files.
(iii) To achieve the same layout on different computers, because the list-directed form is installation dependent.

9 Problems

These problems exploit the fact that FORMAT-directed output will allow you to print as many digits of a result as you want.

Problem 6.1 Stirling's approximation to the factorial of a large number is surprisingly good. Write a program to evaluate this and compare its accuracy with a direct calculation using real arithmetic over the range of your computer.

$$n! \approx \sqrt{2\pi n}\,(n/e)^n$$

Problem 6.2 The library functions of FORTRAN will usually give an accuracy which is close to the limits of the machine's capabilities.
(a) Use the ATN function to find π. How accurate is your ATN function, given that
$\pi = 3.14159\ 26535\ 89793\ 23846$
(b) Similarly find e with EXP. The actual value is $e = 2.71828\ 18284\ 59045\ 23536$

Problem 6.3 Investigate carefully the accuracy of SIN(x) over the range $-\pi < x < \pi$.

Problem 6.4 Investigate the accuracy of SQRT over the entire range of positive real numbers on your machine.

Seven

Program control

1 Exercising control

Computers do not just calculate—they use the results of calculations to decide what a program will do next. This is what makes them really useful. The GO TO statement and the logical IF statement have already been introduced in earlier chapters, and they are examples of control statements. In this chapter and the next, all the useful program control facilities of FORTRAN are covered. You are also warned not to use some of the others which are obsolete. With this information, you can then do almost anything in FORTRAN because the basics of calculation and decision making have been covered.

2 What we know already

The GO TO statement was introduced near the beginning of this course. Some modern computer languages have tried to eliminate the GO TO statement altogether, by providing all the basic control structures that you could ever need in a more lucid form. However in FORTRAN, these structures have not yet been made part of the language, and so we still need GO TO to achieve them. The GO TO statement:

> **GO TO** *label*

causes a program to jump to the statement whose label is *label*. This must exist in the same program unit as the GO TO statement.

We have also met the logical IF statement:

IF (*logical expression***)** *true statement*

This statement examines the *logical expression*, and if it is .TRUE. the *true statement* is executed. The *true statement* can be any FORTRAN executable statement except IF, ELSE (this chapter), END or DO (Chapter 8).

The simplest logical expression is

arithmetic expression   *relational operator*   *arithmetic expression*

as we have seen. In this chapter we will see how to form more complicated logical expressions. The relational operators are:

.GT.	greater than
.LE.	less or equal
.GE.	greater or equal
.LT.	less than
.EQ.	equal to
.NE.	not equal

3 Logical expressions

The logical expressions that we have seen so far have been limited to a comparison of two arithmetic values:

value   comparison   value

We have available in addition five logical operators which are used with logical expressions or logical values to make more complicated expressions:

    .NOT. *logical expression*

If the *logical expression* is .TRUE., the result is .FALSE., and vice versa.

    logical expression **.AND.** *logical expression*

The result is .TRUE. if both *logical expressions* are .TRUE., otherwise .FALSE.

    logical expression **.OR.** *logical expression*

The result is .TRUE. if either or both of the *logical expressions* are .TRUE. This is called the inclusive OR operation.

    logical expression **.EQV.** *logical expression*

The result is .TRUE. if both *logical expressions* are the same (equivalent). If the *logical expressions* are different the result is .FALSE..

    logical expression **.NEQV.** *logical expression*

This is the exclusive OR operation. The result is .TRUE. if the logical expressions are different, i.e. one .TRUE. and the other .FALSE.. It is the opposite of the .EQV. operation. Therefore

a . NEQV. b   means the same as   **.NOT. (a .EQV. b)**

An expression in FORTRAN might include arithmetic operators, relational operators and logical operators. There is also a character operator // for concatenation, introduced in Chapter 18. The overall priority of all FORTRAN operations is:

( )	Expressions in brackets	Highest
★★		
★ or **/**	Arithmetic operators	
+ or **−**		
//	Character Operator	
.GT. .GE. .EQ. .LE. .LT. .NE.	Relational Operators	
.NOT. .AND.	Logical Operators	
.OR. .EQV. or .NEQV.		Lowest

The effect of a mixed expression in FORTRAN is close to what you would expect from common sense. Among themselves, the logical operators obey a priority which resembles that of the arithmetic operations. However as a group they have a lower priority than the arithmetic or relational ones. If you write

```
IF(I.LT.J.AND.J.LT.K.OR.K.LT.J.AND.J.LT.I) PRINT*,'MID IS ',J
```

the logical expression means

```
((I.LT.J).AND.(J.LT.K)) .OR. ((K.LT.J).AND.(J.LT.I))
```

These priorities are not the same as in Pascal. A Pascal programmer is always forced to use brackets in an expression like

```
(i<j) and (j<k)
```

while in FORTRAN you would get what you want by writing

```
I.LT.J .AND. J.LT.K
```

Example Here is a program which finds the middle value of three numbers. It takes care of the possibility that two or three of the given numbers are the same. If you think this is a bit 'brute force', I would agree with you. I will give you some alternatives shortly.

```
C A PROGRAM TO DEMONSTRATE COMPLEX LOGICAL EXPRESSIONS
      PRINT*,'ENTER THREE INTEGERS TO FIND THE MIDDLE VALUE'
      READ*,I,J,K
C PERHAPS THE ANSWER IS I, INCLUDE CASE I=J BUT NOT K
      IF(J.LE.I.AND.I.LT.K.OR.K.LT.I.AND.I.LE.J)
     +  PRINT*,'MID IS ',I
C OR MAYBE IT IS J, INCLUDES CASE J=K BUT NOT I
      IF(I.LT.J.AND.J.LE.K.OR.K.LE.J.AND.J.LT.I)
     +  PRINT*,'MID IS ',J
C OR IT COULD BE K, NO EQUALITIES CONSIDERED
      IF(J.LT.K.AND.K.LT.I.OR.I.LT.K.AND.K.LT.J)
     +  PRINT*,'MID IS ',K
C FINALLY K = I OR ALL THREE EQUAL
      IF(I.EQ.K) PRINT*,'MID IS ',I
      END
```

4 A block IF

The logical IF statement was the workhorse of good old FORTRAN IV, but because it allows only one statement for the .TRUE. condition, it often made programmers with a good sense of structure feel uncomfortable with what they were writing. For example, if you want to switch the variables MAXI and MINI when MAXI is less than MINI, you require three statements to accomplish the switch. The block IF can do it:

```
10 IF(MAXI.LT.MINI) THEN
      ITEMP=MAXI
      MAXI=MINI
      MINI=ITEMP
   END IF
```

In general, you can write

```
IF(logical expression) THEN
```
    a block of statements
```
END IF
```

to have the statements between IF and END IF obeyed if the logical expression is .TRUE. Otherwise the block is skipped. You will notice that I always write the statements between IF and END IF indented to emphasize that they form a block.

Example Let us find the middle of three values again. This time I will put them in order before printing the one in the middle. I call this a data processing approach to the problem:

```
C THE MID VALUE PROBLEM SOLVED BY ORDERING THE DATA
      PRINT*,'ENTER THREE INTEGERS TO FIND THE MIDDLE VALUE'
      READ*,I,J,K
C PERHAPS J IS LESS THAN I
      IF (J.LT.I) THEN
         ISAVE=J
         J=I
         I=ISAVE
      END IF
C PERHAPS K IS LESS THAN J
      IF (K.LT.J) THEN
         ISAVE=K
         K=J
         J=ISAVE
      END IF
C IF WE SWITCHED J AND K, J MIGHT NOW BE LESS THAN I
      IF (J.LT.I) THEN
         ISAVE=J
         J=I
         I=ISAVE
      END IF
C NOW WE KNOW FOR SURE THAT THE MID VALUE IS J
      PRINT*,'AFTER SORTING THE NUMBERS, THE ORDER IS ',I,J,K
      PRINT*,'AND THE MIDDLE VALUE IS ',J
      END
```

Example While we are on the subject of the mid value, this little example has nothing at all to do with IF blocks, but it is a functional approach to finding the middle of three values. Remember the MAX and MIN functions?

```
C THE MID VALUE PROBLEM SOLVED FUNCTIONALLY
      PRINT*,'ENTER THREE INTEGERS TO FIND THE MIDDLE VALUE'
      READ*,I,J,K
      PRINT*,'THE MIDDLE VALUE IS ',
     +   MAX(MIN(I,J),MIN(J,K),MIN(K,I))
      END
```

Explanation The three MINs give the smallest value twice, and the middle value once; we do not care in what order because the MAX of those three is the value we are after!

I have shown you three alternative ways of doing the same thing because I want to help you to develop judgement about the virtues of various approaches to a single problem. So which is best? I know which I like, but I also know that others disagree. I prefer the functional approach because it is efficient and to me it is clear. You have to make up your own mind; just remember there is more than one way to bait a hook if you are trying to catch a computer scientist.

5 An IF with alternatives

The block IF allows you to carry out a block with any number of statements when a condition is .TRUE. The statements which follow END IF are obeyed whether the condition is .TRUE. or .FALSE. Suppose you wanted instead to do one thing on .TRUE. and another on .FALSE.?

This is called an alternative structure. The block IF statement has an ELSE facility for just this situation. You write

```
IF (logical expression) THEN
```
    the .TRUE. block
```
ELSE
```
    the .FALSE. block
```
END IF
```

as in this fragment from a larger example coming in Chapter 9:

```
C C SELECT WHICH SIDE THE MIDPOINT IS ON
C          IF(FMID.EQ.SIGN(FMID,FX1)) THEN
C ON THE X1 SIDE, REPLACE X1
           PRINT*,'THE MIDPOINT REPLACES X1'
           X1=XMID
           FX1=FMID
        ELSE
C ON THE X2 SIDE, REPLACE X2
           PRINT*,'THE MIDPOINT REPLACES X2'
           X2=XMID
           FX2=FMID
        END IF
```

The IF statement here is testing to see if the two real variables FMID and FX1 have the same sign, apparently disregarding my advice against comparing two real values for equality. Refer to the definition of the SIGN function, in Table 3.1, and you will see that it is safe.

You may have the choice of more than two alternatives; then you use the ELSE IF form:

```
IF (decision 1 ) THEN
```
    true block 1
```
ELSE IF (decision 2) THEN
```
    true block 2
```
ELSE IF (decision 3)
```
    true block 3

and so on until the final one can be an ordinary ELSE which means 'none of the above', an option I would have liked when voting in a recent election.

```
ELSE
```
    ordinary ELSE block
```
END IF
```

With an IF block of this type, at most one of the blocks is executed. If an ordinary ELSE is present, exactly one will be obeyed. Without an ordinary ELSE, you can get none or one, depending on how the crispies crunch.

To summarize, a block IF structure:

(i) begins with IF (*logical expression*) THEN
(ii) is followed by any number of optional ELSE IF statements
(iii) is finally followed by at most one optional ELSE statement
(iv) must be closed by an END IF statement.

You can place one IF block inside another. To do this, the inner block must be completely inside one of the true blocks of the outer one. This means it cannot be split by an ELSE IF or ELSE of the outer block.

Example Here is the middle of three values found using an IF block with others 'nesting' inside it. This is the most efficient version yet, because half the time only two comparisons are needed to find the result. However because of its complexity it is probably not a good solution. I did not get it right until the second try, which is not my usual standard:

```
C THE MID VALUE PROBLEM SOLVED BY USING THE BRAIN
      PRINT*,'ENTER THREE INTEGERS TO FIND THE MIDDLE VALUE'
      READ*,I,J,K
      IF (J.LT.I) THEN
        IF (I.LT.K) THEN
C          J LESS THAN I LESS THAN K
           PRINT*,'MID IS ',I
        ELSE
          IF (K.LT.J) THEN
C            K LESS THAN J LESS THAN I
             PRINT*,'MID IS ',J
          ELSE
C            J LESS THAN K LESS THAN I
             PRINT*,'MID IS ',K
          END IF
        END IF
      ELSE
        IF (I.GT.K) THEN
C          K LESS THAN I LESS THAN J
           PRINT*,'MID IS ',I
        ELSE
          IF (K.GT.J) THEN
C            I LESS THAN J LESS THAN K
             PRINT*,'MID IS ',J
          ELSE
C            I LESS THAN K LESS THAN J
             PRINT*,'MID IS ',K
          END IF
        END IF
      END IF
      END
```

If you examine this program, you will see that every nested IF is closed by its own END IF before an ELSE or an ELSE IF of an outer block. From this it follows that END IF, ELSE and ELSE IF always belong to the most recent unclosed IF block.

Exercise Unlike the other versions of the middle value problem, in the incredible IF nest I have not covered the case where two or three of the values are equal. Enjoy yourself getting that right!

6 Other (useful) control statements

There are a number of other control statements of FORTRAN 77. The remaining useful ones are covered in the next few chapters.

(i) The DO statement and its friend CONTINUE are so important that they rate Chapter 8 all to themselves.

(ii) The RETURN statement can be used in FUNCTION and SUBROUTINE subprograms, and is described in Chapter 10.

(iii) The CALL statement activates a SUBROUTINE and is described in Chapter 11.

The STOP statement is very helpful. It is an alternative way of terminating a program before it reaches the final END. The difference is that you can put STOP anywhere in a program, whereas the END statement can only be the final line of a program unit.

The STOP statement is

    STOP [*option*]

where *option* is a number of up to 5 digits or a character string constant:

    IF (IERROR.GT.99) STOP 'SORRY BUDDY, TOO MANY ERRORS'

The END statement

    END

must be the final statement of a program unit. In a main program it executes as STOP, but without the optional message. In a subprogram it behaves like RETURN as we will see in Chapter 10.

The PAUSE statement is available to bring a temporary halt to a program, but is probably not very useful to you. What it does depends on the computer you are using. On your own little machine, it will probably wait for you to do something. On a big machine it may not do anything at all. The PAUSE statement is:

    PAUSE [*option*]

where the option is a number or string constant as for STOP:

    PAUSE 'OVER TO YOU BOO-BOO'

7 To be avoided—useless control statements

Why does FORTRAN 77 have useless statements? It is all historical. These statements once performed useful service in earlier versions of FORTRAN, but should not be used in new programs. They will be eliminated from a future version of FORTRAN. I give no description of them apart from an informal list of their syntax:

(i) The arithmetic IF

    IF (*arithmetic expression*) *minus label, zero label, plus label*

(ii) The computed GO TO

>   **GO TO** (*label for 1*, *label for 2*, ...) [,] *integer expression*

(iii) The assigned GO TO

>   **ASSIGN** *label number* **TO** *integer variable name*
>
>   :
>   :
>
>   **GO TO** *integer variable name*

8 A list of Control statements

Here is a list of all the control statements of FORTRAN 77:

1 **GO TO**	9 **END IF**
2 Computed **GO TO**	10 **DO** (Chapter 8)
3 Assigned **GO TO**	11 **CONTINUE** (Chapter 8)
4 Arithmetic **IF**	12 **STOP**
5 Logical **IF**	13 **PAUSE**
6 Block **IF**	14 **END**
7 **ELSE IF**	15 **CALL** (Chapter 11)
8 **ELSE**	16 **RETURN** (Chapter 10)

9 Problems

Problem 7.1 Write a program which will explore the numerical environment of any computer you run it on. It should report on the range of real and integer numbers. Study the consistency of real precision over the range of real values.

Problem 7.2 Write a program which will evaluate and report on the accuracy of some of the mathematical functions for real numbers as supported by FORTRAN.

Problem 7.3 Computers are widely used to produce various forms of drawings, graphs and other pictorial results. Almost every graphics device moves a 'pen' (which might actually be a point on a screen) by tiny steps in the X or Y direction or both. A typical graphics 'driver' would move in

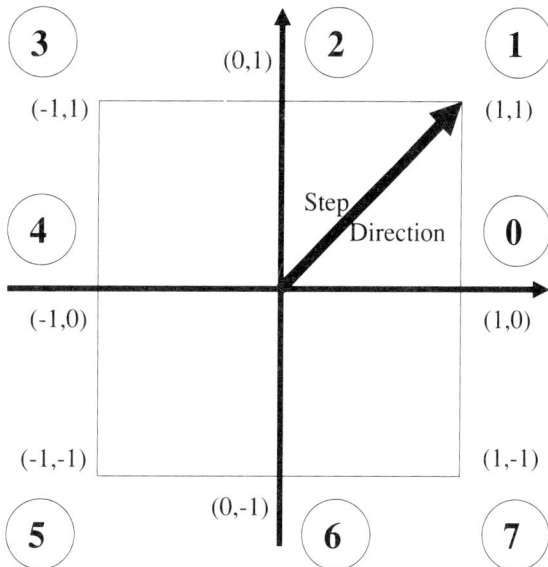

Fig. 7.1. Encode, decode and rotate the step directions.

one of the eight directions shown in Fig. 7.1. Smooth curves are then made up of a very large number of single steps in these eight directions. Programs which control these devices have to be very efficient; although the algebra of the pen motion lends itself to the use of trigonometric functions, these would be too slow in practice. Instead carefully organized logic and arithmetic are used involving the minimum of computation.

(i) Write a program without trigonometric functions which 'encodes' the integer co-ordinates of the endpoints in Fig. 7.1 into a number from 0 to 7 as shown.

(ii) Write a program without trigonometric functions which decodes a number from 0 to 7 into the integer co-ordinates of the endpoints in Fig. 7.1.

(iii) Write programs for rotation of the step direction: given integer end co-ordinates, calculate new ones from them for rotations of 45 or 135 degrees clockwise or anticlockwise. The most efficient schemes would not use the encoding and decoding method.

Problem 7.4 Many games can be devised to be played with the computer. With complex games such as chess, no optimum strategy is known and programming these is a deep study. However for many simple games optimum strategies are possible. Such a game is NIMB, which can always be won by the first player. Write a program to play the simplified version described below. A good program will issue instructions and information as the game proceeds. Furthermore it will never lose if given the first move or if the opponent makes a mistake.

The game in a simplified version begins with the number 15, which could represent, for example, 15 matches on a table. Each of the two players in turn must remove one, two or three from the number available. The loser is the player forced to remove the last one. The winning strategy is very simple.

Problem 7.5 Mastermind was been a popular game a few years ago. Here, in its simpler form, four coloured pegs (which are all different) are chosen from 6 possible colours. You could represent these as a choice of four numbers from 1 to 6. The four pegs are hidden and the player has to discover the colours and their arrangement by trying to match the combination. He is told how many correct colours he has and how many are in the right place. For example if the hidden code is

    4 3 1 5   and the player tries   2 1 3 5

the game reveals that three colours are correct and one is in the right place. Write a program in which the computer sets the problem and you play. The author believes it is always possible to solve the code after the third try if all the colours are different, but he forgets how. Solutions please!

Problem 7.6 Mastermind again. Now you set the code and the computer plays to find it on the third move.

Eight

Repeating

1 Repeat forever

All programming languages have facilities to help you organize repeated processes. Although FORTRAN 77 is not rich in these, all the basic structures can be achieved. We will first describe these structures in 'pseudocode' and then give the FORTRAN implementation.

Pseudocode is an informal way of describing computer programs. It lies somewhere between a natural language of the kind that we speak, and a computer language which is stilted but precise. Pseudocode is not formally defined—you can have yours and I can have mine. In this and the following chapter I will describe structures in my private pseudocode and hope that you can understand them.

In Chapter 4, the GO TO statement was introduced for achieving endless repetition. A description of endless repetition in pseudocode could be:

> repeat
>> *some statements*
> until eternity

This describes a structure which is implemented in FORTRAN 77 using GO TO:

```
C WARNING - THIS PROGRAM WASTES RESOURCES
      PRINT*,'BET YOU CAN''T '
   10 PRINT*,'STOP ME .. '
      GO TO 10
      END
```

This program also illustrates a feature of the 'repeat forever' process; once you have started it, you must intervene to stop it. In Chapter 4 you were invited to find out how to stop an endless repetition like the one above, or in an even more extreme case one like this:

```
   10 GO TO 10
      END
```

The action required to stop a loop which contains a request for input may not be the same:

```
C FIND THE AVERAGE OF TWO NUMBERS
   10 PRINT*,'ENTER TWO REAL NUMBERS TO AVERAGE'
      READ*,XONE,XTWO
      AVG=XONE+XTWO/2.Ø
      PRINT*,'THE AVERAGE = ',AVG
      PRINT*
      GO TO 10
      END
```

2 More about counting

In principle, counting is easy, although there are a number of subtle variations on it. A variable used for the counter is given an initial value before the counting begins, and is altered each time the loop is repeated. This program which counts forever was in Chapter 4:

```
C EINE KLEINE KOUNTINGPROGRAM
      ICOUNT=1
   10 PRINT*,'NEXT IS ',ICOUNT
      ICOUNT=ICOUNT+1
      GO TO 10
      END
```

It is more usual to have a count which stops:

```
C COUNT TO TEN MARK I
      ICOUNT=1
   10 PRINT*,'NEXT IS ',ICOUNT
      ICOUNT=ICOUNT+1
      IF (ICOUNT.LE.10) GO TO 10
      END
```

Example A prime number is an integer which has no factors other than itself and 1. This program tests NUMBER to see if it is prime. To do this, all the integers from 2 to SQRT(NUMBER) could be checked to see if they divide exactly into NUMBER. However only half as much effort is required if only odd numbers are accepted and only odd factors are tried. Notice the use of the MOD function in two places to test for exact division. Notice also the expression SQRT(REAL(NUMBER)). To write SQRT(NUMBER) would be illegal:

```
C TEST A NUMBER TO SEE IF IT IS PRIME
C INSIST ON AN ODD NUMBER GREATER THAN 3
C     10 PRINT*,'ENTER AN ODD NUMBER GREATER THAN 3'
      READ*,NUMBER
      IF ((NUMBER.LE.3).OR.(MOD(NUMBER,2).EQ.0)) GO TO 10
C TEST FOR ALL ODD FACTORS UP TO SQRT(NUMBER)
      ITEST=3
      MAX=SQRT(REAL(NUMBER+1))
   20 IF (MOD(NUMBER,ITEST).EQ.0) GO TO 30
      ITEST=ITEST+2
      IF(ITEST.LT.MAX) GO TO 20
C IF WE GET TO HERE, NO FACTOR HAS BEEN FOUND
      PRINT*,NUMBER,' IS A PRIME'
      GO TO 10
C WE JUMP TO HERE WHEN A FACTOR IS FOUND
   30 PRINT*,NUMBER,' IS NOT A PRIME'
      PRINT*,'ITS SMALLEST FACTOR IS ',ITEST
      GO TO 10
      END
```

Exercise Find all the prime factors of a number. If a factor is repeated, you should find it more than once. This problem is best done by reducing the number each time a factor is found, and then starting to test it all over again.

3 Why not count with reals?

Because a real value is an approximation, that's why. The computer does not necessarily get the exact result when you do real arithmetic. Here are two programs. They are both expected to repeat a counting loop 10 times. One of them probably will, but the other probably won't:

```
C THIS MIGHT QUIT EARLY          C THIS MAY LOOP TOO OFTEN
      X=Ø.1                             X=Ø.Ø
  1Ø PRINT*,X                       1Ø X=X+Ø.1
      X=X+Ø.1                           PRINT*,X
      IF(X.LE.1.)GO TO 1Ø               IF(X.LE.1.)GO TO 1Ø
      END                               END
```

This is because the value of 0.1 is not exact in your computer. If it is too large, the program on the left will fail to print the value 1.0. If the value of 0.1 is too small, the program on the right will produce an extra value, 1.1.

This is why we never count with reals: You can never rely on a real value to be exact!

The only safe way to make a real counter is to count with an integer and generate the desired real value from it:

```
C THIS WILL LOOP 1Ø TIMES
      I=1
  1Ø X=REAL(I)/1Ø.Ø
      PRINT*,X
      I=I+1
      IF(I.LE.1Ø) GO TO 1Ø
      END
```

4 Test after (REPEAT)

All the loops we have seen in this text so far have the test for stopping applied at the end, which can be described by the repeat .. until pseudocode structure:

repeat
    some statements
until *some condition*

Unfortunately, FORTRAN 77 does not have an explicit implementation of this structure so we have to simulate it. The FORTRAN version is:

    labelled statement
        some statements
  IF (**.NOT.** *some condition*) **GO TO** *label*

In the test that terminates the loop, we always write the opposite of the condition used in the pseudocode description. Of course we do not usually use the .NOT. to express this.

Example In the program earlier in this chapter which tested to see if a number was prime, we used this structure:

repeat

    request a number

until (number is odd) or (number < 3)

In FORTRAN this was

```
C INSIST ON AN ODD NUMBER GREATER THAN 3
   1Ø PRINT*,'ENTER AN ODD NUMBER GREATER THAN 3'
      READ*,NUMBER
      IF ((NUMBER.LE.3).OR.(MOD(NUMBER,2).EQ.Ø)) GO TO 1Ø
```

5 Test before (WHILE)

Sometimes it is better to test a loop at the beginning. The pseudocode for this is:

    while *condition* do

        some statements

    end while

The FORTRAN model is more awkward and so less likely to be used:

start label   **IF(.NOT.** *condition*) **GO TO** *final label*

                    some statements

              GO TO *start label*

final label   *final statement*

              program carries on

Example The while structure is a useful way of expressing the computation of a factorial if we wish to include the calculation of factorial zero. In pseudocode, this is the requirement:

    factorial=1

    counter=number

    while counter > 0 do

        factorial=factorial*counter

        counter=counter-1

    end while

which we can implement in FORTRAN as:

```
C FORM THE PRODUCT 1*2* ... *NUMBER
      NFACT=1
      I=NUMBER
   2Ø IF(I.LE.Ø) GO TO 3Ø
         NFACT=NFACT*I
         I=I-1
         GO TO 2Ø
   3Ø PRINT*,' THE FACTORIAL OF ',NUMBER,' IS ',NFACT
```

6 Automatic counting—the DO and CONTINUE statements

Until now we have been counting the hard way, using IF and GO TO statements to simulate the repeat and while constructions. Because so many calculations involve counting, all languages have special structures to meake it easier for you. In FORTRAN, you can count to 10 by saying:

```
C COUNT TO TEN WITH DO
      DO 5 I=1,1Ø
         PRINT*,'NEXT IS ',I
    5 CONTINUE
      END
```

The DO statement

> **DO** *label variable* = *start*, *finish*
> *statements*
> *label final statement*

causes all the statements between the DO and the *final statement* to be repeated. The index *variable* takes all the values from the expression *start* and increases in steps of 1 until it exceeds the final value *finish*. Not all statements qualify as the *final statement* of a DO loop—most of the control statements are banned. Rather than memorize the forbidden ones, use the CONTINUE statement, which does nothing except provide you with a handy place for a label:

[*label*] **CONTINUE**

You can have other steps than 1 by including the optional *increment* in the DO statement:

DO *label variable* = *start*, *finish* [, *increment*]

Example In the prime number example, we wished to try dividing the given number by all the odd numbers from 3 to SQRT(number). We can easily do this with a DO loop:

```
C TEST FOR ALL ODD FACTORS UP TO SQRT(NUMBER)
      DO 2Ø ITEST = 3, SQRT(REAL(NUMBER+1)), 2
         IF (MOD(NUMBER,ITEST).EQ.Ø) GO TO 3Ø
   2Ø CONTINUE
C IF WE GET TO HERE, NO FACTOR HAS BEEN FOUND
```

7 How the DO loop works

You might think that is obvious. Well it isn't. Consider these two loops:

```
C COUNT TO TEN WITH DO              C SO WHAT DOES THIS DO
      DO 5 I=1,1Ø                         DO 5 I=1Ø,1
         PRINT*,'NEXT IS ',I                 PRINT*,'NEXT IS ',I
    5 CONTINUE                          5 CONTINUE
      END                                 END
```

We know what the one on the left does. So what about the one on the right? Is a DO loop tested at the end like the repeat structure, or is it like while which is tested at the beginning?

Well, most versions of FORTRAN IV would have treated this like repeat. In the example on the right, FORTRAN IV would probably have executed the loop once. However FORTRAN 77 is most definitely like a while. A FORTRAN 77 program will not execute the loop on the right at all. So much for compatibility. The best way to understand a FORTRAN 77 loop is to consider how it actually works. In the DO statement

> **DO** *label variable* = *start*, *finish* [, *increment*]

the *variable* can be either real, integer or double precision (Chapter 19). The values *start*, *finish* and *increment* can be expressions of any of these types, but after evaluation they are converted to the type of the DO *variable*.

The number of times the loop will be repeated is determined before the loop commences, as

MAX ((*finish – start + increment*) / *increment* , 0)

and held in a secret integer variable which you cannot alter, so don't bother to try. The *increment* is also copied into a secret place. Fooling around with *start, finish* or *increment* within the loop will not change the number of times the loop is repeated.

You are also not permitted to alter the value of the DO *variable* inside the loop. At the end of the loop it is incremented for you, by adding on the secret *increment*.

8 Adding up—summation and recurrence

A most important use of loops is in organizing the calculation of a sum. The DO loop takes care of the counting, but to add up anything more complicated, your program has to do all the work. As with counting, you use a variable for summing—set its initial value before the loop, and accumulate the sum in the loop.

Example Sum the numbers from 1 to n. This predicts how many presents will arrive on the nth day of Christmas:

```
      PRINT*,'THIS PROGRAM SUMS THE NUMBERS FROM'
      PRINT*,'1 TO THE LIMIT YOU ENTER.'
      PRINT*
   10 PRINT*,'ENTER INTEGER LIMIT .GT. Ø'
      READ*,LIMIT
      IF(LIMIT.LT.1) GO TO 10
C INITIALIZE THE SUMMING VARIABLE
      ISUM=1
C THEN CARRY OUT THE SUMMATION
      DO 20 K=2,LIMIT
         ISUM=ISUM+K
   20 CONTINUE
      PRINT*,' THE SUM IS ',ISUM
      END
```

Computer people use some fancy words. A process which loops is said to be *iterating*. If it builds on the same values as it iterates, it is called a *recurrence*. (A *recursion* is different again, although they are often confused. I deal with recursion in Chapter 14.) Counting is a recurrence, because it increments a variable. In the program

```
C COUNT TO TEN MARK I
      ICOUNT=1
   10 PRINT*,'NEXT IS ',ICOUNT
      ICOUNT=ICOUNT+1
      IF(ICOUNT.LE.1Ø) GO TO 10
      END
```

a recurrence relationship exists which describes the effect of the recurrence on ICOUNT between a stage $k-1$ and its successor k:

$$ICOUNT_k = ICOUNT_{k-1} + 1$$

Similarly , the sum of numbers from 1 to LIMIT uses a recurrence:

$$\text{ISUM}_k = \text{ISUM}_{k-1} + k$$

Example Recurrence is sometimes a very efficient thing to do, as it can save many steps in a calculation. For example, the power series

$$e^x = 1 + x + x^2/2 + x^3/3! + \dots$$

can be evaluated by following the definition blindly. We are doing a recurrence in evaluating the sum:

$$\text{sum}_k = \text{sum}_{k-1} + \text{term}_k$$

as in this program fragment to evaluate ESUM as a sum of ten terms:

```
C INITIALIZE THE SUM
      ESUM=1.Ø
      DO 1Ø K=1,1Ø
C COMPUTE THE FACTORIAL IN A LOOP
      FACTK=1.Ø
      DO 2Ø L=1,K
        FACTK=FACTK*L
  2Ø    CONTINUE
      POWX=X**K
      TERM=POWX/FACTK
      ESUM=ESUM+TERM
  1Ø CONTINUE
      END
```

Notice that this program puts a loop to evaluate a factorial inside the one which counts the ten terms of the power series. There is nothing wrong with using 'nested loops' in a FORTRAN 77 program, but in this one it is a silly thing to do. The calculation of a fresh factorial for each term is unnecessary and also dangerous.

Look at a term of the sum. To make it, we are dividing a huge power by a huge factorial, even though the term itself is probably not very large. If we have to use a lot of terms, we could get into trouble, particularly with the large factorial. Fortunately, there is a very nice relationship between a term and its predecessor to keep us out of trouble:

$$\text{term}_k = \text{term}_{k-1} * x / k$$

if we call term_k the one which contains x^k. This is how to evaluate this power series:

```
C QUITE SMART SUM OF POWER SERIES FOR EXP(X)
      PRINT*,'ENTER X TO GET POWER SERIES FOR EXP(X)'
      READ*,X
C INITIALIZE THE SUM AND TERM
      ESUM=1.Ø
      TERM=1.Ø
      DO 1Ø K=1,1Ø
C COMPUTE THE NEW TERM FROM THE PREVIOUS ONE
      TERM=TERM*X/K
      ESUM=ESUM+TERM
      PRINT *,'TERM NUMBER ',K
      PRINT*,'    FACTORIAL = ',FACTK
      PRINT*,'    POWER OF X = ',POWX
```

```
        PRINT*,'          TERM = ',TERM
        PRINT*,'          SUM  = ',ESUM
   10 CONTINUE
      END
```

Exercise If you select r items from a choice of n, the number of different combinations you can get is called $_nC_r$, which you can find by the formula

$$_nC_r = \frac{n!}{r!\ (n\text{-}r)!}$$

which is full of factorials. There are a number of ways of working this out without ever computing a factorial or getting big numbers. The result is always an integer, so work entirely in integers. Go for it.

9 About efficiency

Good programmers try to write legibile, concise and efficient code. With experience it is possible to achieve all three at once. With inexperience, you may become obsessed with one of these objectives. Please do not make your programs either overlong or incomprehensible just because I am about to emphasize the importance of efficiency.

Programs containing loops probably spend most of their time in repeated calculations. The optimization of loops is the best way of making programs run faster, assuming the algorithm being used is the correct one. One approach can be the use of sensible recurrence relationships, as discussed in the previous section. Another optimization that is helpful in making loops faster is to remove calculations that are the same every time around. I present here an example of this process. If you are not familiar with the Fourier series, do not worry because it is the method of optimizing the program that matters, not the mathematics behind the example.

The little program which follows is intended to compute a Fourier series coefficient according to the formula

$$a_n = 2/M \sum_{k=0}^{M-1} f(x_k)\ \cos(2nk\pi/M)$$

using M values of function $f(x_k)$ which is a little 'ramp' defined by

$$f(x_k) = 2k/(M\text{-}1)$$

This program is more or less a literal translation of the formula:

```
C FOURIER COSINE COMPONENT A(N) OF M TERM SAWTOOTH
        PRINT*,'COMPUTES FOURIER COSINE COEFFICIENT OF'
        PRINT*,'A SAWTOOTH WAVE WHICH REPEATS EVERY M SAMPLES'
        PRINT*
        PRINT*,'ENTER NUMBER OF SAMPLES IN PERIOD, M'
        READ*,M
   10 PRINT*,'ENTER DESIRED COSINE COEFFICIENT, N'
        READ*,N
C DO THE FOURIER SUMMATION
        AN=Ø.Ø
        DO 2Ø K=Ø,M-1
          ANGLE=(4.Ø*ATAN(1.Ø)*N*K)*2.Ø/M
```

```
      FK=(2.Ø/M)*K-1.Ø
      AN=AN+FK*COS(ANGLE)*2.Ø/M
 2Ø CONTINUE
      PRINT*,'COEFFICIENT IS ',AN
      PRINT*
      GO TO 1Ø
      END
```

The loop that does the summation is inefficient because it repeats identical or 'invariant' calculations each time through. The worst feature is the way that the ATAN function is used every time to find the value of π. In fact the only item that varies in that statement is the value of K. The rest of it can be computed before the loop. Also, the multiplier 2/M is used in three different statements, which is wasteful. Furthermore, every time M and K are used they are converted from integer to real. Finally, every term that is used in the sum is multiplied by 2/M, so we should multiply the sum by 2/M after the loop. With all the redundant operations removed from the loop, we would have this replacement:

```
C DO THE FOURIER SUMMATION
      X2M=2.Ø/M
      ANGLE=X2M*N*4.Ø*ATAN(1.Ø)
      SUM=Ø.Ø
      DO 2Ø K=Ø,M-1
        XK=K
        FK=X2M*XK-1.Ø
        SUM=SUM+FK*COS(XK*ANGLE)
 2Ø CONTINUE
      AN=SUM*X2M
```

Exercise Actually there is a recurrence by which $\cos(2nk\pi/M)$ can be computed from $\cos(2n(k-1)\pi/M)$. Discover and implement it.

10 Nesting structures

In the inefficient power series for EXP(X), I used a nested loop structure, in which one DO loop appeared entirely inside another. Any number of loops can be used in a program as long as they do not cross over each other—in other words they have to be entirely inside one another, or entirely outside one another. If they are inside, they can share the same terminating statement, although it is better style if they do not.

Example This program finds all the primes less than 100 by putting the test for primeness into an outer loop:

```
C FIND ALL PRIMES FROM 1 TO 1ØØ
      PRINT*,'HERE ARE THE PRIMES FROM 1 TO 1ØØ'
C WE KNOW THE FIRST FEW
      PRINT*,1
      PRINT*,2
C NOW TRY ALL THE ODD NUMBERS FROM 3 ONWARDS
      DO 2Ø ITRY=3,99,2
C BY TESTING ALL THE ODD NUMBERS FROM 3 TO SQRT(ITRY)
        DO 1Ø ITEST=3,SQRT(REAL(ITRY)),2
```

```
        IF (MOD (ITRY, ITEST) .EQ.Ø) GO TO 2Ø
   1Ø   CONTINUE
C IF WE COME TO HERE, ITRY IS PRIME
        PRINT*, ITRY
   2Ø CONTINUE
     END
```

You will recall that there were also nesting rules which prevented IF or ELSE blocks from cross-ing over. In general, the block of an IF or an ELSE, and the statements in a DO loop (includ-ing the terminating statement) form blocks which must not overlap. Either they are completely separate, or they are completely enclosed by one another. In addition, a GO TO statement may leave one of these blocks, but a GO TO statement may not jump into one of these blocks. This is common sense—when you jump into the middle of a block, how is the computer supposed to know what to do when it gets to the end of it?

11 Problems

Problem 8.1 In 1202 the mathematician Fibonacci solved the problem of how many pairs of rabbits can be produced from a single pair after k breeding cycles by proposing the series

0, 1, 1, 2, 3, 5, 8 ...

in which it is assumed that a pair born at cycle k does not breed until cycle $k+2$, but then produces another pair in every cycle thereafter (Fibonacci rabbits are long lived). The series is

$$F_k = F_{k-1} + F_{k-2}$$

Write a program to evaluate it.

Problem 8.2 All the factors (prime or otherwise) of a 'perfect number' add up to the number itself, for example

$$6 = 1 + 2 + 3 \qquad 28 = 1 + 2 + 4 + 7 + 14$$

Euclid spoiled a lot of fun by giving a formula for all the even ones. Find some odd perfect numbers.

Problem 8.3 Using loops, find all right angled triangles with integer sides of length <1000.

Problem 8.4 The power series expansions of some common functions are surprisingly effi-cient, while others are surprisingly inefficient. Most can be evaluated using recurrence. Write programs to evaluate:

$$\ln(1 + x) = x - x^2/2 + x^3/3 - x^4/4 + \dots$$
$$\sin x = x - x^3/3! + x^5/5! - x^7/7! + \dots$$
$$\cos x = 1 - x^2/2 + x^4/4 - x^6/6 + \dots$$

Which of these are efficient and which are inefficient? Do the recurrence relationships give any guidance in estimating the residual errors after n terms, or the expected rate of convergence? Would you use any of them if you had to write your own mathematical functions to find results to 6 decimal places?

Nine

Structured Programming

1 Yes you can

This Chapter is about the organization of well-structured programs. We already know a great deal about the program control statements and the structures that can be created using them. The critics say that structured programming is not possible in FORTRAN. They are wrong. I have been emphasizing good program structure and the means of achieving it in FORTRAN from the very beginning of this course.

The basic idea behind structured programming is that any program, however complex, should be written so that it can be read and understood by a human who starts at the beginning and follows it through from top to bottom. Computer scientists have identified a fundamental set of control structures which make this possible. No computer language yet invented reads like a novel by Dickens, but by following certain principles we can make programs more intelligible. An obvious feature of a well-structured program is that it does not contain a lot of jumps from here to there. In other words the GO TO statement is used sparingly, if at all.

The critics have a point, because the ideal control structures are not present in FORTRAN 77, and a GO TO statement is often necessary to implement a structure. That is why we have used pseudocode to express some control structures for loops.

2 One by one

The simplest structure occurs when a series of operations are carried out one after the other, in sequence. A FORTRAN program is obeyed in the order that the statements occur, and so a series of statements with no branching or jumping forms a sequence. A tidy sequence of operations makes a program readable, and is ruined by any unnecessary jumping around. If you find that an identical process is being used in various places, and is more than a few statements long, do not start jumping around. Later, you can consider making it a FUNCTION subprogram, as described in Chapter 10, or a SUBROUTINE subprogram, as described in Chapter 11.

Example Suppose we intend to evaluate the binomial coefficient $_nC_r$, which is the number of combinations of n things taken r at a time:

$$_nC_r = n! / \{ n! (n\text{-}r)! \}$$

To demonstrate, I will use the obvious method of computing the result. There are safer and more efficient ways which you may know already if you did the $_nC_r$ exercise in the previous chapter. I hope you structured it well! The obvious method can be expressed in pseudocode:

> Evaluate n !
> Evaluate r !
> Evaluate $(n\text{-}r)$!
> Combine the results to form $_nC_r$

The following is a well-structured program fragment to do this:

```
C EVALUATE NCR FROM PREDEFINED N = IN AND  R = IR.
C
C FIRST GET THE FACTORIAL OF IN
      IFACN=1
      DO 10 K=2,IN
         IFACN=IFACN*K
   10 CONTINUE
C SECOND THE FACTORIAL OF IR
      IFACR=1
      DO 20 K=2,IR
         IFACR=IFACR*K
   20 CONTINUE
C THIRD THE FACTORIAL OF (IN-IR)
      IFACNR=1
      DO 30 K=2,IN-IR
         IFACNR=IFACNR*K
   30 CONTINUE
C FINALLY MAKE THE ANSWER NCR
      NCR=IFACN/(IFACR*IFACNR)
```

It is well-structured because it does one thing at a time, and we can follow its steps easily. In the next chapter we will find that we can write our own functions, and we can then avoid repeated code and still have a nice sequential structure:

```
C EVALUATE NCR FROM PREDEFINED N = IN AND  R = IR.
C
C FIRST GET THE FACTORIAL OF IN
      IFACN=IFACT(IN)
C SECOND THE FACTORIAL OF IR
      IFACR=IFACT(IR)
C THIRD THE FACTORIAL OF (IN-IR)
      IFACNR=IFACT(IN-IR)
C FINALLY MAKE THE ANSWER NCR
      NCR=IFACN/(IFACR*IFACNR)
```

You will find the function IFACT used as an illustration in the next chapter, and also a superb function for $_nC_r$.

Most people of any experience would, of course, have seen the need for a function immediately in this example. Naturally enough, the computation reduces to:

```
C EVALUATE NCR FROM PREDEFINED N = IN AND  R = IR.
      NCR=IFACT(IN)/(IFACT(IR)*IFACT(IN-IR))
```

which still is not the best solution.

Exercise Examine the formula for $_nC_r$ and you will see that some of the multiplications are common to the numerator and denominator. You can write it out in sequential form using only two loops. Do it.

3 To do or not to do

The elementary sequential structure of a program can be altered by a number of control state-ments. One of the most common is a decision to be taken using an IF statement. With it, a series of operations can be made dependent on some condition. Therefore in pseudocode we can define a conditional structure:

>   if *condition* then do *some process*

Notice that the pseudocode in this case resembles FORTRAN very closely. My personal preference for a conditional structure lies very close to what is actually done in FORTRAN.

A straightforward logical IF statement in FORTRAN covers the special case where the condi-tional process can be expressed by one statement. For example, suppose XMAX is to be the greater of X1 or X2. We could write:

```
    XMAX=X1
    IF (XMAX.GT.X2) XMAX=X2
```

Very often the conditional process involves a series of steps. For this we use the block IF state-ment, as in one of the mid value programs in Chapter 7:

```
C PERHAPS J IS LESS THAN I
      IF (J.LT.I) THEN
         ISAVE=J
         J=I
         I=ISAVE
      END IF
```

4 Tweedle this or tweedle that

It is fashionable to criticize the structures of FORTRAN 77, but the block IF, with or without ELSE is as good as you will find in any language. If you wish to select from one of two alter-natives, then the basic structure is

>   if *condition* then
>   *true process*
>   else
>   *false process*
>   end if

For example, from Chapter 7:

```
C SELECT WHICH SIDE THE MIDPOINT IS ON
C        IF (FMID.EQ.SIGN(FMID,FX1)) THEN
C ON THE X1 SIDE, REPLACE X1
         PRINT*,'THE MIDPOINT REPLACES X1'
         X1=XMID
         FX1=FMID
      ELSE
C ON THE X2 SIDE, REPLACE X2
         PRINT*,'THE MIDPOINT REPLACES X2'
         X2=XMID
         FX2=FMID
      END IF
```

5 Make a choice

Moving on from a choice between two alternatives, we may want to choose one course of action from a number of alternatives. FORTRAN 77 does not have the so-called case structure, which we could express by the pseudocode:

> case *expression* from
>> choose *choice*
>>> *process*
>> end choice
>> choose *choice*
>>> *process*
>> end choice
>> and so on . . .
> end case

However, a series of IF and ELSE IF blocks does the job very nicely.

Example This program tells you which of the London telephone directories to find the letter LETTER in. LETTER, L1 and L2 are variables of type CHARACTER and you will have to wait for Chapter 18 to find out all about using them:

```
IF(LETTER.GE.'A'.AND.LETTER.LE.'D') THEN
  L1='A'
  L2='D'
ELSE IF (LETTER.GE.'E'.AND.LETTER.LE.'K') THEN
  L1='E'
  L2='K'
ELSE IF (LETTER.GE.'L'.AND.LETTER.LE.'R') THEN
  L1='L'
  L2='R'
ELSE
  L1='S'
  L2='Z'
END IF
PRINT*,'USE THE ',L1,' TO ',L2,' DIRECTORY'
```

6 Over and over

The previous chapter introduced three structures for iteration, the while, repeat and counting DO loop. The while structure decides at the beginning whether a process is to be carried out:

> while *condition* do
>> *process*
> end while

In FORTRAN we need to use GO TO to achieve this, as we did when finding a factorial in Chapter 8:

```
C FORM THE PRODUCT 1*2* ... *NUMBER
      NFACT=1
      I=NUMBER
   2Ø IF(I.LE.Ø) GO TO 3Ø
```

```
      NFACT=NFACT*I
      I=I-1
      GO TO 20
   30 CONTINUE
```

The repeat structure will always carry out a process once because it tests the condition afterwards:

repeat
>   *process*
until *condition*

Again in FORTRAN a GO TO is required to construct the repeat loop. This is how to insist that correct data is entered to a program:

```
   10 PRINT*,' ENTER AN INTEGER .GE. 0'
      READ*,NUMBER
      IF(NUMBER.LT.0) GO TO 10
```

A counting loop is established by the DO statement:

>   DO *label variable* = *start, finish* [*, increment*]
>   *some statements*
label   final statement

as we did in testing for prime numbers, from Chapter 8:

```
C TEST FOR ALL ODD FACTORS UP TO SQRT(NUMBER)
      DO 20 ITEST = 3, SQRT(REAL(NUMBER+1)), 2
         IF (MOD(NUMBER,ITEST).EQ.0) GO TO 30
   20 CONTINUE
```

The GO TO statement in this example escapes from the loop—which is a legitimate use of GO TO, one that is also necessary in the Pascal language. It is important to remember that the DO loop is like the while structure. The process in the loop may not be carried out at all, depending on the value of start compared with finish, and taking the sign of increment into account.

7 We're stuck with GO TO

Some computer scientists have been known to refer to structured programming as programming without GO TO. In FORTRAN the GO TO statement should only be used to simulate a respectable program control structure, such as the repeat or while constructions.

In practice there are a few situations where a GO TO is not as bad as all that. A GO TO is useful to escape from a DO loop or IF block to somewhere further down the program. It should then never transfer in an upwards direction against the flow of the program except where a repeat construction is being simulated. This permissible use is illustrated in the program to find all the primes from 1 to 100, at the end of the previous chapter. Arguably, even the GO TO statement in that program could be eliminated.

Throughout this book, the preferred structures are used, and the GO TO is only used to simulate them or to escape from a loop. In your FORTRAN career, try to do the same.

Exercise Eliminate the GO TO statement from the prime number example. Make sure that it works. Do you prefer it with or without the dreaded GO TO?

8 An actual calculation—developing real programs

Now we can undertake a serious calculation, and at the same time illustrate the program development process, in which we design, implement, test and apply a program, not forgetting to document it carefully.

Suppose a real distinct root is sought of an equation

$$f(x)=0$$

We are going to use the method of successive approximation, in which we begin with initial guesses of x which enclose the solution, and zoom in on the answer by halving the interval between our guesses each time. If the guesses are x_1 and x_2 as in Fig. 9.1, and we know that $f(x_1)$ has the opposite sign to $f(x_2)$, then we divide the interval from x_1 to x_2 in two by finding the midpoint, $xmid$:

$$xmid = (x_1 + x_2) / 2$$

By inspecting the sign of $f(xmid)$, we know which half of the interval to look at further. If the sign of $f(xmid)$ is the same as the sign of $f(x_1)$, then we can select the interval from $xmid$ to x_2 as the target zone. We replace the value of x_1 by $xmid$, and do it all again. Similarly if the target zone is from x_1 to $xmid$, the sign of $f(xmid)$ is the same as the sign of $f(x_2)$ and we proceed by replacing x_2 by $xmid$.

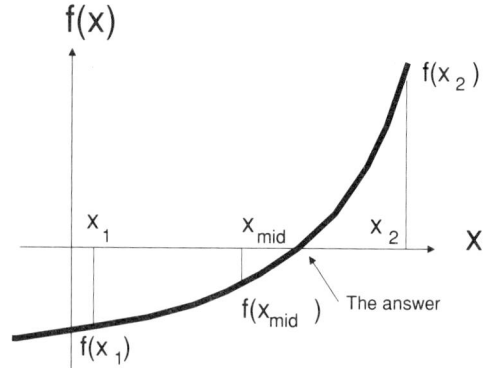

Fig. 9.1. Finding a root by successive approximation.

In a computer program, therefore, the steps are:

(i) Establish the initial guesses x_1 and x_2 so that $f(x_1)$ and $f(x_2)$ have opposite sign.

(ii) Calculate $xmid$, and evaluate $f(xmid)$.

(iii) Replace one of x_1 or x_2 by xmid, depending on the sign of $f(xmid)$.

(iv) Return to step (ii) if further improvement is required.

The diagram in Fig. 9.2 is an outline flowchart which describes the process graphically. I have more to say about flowcharts a bit later.

In order to realize this process in a FORTRAN program, we elaborate on the details.

(i) Initial guesses

We should choose x_1 and x_2 so that $f(x_1)$ and $f(x_2)$ are of opposite sign. Assuming this is an interactive program, we will prompt the user until this condition is met. We could describe this by the 'pseudocode':

repeat
    prompt the user for x_1 and x_2
    work out $f(x_1)$ and $f(x_2)$
until sign of $f(x_1)$ is different from sign of $f(x_2)$

Let us think carefully how we will decide when the signs are different. You could do this with a number of IF statements, but I prefer a particular use of the SIGN function. This logical expression is .TRUE. when the signs are the same:

$f(x_1).EQ.SIGN(f(x_1),f(x_2))$

(ii) Calculate the midpoint of the interval x_1 to x_2

$xmid = (x_1 + x_2) / 2$

We also want the sign of f(*xmid*). At this point in the program we will want to follow the progress of the calculation, at least while we are testing it, so I will include some printing.

(iii) Replace x_1 or x_2 by *xmid*

We can make the same use of the SIGN function, to check if f(*xmid*) has the same sign as f(x_1). If it does, replace x_1. Otherwise replace x_2. This is a structure in which we choose from two alternative blocks, as supported by the IF. . . THEN with ELSE facility. This is the only tricky bit. Be sure you understand it. In pseudocode

```
if sign of f(x₁) = sign of f(xmid) then
        replace x₁ by xmid
        update f(x₁)
else
        replace x₂ by xmid
        update f(x₂)
end if
```

(iv) Is further improvement desired?

We must decide when to be satisfied with the answer. Sometimes this is a complicated question. In this program I duck the issue by comparing abs($x_2 - x_1$) with a variable *small* which is given a suitable initial value. When we are satisfied, we print the answer and stop. The pseudocode for the whole problem is then:

```
begin
    set small
    repeat
            prompt the user for x₁ and x₂
            work out f(x₁) and f(x₂)
    until sign of f(x₁) is different from sign of f(x₂)
```

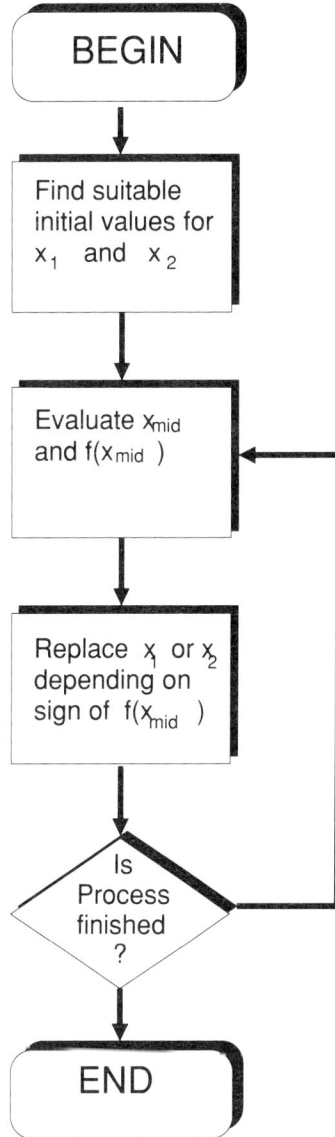

Fig. 9.2. Outline flowchart for the method of successive approximation.

> repeat
>> compute *xmid* and f(*xmid*)
>> print some results
>> if sign of f(*x₁*) = sign of f(*xmid*) then
>>> replace *x₁* by *xmid* and update f(*x₁*)
>> else
>>> replace *x₂* by *xmid* and update f(*x₂*)
>> end if
> until abs(*x₂* − *x₁*) *small*
> print the result
end

Supposing finally that the function is $f(x) = x^3 - 7.8\,x^2 + 18.5\,x - 9.1$, I can now easily write the program out in FORTRAN. It is best to pick variable names that relate to the meaning of the values they represent. With a limit of six letters in a FORTRAN name, this is not always easy, but we should try. In this example I select the obvious:

X1 for x_1 and FX1 for f(x_1)   X2 for x_2 and FX2 for f(x_2)
XMID for the midvalue of x_1 and x_2,   FMID for f(XMID)
SMALL for the acceptable interval between x_1 and x_2 which will stop the calculation.

Here it is. Note particularly how GO TO is necessary in the implementation of the structure which was expressed as repeat..until in the design:

```
C SOLVE AN EQUATION BY SUCCESSIVE APPROXIMATION
C
C SET SMALL HERE - THE PRECISION REQUIRED IN X
      SMALL=1E-5
C FIRST GET GUESSES OF OPPOSITE SIGN
      PRINT*,'TO SOLVE X**3 - 7.8 X**2 + 18.5 X - 9.1,'
      PRINT*,'ENTER X1, X2 WHICH ARE TWO GUESSES OF F(X)=Ø'
      PRINT*
      PRINT*,'F(X1) AND F(X2) SHOULD BE OF OPPOSITE SIGN'
   1Ø READ*,X1,X2
      FX1=((X1-7.8)*X1+18.5)*X1-9.1
      FX2=((X2-7.8)*X2+18.5)*X2-9.1
      PRINT*,'AT X1 = ',X1,' F(X) IS ',FX1
      PRINT*,'AT X2 = ',X2,' F(X) IS ',FX2
C IF THESE GIVE THE SAME SIGN, TRY AGAIN
      IF(FX1.EQ.SIGN(FX1,FX2)) THEN
         PRINT*,'THE SIGNS OF F(X) ARE THE SAME. TRY AGAIN.'
         GO TO 1Ø
      END IF
C FIND THE MIDPOINT BETWEEN X1 AND X2, AND COMPUTE F(X) THERE
   2Ø PRINT'(1X,5Ø(''*''))'
      PRINT*
      XMID=(X1+X2)/2.Ø
      FMID=((XMID-7.8)*XMID+18.5)*XMID-9.1
      PRINT*,'AT THE MIDPOINT ',XMID,' F(X) IS ',FMID
```

```
C SELECT WHICH SIDE THE MIDPOINT IS ON
      IF(FMID.EQ.SIGN(FMID,FX1)) THEN
C ON THE X1 SIDE, REPLACE X1
         PRINT*,'THE MIDPOINT REPLACES X1'
         X1=XMID
         FX1=FMID
      ELSE
C ON THE X2 SIDE, REPLACE X2
         PRINT*,'THE MIDPOINT REPLACES X2'
         X2=XMID
         FX2=FMID
      END IF
      PRINT*,'NOW WE HAVE'
      PRINT*,'AT X1 = ',X1,' F(X) IS ',FX1
      PRINT*,'AT X2 = ',X2,' F(X) IS ',FX2
C IF THE ANSWER IS NOT YET SMALL ENOUGH, GO BACK
      IF(ABS(X2-X1).GT.SMALL) GO TO 20
C ANSWER IS ACCEPTED, PRINT IT
      PRINT*
      PRINT*,'AN ACCEPTABLE ROOT IS ',XMID
      END
```

Exercise Try it. Test it thoroughly with different functions, checking the results by hand or calculator. Under what conditions will it work?

So now we have a useful piece of software. We can use it to solve equations whenever we want. In Chapter 10 we will see how to define the function separately, so that we do not have to alter the program every time a new equation is to be solved.

This section has been a model of the software development process, illustrating the same steps that we would follow in solving a much larger problem:

(i) Design—the problem was stated and analyzed. The solution was outlined and elaborated until it was ready for:

(ii) Implementation by translating the design into FORTRAN 77. Then we did:

(iii) Testing and

(iv) Application. I asked you to do that.

(v) Documentation. What's that you say? Oh yes we have. This whole section is the documentation.

Careful programmers follow similar steps in developing programs. Although errors are always possible, there will be fewer if a programmer is systematic in the development process. Although this may seem an obvious way to organize a programming task, it has been given a name: *Stepwise Refinement*. We work from the general to the particular, deciding how each part of the task is done in detail after the more general outline is known.

The most difficult part of programming occurs when a program does not work and the errors in it have to be found. They could be errors in conception, design, details, coding or (very unlikely) the computer system. The job of finding errors is the nearest programming comes to being an art rather than a craft; experience and inspiration always help. That is why I have tried to encourage you to get lots of practice.

9 Flowcharts or pseudocode

Traditionally, FORTRAN programs have been documented by using flowcharts. These are diagrams which illustrate the flow of control through a program to help us follow its structure. They are now less popular than before, because the control structures which are now thought to be fundamental to programming do not express themselves as well in flowcharts as they do in pseudocode.

Figure 9.3 illustrates some of the standard flowcharting symbols, and Fig. 9.4 is a flowchart of the program we have developed in the previous section. I leave it to you to decide whether pseudocode or flowcharts are the better form of description. Documentation of large programs ought to include one of these, or even both.

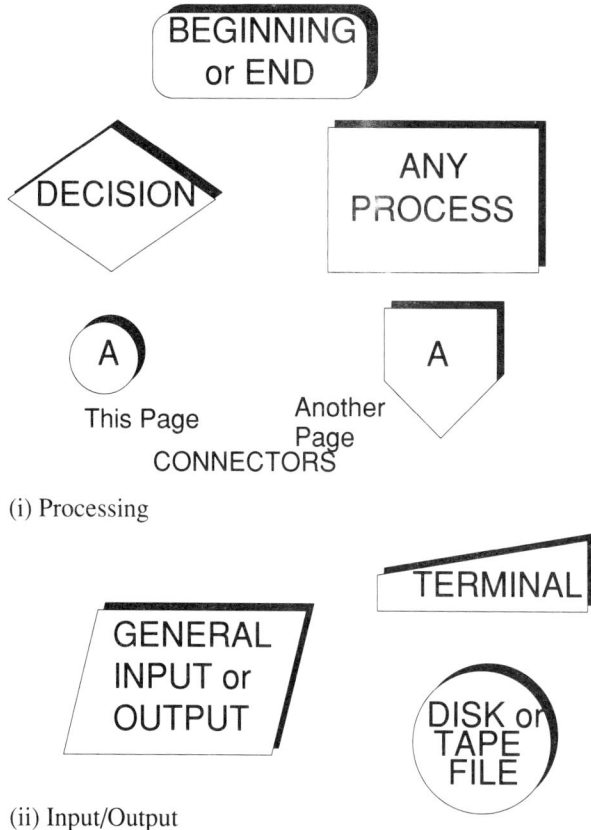

(i) Processing

(ii) Input/Output

Fig.9.3. Some standard flowchart symbols.

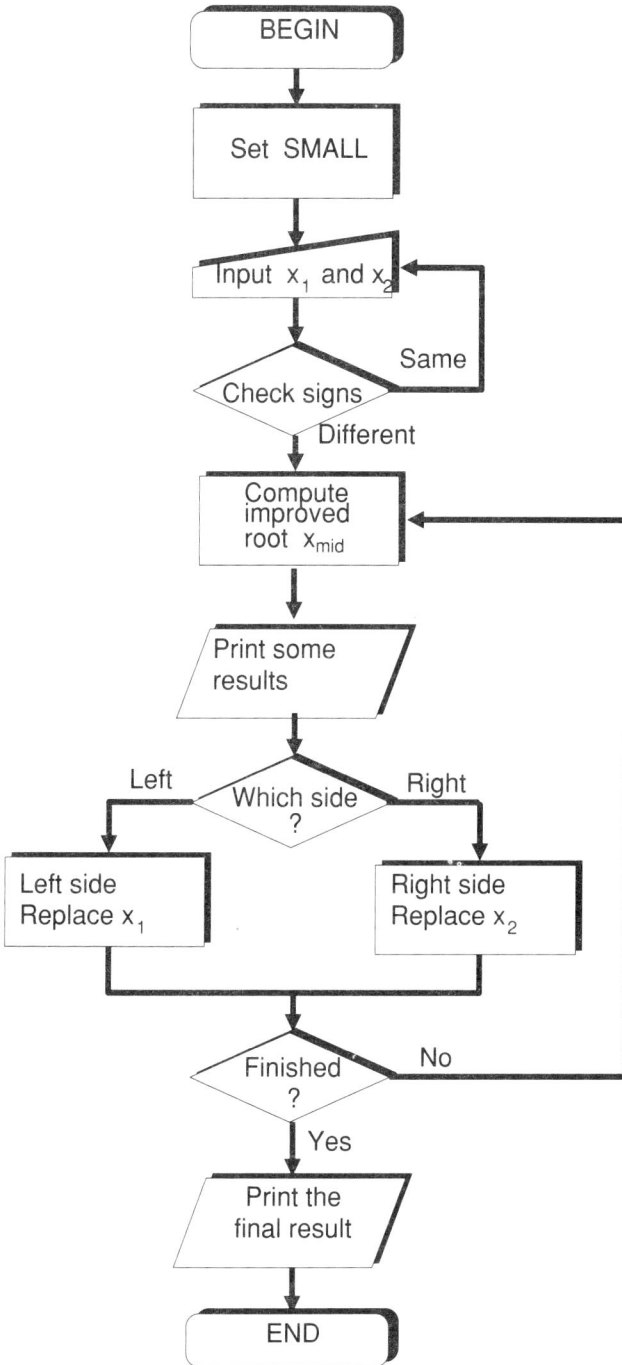

Fig. 9.4. Detailed flowchart for the method of successive approximation.

10 Problems

Problem 9.1 The basic requirement of calendar calculations is to convert back and forth between a day number relative to some time in the distant past, and the date. By doing this in various combinations some useful results can be obtained. We discussed some of this in Chapter 4. Write a calendar utility which presents your user with a number of options; displayed as a list we call this a menu.

There are any number of useful things that you could include:

1. The day of the week for a given date.

2. The number of days between two dates.

3. The date we get if we add a certain number of days to a given starting date.

4. The date of a particular occurrence of a particular weekday in a particular year or month. (For example, my running club has a handicap race around Hyde Park on the first Friday of every month. Give me the dates for 1997.)

5. Occurrences of certain combinations (for example Friday the 13th in 1492).

And so on. Use your imagination. Of course you do.

Problem 9.2 Discover the algorithm for public holidays in your country, assuming there are some. Write a program to print a calendar for any given year with the public holidays indicated in some useful way. Easter is very tricky, but the first Monday in May is easier.

Problem 9.3 The method of False Position is another way of solving equations, similar to successive approximation as programmed in this chapter. From the initial guesses x_1 and x_2 on either side of the root, we use the secant joining the function values $f(x_1)$ and $f(x_2)$ to compute where the solution would be if the function were a straight line, as in Fig. 9.5. By elementary algebra, the improved guess using this method is:

$$xmid = x_1 + f(x_1)\,(x_2 - x_1) / (f(x_2) - f(x_1))$$

Write a program to solve equations using the False Position method. Solve

(i) $x^3 - 7.8\,x^2 + 18.5\,x - 9.1 = 0$

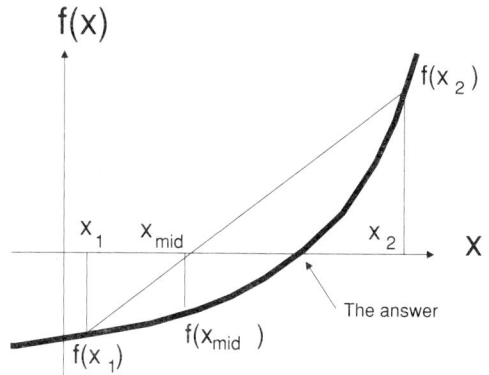

Fig. 9.5. Finding a root by the method of false position.

to check the correctness of your solution against the successive approximation program. Also solve

(ii) $\ln(x) + 1 = 0$ (the answer is of course $1/e$ or 0.3679)

(iii) $x^3 - 3x^2 + 2.5x - 0.5 = 0$ (there are three roots, all real)

Compare the speeds of convergence of the two methods, i.e. how fast they get to the answer from some reasonable starting position .

Problem 9.4 The Newton-Raphson method will converge more rapidly than either successive approximation or False Position, if it converges at all. This method requires only a single guess, x_1 and uses the slope of the function at x_1 to predict an improved root. In Fig. 9.6,

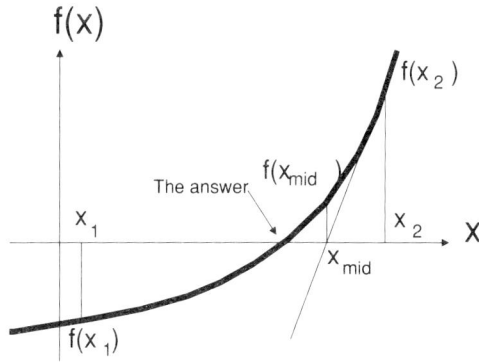

Fig. 9.6. Finding a root by the Newton-Raphson iteration.

$$x_2 = x_1 - f(x_1)/f'(x_1)$$

If you don't know how to calculate the slope, $f'(x)$, ask someone who knows more mathematics than you do to work out the formula for $f'(x)$ for you. Write a nicely structured program and solve the same three equations by this method. Investigate how fast it converges compared to the other methods. For equation (iii) investigate how the choice of initial guess affects the stability of the method (i.e. its ability to get on the right track for each root).

Problem 9.5 Don't be afraid of this one—tackle it systematically.

The speed of convergence of some numerical methods can be accelerated by a procedure known as Aitken's delta-squared extrapolation. If three successive improved estimates of a root are known, say r_1, r_2 and r_3, then a further improvement is

$$z = (r_1 r_3 - r_2^2)/(r_3 - 2r_2 + r_1)$$

This acceleration can easily be built into either of the methods of successive approximation or False Position. The complication is that r_1, r_2 and r_3 must be estimates from the same side of the root. Integer variables can be used to count how many estimates are available on each side and so the extrapolation can be used at the right point. Each time the Aitken formula is used, the improved estimate z becomes r_1 for that side of the root for the next round, and you start counting again for that side. Therefore the Aitken formula is used after the first three estimates (on a given side of the root) and then after every further two estimates on that side. The whole procedure can be added to the flow diagram of Fig. 9.4 as a simple elaboration, i.e no major change to the program structure is required.

By incorporating Aitken's extrapolation solve the same three equations again. Compare the speed of convergence and stability with the given program for successive approximation. Also compare with the programs you used in Problems 9.3 and 9.4. Which of the three would you use for tackling an unknown function? If you have done these three problems well you now have quite a useful function solving kit.

Ten

Make some functions

1 Statement functions

The FORTRAN language provides you with a number of built-in functions. However it is very likely that you will want to define some private functions to meet your own requirements. If you can express your function in a single assignment statement, then you can put it directly into your program by defining it near the beginning. However if it is complicated enough to need several statements, as is usually the case, you have to write it out as an independent program unit, as we will see in the next section. This is our first encounter with rules about the order of statements, other than END, and we will see that there are others to come.

Suppose you wanted to compute the hypotenuse of a right angled triangle whose other sides have lengths A and B. You can do this in one line by saying

```
HYP(A,B)=SQRT(A*A+B*B)
```

This defines how the computer is supposed to work out the hypotenuse when given the two values A and B. You can then say later in the program something like

```
PRINT*,'THE THREE SIDES ARE ',X,Y,HYP(X,Y)
```

or even

```
PRINT*,'THE THREE SIDES ARE ',1.Ø,1.Ø,HYP(1.Ø,1.Ø)
```

because the computer will substitute the actual values you have given in place of the variables A and B in the function definition. If you want to do this, you must put the definition of your function at the beginning of the program, before any executable statements. It waits there to be used any number of times by expressions in the executable part of your program unit:

```
C DEFINE A STATEMENT FUNCTION
      HYP(A,B)=SQRT(A*A+B*B)
C AND USE IT
      PRINT*,'THIS PROGRAM FINDS THE HYPOTENUSE'
      PRINT*,'ENTER TWO SIDES ADJACENT TO THE RIGHT ANGLE'
      READ*,X,Y
      PRINT*,'THE THREE SIDES ARE ',X,Y,HYP(X,Y)
      END
```

In general a statement function is the single line:

name (*dummy arguments*) = *expression*

The types of the function and its arguments are implied by their names in the usual way, and the type of the expression follows the rules for expressions. HYP(A,B) is a real function of two real arguments, which has a real value assigned to it. We will see in Chapters 18 and 19 that other types can be used. The arguments, separated by commas, are called 'dummy arguments' because when the function is used actual values are substituted in their place. These actual values have to match exactly with the types and order of the dummy arguments.

The names of dummy arguments are meaningful only to the statement function. In other words the 'scope' of the dummy argument is limited to the statement function definition. You can reuse the argument names elsewhere to mean other things, for example as actual variables or dummy arguments in other functions.

It is possible that other names are used in the expression which you have not given as dummy arguments. If so, they are not dummy arguments, but the names of actual values.

There is no reason why one statement function should not refer to another, but if you set up a loop of function references you are in trouble:

```
FUNCA (X) =X*FUNCB (X-1.Ø)
FUNCB (Q) =Q*FUNCA (Q-1.Ø)
```

If there is no argument at all, you must identify your name as a function, both when you define it and when you use it, by giving empty brackets for the list of arguments:

```
PIE () =4.Ø*ATAN (1.Ø)
PRINT*,'THE VALUE OF PIE IS ',PIE ()
END
```

Example Finding the middle of three values was flogged to death as an example of the diversity of approaches to an apparently simple problem. Our functional solution can be expressed in a statement function MID(I,J,K):

```
C DEFINE THE MID VALUE AS A FUNCTION
      MID (I,J,K) =MAX (MIN (I,J) ,MIN (J,K) ,MIN (K,I) )
C THE MID VALUE PROBLEM SOLVED FUNCTIONALLY
      PRINT*,'ENTER THREE INTEGERS TO FIND THE MIDDLE VALUE'
      READ*,I1,I2,I3
      PRINT*,'MID VALUE OF ',I1,I2,I3,' IS ',MID (I1,I2,I3)
      END
```

Exercise Write a statement function MYSIGN(J) which returns the value 1 if J is greater than zero, 0 if J is zero, and-1 if it is less than 0. Test it, of course.

2 A separate module—FUNCTION and RETURN

Most useful functions will involve more than one statement. In FORTRAN, you can define a separate program unit enclosed by its own FUNCTION and END statements. This is a powerful feature in FORTRAN because the FUNCTION is self-contained and can be moved from one program to another, or compiled separately and put into libraries. One of the disadvantages of the language Pascal is that separate compilation is not provided in the standard language.

The FUNCTION statement defines the name, type and dummy arguments of a function:

FUNCTION *name* (*dummy arguments*)

The type is defined as real or integer by the usual spelling convention, or you can over-ride it (not a good idea for reals and integers, but essential with the other types as we shall see in Chapters 18 and 19).

REAL FUNCTION *name* (*dummy arguments*)

A FUNCTION is a separate program unit, often called a *subprogram*, which ends with its own END statement. Within the function, we must associate the result of the function with its name, in an assignment statement:

    name = *value*

Indeed, we can use the *name* as if it were a variable within the function. Here is a function for evaluating the factorial of any integer.

```
      FUNCTION IFACT(N)
C A FUNCTION FOR FACTORIAL N
C CHECK TO SEE IF N IS LEGAL
      IF(N.LT.Ø) THEN
         PRINT*,'ILLEGAL FACTORIAL - RESULT ZERO'
         IFACT=Ø
         RETURN
      END IF
C CALCULATE THE FACTORIAL
      IFACT=1
      DO 1Ø K=2,N
         IFACT=IFACT*K
   1Ø CONTINUE
      END
```

IFACT is an integer function of an integer argument N. To use it we write references to IFACT in another program unit, providing actual values in place of the argument N:

```
C USE A FUNCTION SUBPROGRAM TO FIND A FACTORIAL
   1Ø PRINT*,'ENTER A POSITIVE INTEGER TO FIND ITS FACTORIAL'
      READ*,NUMB
      PRINT*,'THE FACTORIAL OF ',NUMB,' IS ',IFACT(NUMB)
      GO TO 1Ø
      END
```

All we have to do to make this work is arrange for the 'main' program to be able to find the function. Most of the time you will present your program units to the computer as one file, with the self-contained main program and each self-contained subprogram occurring in any order. Then when you run the program, they find one another because they are in the same file. If there are subprograms referred to but not found, the computer begins to search various libraries. How to organize libraries varies between computer systems. All computer systems will search FORTRAN's own library, which is how it finds things like SQRT and MAX. This means that you can provide your own versions of any library function by arranging for it to find your version first; usually you would do this by including your functions in the 'source' program file.

You will notice the RETURN statement in the factorial function. The termination of a function is indicated by the END statement, but you may sometimes wish to complete your function earlier. To do this you write RETURN:

    RETURN

In a main program, the END statement acts like STOP—the termination of your program.

In a subprogram, END behaves like RETURN—terminates the function (or subroutine) and carries on in the program that used it.

Example There is a safe and fast way of evaluating $_nC_r$. The key is in the recurrence:

$_nC_r = n! / \{ (n-r)! \ r! \} \ _nC_{r-1}$

Using this the result can be accumulated in one loop. Since individual factorials are not calculated, you are much less likely to the result spoiled by huge or incorrect factorials. Here is a function for combinations together with a little program for testing it. The two program units, the main program and the function, are presented to the computer exactly like this:

```
      PRINT*,'TESTING BINOMIAL COEFFICIENTS'
   1Ø PRINT*,'ENTER IN AND IR, BOTH POSITIVE INTEGERS'
      PRINT*,'IN MUST BE GREATER THAN OR EQUAL TO IR'
      READ*,I,J
      PRINT*,I,' C ',J,' IS ',NCOMBS(I,J)
      GO TO 1Ø
      END


      FUNCTION NCOMBS(IN,IR)
C A FUNCTION FOR COMBINATIONS BY D. M. MONRO
C INPUT PARAMETERS
C    IN, IR INTEGER VALUES NOT ALTERED BY SUBPROGRAM
C    THE NUMBER OF COMBINATIONS OF IN ITEMS TAKEN IR
C    AT A TIME IS COMPUTED
C OUTPUT PARAMETERS
C    THE OUTPUT VALUE IS ASSIGNED TO THE FUNCTION NCOMBS
C CHECK TO SEE IF DATA IS LEGAL
      IF(IN.LT.Ø .OR. IR.LT.Ø .OR. IN.LT.IR ) THEN
         PRINT*,'ILLEGAL DATA - RESULT ZERO'
         NCOMBS=Ø
         RETURN
      END IF
C CALCULATE THE COMBINATIONS BY RECURRENCE
      NCOMBS=1
      DO 1Ø K=1,IR
         NCOMBS=(IN-K+1)*NCOMBS/K
   1Ø CONTINUE
      END
```

Like a statement function, a FUNCTION subprogram might have no arguments at all. If so, empty brackets are required in the FUNCTION statement:

```
      FUNCTION EEUGH()
      EEUGH=EXP(1.Ø)
      END
```

In referring to a FUNCTION subprogram with no arguments, empty brackets are used:

```
      YILSL=EEUGH()**2
```

Exercise You should already know the largest integer whose factorial you can find. Alter the factorial function so that it prevents you from computing one that is too large. Similarly, find the limits on the function NCOMBS, and alter it so that it prevents you from exceeding them. Now do both functions again using reals, and deal sensibly with the available range.

3 About scope

A feature of subprograms is the way variable names are treated. The FUNCTION IFACT is a separate program unit, and all the variable names which appear as dummy arguments are given actual values by another program which uses the function. This is a shortened version:

```
      FUNCTION IFACT(N)
C A FUNCTION FOR FACTORIAL N (SHORTENED)
      IFACT=1
      DO 1Ø K=2,N
        IFACT=IFACT*K
  1Ø CONTINUE
      END
```

The dummy arguments are the only values which are shared between the function and a program which uses it. In IFACT, only N is a value from the main program. All the other names are local names whose scope is limited to IFACT. It is not possible for a name to be known everywhere, or have 'global' scope. There is a mechanism for sharing values with other program units, but it is not through their names as we will see later.

In IFACT a variable K was used, which is a private variable belonging to IFACT, unrelated to any variable K which may exist in the program which uses IFACT. This makes IFACT highly portable; you know that it will not interfere with any K used elsewhere. This is one of the strengths of FORTRAN—program units respect each other's privacy.

A FUNCTION subprogram can have statement functions inside it. If this is the case, they belong (for the present) immediately following the FUNCTION statement. Their scope is also limited to the program unit in which they are defined. Therefore to use the same statement function in a number of program units, you would have to redefine it in each program unit. It would probably be better to make it a FUNCTION subprogram, even though its definition needs only one line, because all program units in the same program file will be able to find it.

Once a name has been used for a function the same name cannot be given to a variable or to anything else in that program unit (except a COMMON block, Chapter 17).

4 Defining values—PARAMETER and DATA

Every time you have used a constant until now, you have written it out, for example:

```
      RMILES=RKILOS/1.6Ø934
```

which converts kilometres to miles. There are advantages to giving names to constants, for example in calling the conversion factor 1.60934 by the name TOMILE:

```
      PARAMETER (TOMILE=1.6Ø934)
      RMILES=RKILOS/TOMILE
```

This way it is much easier to change the value of a constant which occurs many times in the program. The PARAMETER statement allows you to give a name to a constant:

PARAMETER (*name=constant,* [*name=constant, . . .*])

Quite obviously, *name* is the name you are giving the constant and *constant* is its value, which might be a name of a constant as long as it is defined in an earlier PARAMETER statement, or even earlier in the same one. The type is implied by the spelling of the name as usual, and the constant may be converted to give you that type. An expression is not permitted.

Example

```
PARAMETER (ONE=1.Ø)
PARAMETER (X=5, PIE=3.1415926543)
PARAMETER (IONE = ONE)
```

defines ONE as the real constant 1.0, X as the real constant 5.0 (after conversion), PIE as the real constant 3.1415926543 and IONE as the integer constant 1 (after conversion).

Example Here is a function subprogram for reducing an angle ANGLE to an equivalent one in the range 0 to 2π. This is important in evaluating functions which are periodic, like sin or cos. It may take a lot of terms to evaluate the sine of a large angle by a power series, while the equivalent one has the same sine and can be evaluated in fewer terms. The subprogram is given the value of π in a PARAMETER statement. Therefore in this example PIE is a constant:

```
      FUNCTION PANGLE (ANGLE)
C A FUNCTION TO FIND THE PRINCIPAL ANGLE OF THE GIVEN
C ANGLE IN THE RANGE Ø TO 2*PIE
C THE PARAMETER STATEMENT
      PARAMETER (PIE=3.1415926543)
C A STATEMENT FUNCTION
      RMOD (X,Y)=X-Y*INT(X/Y)
C THE EXECUTABLE PROGRAM STARTS HERE
      PANGLE=RMOD (ANGLE,2.Ø*PIE)
      END
```

The DATA statement does a similar (but not identical thing) for variables. We know that variables are undefined at first, and it is an error to use them until you give them a value. Mostly we have done this with assignment or READ statements. The DATA statement allows us to give them an initial value, which is available as soon as the program commences:

DATA *names* /*constants*/ [,*names*/*constants*/,...]

as in

```
DATA ONE, IONE /1, 1/
DATA X, PIE /5, 3.1415926543/
```

Remember: PARAMETER defines constants
            DATA assigns initial values to variables

The types of the variables depend on their names, and the constants might be converted to the correct type. DATA and PARAMETER use different punctuation, which might seem strange. Committees are like that—PARAMETER was invented twenty years later than DATA.

5 Preserving values—use SAVE for safety

The DATA statement used in a subprogram presents us with an important question. Do you think that this program will count, or will it always print the value 1?

```
C MYSTERY COUNTING PROGRAM        FUNCTION NEXT ()
      DO 1Ø K=1,2Ø                 DATA INEXT /1/
        PRINT*,NEXT ()             NEXT = INEXT
  1Ø CONTINUE                      INEXT=INEXT+1
      END                          END
```

The answer is not as easy as you might think. Most FORTRAN implementations are static—when you come back to a subprogram it is likely that the values you left behind are still there, but you cannot be sure. To be certain that some named variables are preserved, write:

>   **SAVE** *names*

To save everything in sight, just write:

>   **SAVE**

Example This function will count for sure; Pascal persons please note:

```
C MYSTERY COUNTING PROGRAM          FUNCTION NEXT()
        DO 1Ø K=1,2Ø                SAVE
           PRINT*,NEXT()            DATA INEXT /1/
     1Ø CONTINUE                    NEXT = INEXT
        END                         INEXT=INEXT+1
                                    END
```

6 The order of some statements

In this chapter we have seen a number of statements which share two new properties. First of all they do not actually execute instructions themselves, and secondly they have to go in some special order near the beginning of the program. Here is a diagram which summarizes how the principal statements we know so far have to be positioned in a program unit

Comments can go anywhere before END	Heading: PROGRAM (optional) or FUNCTION or SUBROUTINE (next chapter)		
	FORMAT statements can go after heading, before END	PARAMETER or SAVE	
		DATA statements	Statement functions
			Executable Statements
END is always the very end			

As an example, look at the DATA statement. It must go after PARAMETER or SAVE, and it must go before END. Apart from that, it can go anywhere and be freely mixed with statement function definitions or executable statements. Where two kinds of statements are shown in the same box, they can be mixed, for example PARAMETER and SAVE. Where they are shown above or below others they must go in that order. There are more statements like these to come before the order of all statements is summarized in a similar way in Chapter 17.

7 Variable and value arguments—be careful

The dummy arguments of a subprogram are treated in the subprogram as if they were variables. Their values are available (if they have one) and you can alter them. In the same way you can use the name of a function as if it were a variable. This will not surprise anyone. What will surprise the Pascal people, however, is that FORTRAN has no way of checking whether an actual argument is something that can be safely altered. An actual argument can be the name of a variable (no problem), an expression (no problem, as we will see) or a constant (ouch)! Consider a nasty little function, ISUCK which computes the successor of its integer argument:

```
      FUNCTION ISUCK(I)
C DEMONSTRATES A DANGEROUS SIDE EFFECT:
C RETURNS THE SUCCESSOR OF INTEGER VARIABLE I,
C AND ALSO REPLACES I WITH ITS SUCCESSOR, I+1
      I=I+1
      ISUCK=I
      END
```

This main program is clearly not a problem:

```
C SAFELY SUCKS A VARIABLE ARGUMENT
      I=1
   10 PRINT*,'SUCCESSOR OF ',I,' IS ',ISUCK(I)
      IF (I.LE.1) PRINT*,'ZOWIE!'
      IF (I.LE.5) GO TO 10
      END
```

But what about this next one. How many times does it print zowie!? The answer is 5!

```
C INSANELY SUCKS A CONSTANT ARGUMENT
      PARAMETER (ONE=1, FIVE=5)
      I=ONE
   10 PRINT*,'SUCCESSOR OF ONE IS ',ISUCK(ONE)
      IF (I.LE.ONE) PRINT*,'ZOWIE!'
      I=I+1
      IF (I.LE.FIVE) GO TO 10
      END
```

This is because the SUCK program has altered the constant ONE. You do not have this problem if the argument is an expression, because FORTRAN works out the value and places it in a temporary memory store. This is what we mean by a 'value argument'. When the function treats this as a variable it is not harming anything. To make a constant argument safe, place an extra pair of brackets around it, transforming it into an expression. This prints zowie! once:

```
C SAFELY SUCKS A VALUE ARGUMENT
      PARAMETER (ONE=1, FIVE=5)
      I=ONE
   10 PRINT*,'SUCCESSOR OF ONE IS ',ISUCK((ONE))
      IF (I.LE.ONE) PRINT*,'ZOWIE!'
      I=I+1
      IF (I.LE.FIVE) GO TO 10
      END
```

This problem is not a brilliant feature of FORTRAN—it leads to unexpected errors which are very difficult to find. Be careful.

In a similar way, the people who wrote the FORTRAN 77 standard have taken great care to spell out what can happen if a function changes one of its arguments which is a variable at an embarrassing moment, for example in the middle of an input/output list. I think that this is bad programming. It is strongly suggested that the purpose of a FUNCTION is to return a single result, and that no FUNCTION should modify its arguments; SUBROUTINEs should be used for that purpose.

DO NOT WRITE A FUNCTION THAT MODIFIES ITS ARGUMENTS

8 Recursion—difficult

We know about *recurrence*. For example, the sum of all numbers from 1 to some limit is

sum to limit = limit + sum to (limit-1)

Can you do the sum this way?

```
      FUNCTION ISUMTO(LIMIT)
C ATTEMPT TO USE ILLEGAL RECURSION
      IF (LIMIT.GT.Ø) THEN
         ISUMTO=LIMIT+ISUMTO(LIMIT-1)
      ELSE
         ISUMTO=Ø
      END IF
      END
```

Here we are expressing the recurrence recursively. A *recursive* program contains procedures which call themselves. The line

```
      ISUMTO=LIMIT+ISUMTO(LIMIT-1)
```

tries to use the function ISUMTO—but we are already inside it. You cannot do this in FORTRAN. A FUNCTION or SUBROUTINE may not call itself directly. This is called *recursion* and will be prevented by FORTRAN, which can detect that you are trying to do it, as in the example above. It is also wrong for a subprogram to call itself through a chain of other FUNCTIONs or SUBROUTINEs. This is called *mutual recursion*, and the computer system cannot prevent it, but your program will fail if you try it:

```
      FUNCTION ONE(I)              FUNCTION TWO(I)
      ONE=TWO(I)                   TWO=ONE(I)
      END                          END
```

FORTRAN SUBPROGRAMS ARE NOT RECURSIVE

That does not mean that you cannot do recursion. In a later chapter I will show you how to simulate recursion using a 'stack'. In a number of applications, recursion is useful (but not as often as some false prophets would maintain). Recurrence and recursion are not the same thing. A *recurrence* is any process of repetition which modifies data. *Recursion* is just one mechanism for achieving recurrence, often elegant but usually inefficient.

9 Problems

Problem 10.1 The saturating ramp function illustrated by Fig. 10.1 is

$f(x) = -1$ for $x < -1$
$f(x) = x$ for $-1 < x < 1$
$f(x) = 1$ for $x > 1$

Write a FUNCTION RAMP(x) to evaluate this.

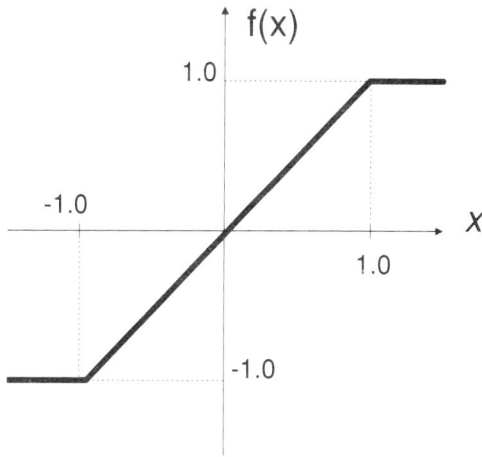

Fig. 10.1. A symmetric saturating ramp function.

How would you evaluate a more complicated one, as in Fig. 10.2 with

$f(x) = a$ for $x < b$
$f(x) = c$ for $x > d$
$f(x) = $ a straight line for $b < x < d$.

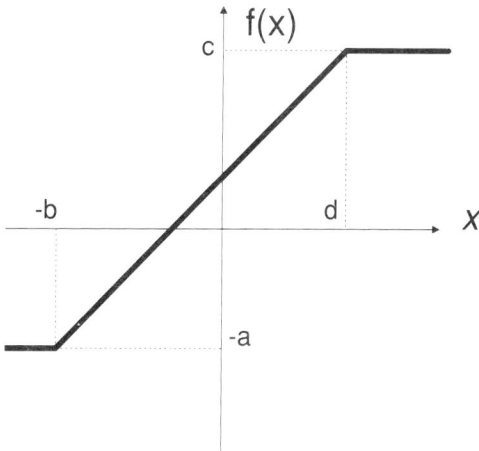

Fig. 10.2. A non-symmetric saturating ramp function.

Problem 10.2 This had to come eventually. Write a program to find the roots of the quadratic equation

$$ax^2 + bx + c = 0$$

covering all cases. How would you solve a general cubic?

Problem 10.3 A computer is supposed to produce predictable results. You may think it strange that a lot of research has been devoted to making them generate numbers which are unpredictable—these are called pseudorandom numbers.

Start with s, a starting number, or seed. Choose a multiplier m so that m^2 is not out of the computer's range, but m^2 is large compared to an upper limit r. For safety at least one of m or r should be odd. Then a formula like

$$n = (s * m) \bmod r$$

will produce an apparently random integer in the range 1 to $r-1$, although not all the integers from 1 to $r-1$ will occur. Turn this into a recurrence which replaces s by n on each iteration, and you have a random number generator.

Write a FUNCTION subprogram to do this. Give the initial value of s in a data statement. Use SAVE to ensure that the replacement for s becomes available next time around.

Problem 10.4 If you make a new sequence of numbers by summing 12 successive random numbers in the range 0.0 to 1.0, the distribution of these summed values is almost indistinguishable from the Gaussian distribution ('bell' curve) with mean 6 and standard deviation 1. Subtract 6 and the mean is 0. Write a function which generates random numbers with a Gaussian distribution. To do it you have to cope with the problem of making real random numbers from 0.0 to 1.0. If you know enough about statistics to handle the scaling, give the desired mean and standard deviation as arguments.

Problem 10.5 Surely you know about binary numbers? A positive integer can be decomposed into its binary bits. Write a function IREV(NUMB,N) to find an integer whose N least significant bits are the reverse of the same bits in a given integer NUMB. Think!

Problem 10.6 If you can do the previous problem, then try to write two functions:

IRVSUC (NUMB, N) and IRVBLO (NUMB, N)

IRVSUC gives the same as IREV (IREV (NUMB , N) + 1 , N), meaning the next number (successor) after NUMB in the bit reverse counting sequence. But look for a more efficient way of doing it than that. Similarly IRVBLO is the predecessor of NUMB. Well you want some challenging problems, don't you?

Eleven

Subroutines

1 Portability—the power and the glory

FORTRAN has been a durable computing language. It was one of the first, and more people than ever are using it as the main language for scientific and technical calculation. One reason is the straightforwardness of the FUNCTION and SUBROUTINE facilities. It is easy to gather algorithms into independent modules, which can be shared through program libraries. Often a FORTRAN module can be added to a new program without change. By contrast, a Pascal procedure usually requires both the host program and the procedure to be altered.

The FUNCTION and SUBROUTINE are modules or 'units' which do not share values with other program units except through their argument lists, (and through the COMMON area, yet to be introduced). These are the interfaces between program modules, which allow you to create any number of FORTRAN modules, and use them in any number of programs.

2 Use a subroutine

A SUBROUTINE subprogram begins with the SUBROUTINE statement, and ends with END. In between it can RETURN, just like a function, and it returns at the END anyway:

> **SUBROUTINE** *name* [(*dummy arguments*)]
> *lots of statements*
> *perhaps some* **RETURN**s
> **END**

There need not be any arguments. A main program, or another subroutine, or even a function invokes a subroutine through the CALL statement:

> **CALL** *name* [(*actual arguments*)]

The *name* follows the same rules as the names of variables and other items, but there is no type associated with that name. The arguments operate in the same way as for functions.

Example Here is a subroutine which is passed two integer arguments, I and J, and places them in order so that I is not greater than J:

```
      SUBROUTINE IORDER(I,J)
C PLACES THE INTEGER ARGUMENTS I AND J IN ORDER  I.LE.J
      IF(J.LT.I) THEN
         ITEMP=I
         I=J
         J=ITEMP
      END IF
      END
```

Now we can beautify one way of finding the middle of three values from Chapter 7, which place the values in order:

```
      FUNCTION MID(I1, I2, I3)
C FIND THE MIDDLE VALUE OF THE ARGUMENTS I1,I2,I3
C INPUT PARAMETERS
C    I1,I2,I3 INTEGER VARIABLES
C OUTPUT PARAMETERS
C    I1,I2,I3 INTEGER VARIABLES PLACED IN INCREASING ORDER
C    MID IS THE MIDDLE OF THE THREE VALUES
C PERHAPS I2 IS LESS THAN I1
      CALL IORDER(I1,I2)
C PERHAPS I3 IS LESS THAN I2
      CALL IORDER(I2,I3)
C IF WE SWITCHED I2 AND I3, I2 MIGHT NOW BE LESS THAN I1
      CALL IORDER(I1,I2)
C NOW WE KNOW FOR SURE THAT THE MID VALUE IS I2
      MID=I2
      END
```

Here is the main program for trying this out:

```
      PRINT*,'ENTER THREE INTEGERS TO FIND THE MIDDLE VALUE'
      READ*,I,J,K
      PRINT*,'THE MIDDLE VALUE IS ',MID(I,J,K)
      PRINT*,'AFTER FINDING THAT, THE ORDER IS ',I,J,K
      END
```

Notice that actual arguments are passed to the subroutine in the CALL statement. As with a function, the actual values are substituted for the dummy arguments I and J within the subroutine. The I, J and K of the main program are not the same variables as the I and J used in subroutine IORDER.

3 Danger—shared arguments

In the program just considered the values of I and J are often exchanged. When the function MID has called the subroutine IORDER three times, its arguments I1, I2 and I3 have been placed in order. But suppose they were not variables. This is lethal:

```
      PRINT*,'WHEN WE START, THE ORDER IS ',1,2,3
      PRINT*,'THE MIDDLE VALUE IS ',MID(3,1,2)
      PRINT*,'AFTER FINDING THAT, THE ORDER IS ',1,2,3
      END
```

We discussed this in the previous chapter. A FORTRAN module trusts you to use its interface correctly. This is both a strength and a weakness of FORTRAN. You are not protected from getting the interface wrong, and if you do your program can self-destruct. It won't hurt the computer, just your pride.

You must be careful that any argument altered by the subprogram is a variable (if you want the value carried back) or an expression (if you don't care). Do not use a constant (or the name of a constant) as an actual argument if it can be altered by the subprogram.

You can always make a constant into an expression by placing it in brackets:

```
PRINT*,'WHEN WE START, THE ORDER IS ',1,2,3
PRINT*,'THE MIDDLE VALUE IS ',MID((3),(1),(2))
PRINT*,'AFTER FINDING THAT, THE ORDER IS ',1,2,3
END
```

4 Some examples

The position of a point in a plane is given by two numbers. It might be expressed as Cartesian (x, y) co-ordinates or in the polar form (*radius, angle*) as in Fig. 11.1. A FUNCTION subprogram can return only a single value, so we convert (x, y) to (*radius, angle*) using a SUBROUTINE. With the angles in radians, this converts one way:

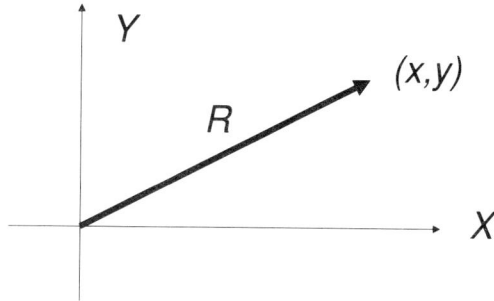

Fig. 11.1. Polar and Rectangular Co-ordinates.

```
      SUBROUTINE TOPOLE(A,B)
C CONVERT REAL RECTANGULAR CARTESIAN CO-ORDINATE (A,B)
C TO POLAR FORM AS (A=RADIUS, B=ANGLE IN RADIANS)
C THIS SUBROUTINE REPLACES ITS INPUT PARAMETERS
C SOME STATEMENT FUNCTIONS
      RAD(X,Y)=SQRT(X*X+Y*Y)
      ANG(X,Y)=ATAN2(Y,X)
C DO IT - NOTICE THE TEMPORARY VARIABLE
      TEMP=RAD(A,B)
      B=ANG(A,B)
      A=TEMP
      END
```

Exercise Write a subroutine to convert the other way. Add a new argument MODE to both your new subroutine and the example above. If MODE is 0, you use angles in radians. If MODE is 1 they are in degrees. I used some statement functions; you do not have to use those. Perhaps you will write some others to help with the degrees/radians conversion.

5 Solve some differential equations

It is much easier to solve a differential equation on a computer than by analytical methods. The Euler method is one of the simplest ways. If you know the value of a variable y at some time t, then you can predict its value a bit later at time $t +h$ as

$$y(t+h) = y(t) + h \, dy(t)/dt$$

where h is the time step. That is all there is to it! If you can differentiate a function, you can work out its behaviour at a series of time steps one after the other, and you have a model of the real behaviour. The solution is the value of y at the instants of time chosen.

Most interesting equations involve several variables. If there are two, which we will call Y1 and Y2, here is a subroutine to compute a step in the solution using the Euler method. Yes, it really is this easy. If you ignore the comments, this subroutine has five lines including SUBROUTINE and END:

```
      SUBROUTINE STEP(Y1,Y2,H)
C TAKE A STEP OF REAL LENGTH H BY EULER METHOD, REPLACING
C REAL INPUTS Y1 AND Y2 BY THE EULER PREDICTION. THE EQUATION
C BEING SOLVED IS DEFINED BY THE SUBROUTINE SLOPES WHICH
C IS CALLED FOR THE DERIVATIVES OF Y1 AND Y2.
C INPUT PARAMETERS
C    Y1, Y2 = REAL VARIABLES, THE STATE OF THE SOLUTION AT THE
C                BEGINNING OF THE TIME STEP. THEY ARE REPLACED BY
C                THE PREDICTED STATE AFTER TIME STEP OF LENGTH H.
C    H = REAL VALUE, THE DESIRED TIME STEP.
C OUTPUT PARAMETERS
C    Y1, Y2 = REAL VARIABLES, THE PREDICTED STATE OF THE
C                SOLUTION AFTER THE TIME STEP OF LENGTH H.
C FIRST GET THE DERIVATIVES
      CALL SLOPES(Y1,Y2,DY1,DY2)
C THEN IMPLEMENT THE EULER STEP
      Y1=Y1+H*DY1
      Y2=Y2+H*DY2
      END
```

To solve an equation, write subroutine SLOPES to differentiate the variables. For example,

$$d^2y/dt^2 = -y$$

is the equation of the displacement of a pendulum, or of a mass on the end of a spring, or of the oscillations in an electric circuit with no resistance. Everyone knows the solution is like:

$$y(t) = a \cos(t) + b \sin(t)$$

where the values of a and b depend on the initial values given to y and dy/dt. To solve it, use one variable to represent y and another to represent dy/dt, for example P and Q. Then

$dy/dt = Q$ (the definition of Q)
$dQ/dt = -P$ (from the differential equation)

defines the computer model. Subroutine SLOPES is again simple (four actual statements):

```
      SUBROUTINE SLOPES(P,Q,DP,DQ)
C THIS ROUTINE DEFINES SECOND ORDER EQUATION BEING SOLVED BY
C WORKING OUT DERIVATIVES OF ITS STATE VARIABLES. IT CAN BE
C USED BY VARIOUS METHODS OF SOLVING DIFFERENTIAL EQUATIONS.
C INPUT PARAMETERS
C    P,Q = REAL VALUES, THE STATE OF THE SECOND ORDER SYSTEM
C OUTPUT PARAMETERS
C    DP,DQ = REAL VARIABLES GIVING DERIVATIVES OF X AND Y.
C THE DIFFERENTIAL EQUATION OF SIMPLE HARMONIC MOTION.
      DP=Q
      DQ=-P
      END
```

Using this main program, you could test the solution:

```
      PROGRAM EULEY
C SOLVES SECOND ORDER DIFFERENTIAL EQUATION, STEP LENGTH H
C USER IS PROMPTED FOR INITIAL CONDITIONS, NUMBER OF STEPS
C AND STEP LENGTH. METHOD USED IS DEFINED BY SUBROUTINE STEP.
C OBTAIN THE INPUT DATA
      PRINT*,'SOLUTION OF SECOND ORDER DIFFERENTIAL EQUATION'
      PRINT*,'ENTER INITIAL Y AND DY/DT, BOTH REAL '
      READ*,Y,DYDT
      PRINT*,'ENTER NUMBER OF STEPS, INTEGER '
      READ*,NSTEPS
      PRINT*,'ENTER STEP LENGTH, REAL '
      READ*,H
C PRINT SOME HEADINGS
      PRINT 1Ø
   1Ø FORMAT(7X,'TIME',7X,'Y',7X,'DY/DT')
C DO THE SOLUTION
      DO 3Ø K=1,NSTEPS
         T=K*H
         CALL STEP(Y,DYDT,H)
         PRINT 2Ø,T,Y,DYDT
   2Ø FORMAT(1X,3F1Ø.2)
   3Ø CONTINUE
      END
```

Exercise By trying some different step sizes with this program, you will see an important aspect of solving differential equations on computers. The solution Y of the given equation with Y=1 and DYDT=0 at time 0 should return to the initial state at $t = 2\pi$. Try to achieve this with step sizes H of 1, 2, 4 ... Observe the solution and discover how many steps you need for 1% accuracy at $t = 2\pi$. Well, Euler's method is beautifully simple, but not accurate. It isn't stable either, but we won't go into that. A more accurate method is suggested in Problem 11.5.

6 How about some graphics

Nearly every computer has some graphics facilities. Almost certainly it is possible to draw lines on a plotter or screen. To exploit this all you usually need is these three subroutines to exist in the library of your computer:

```
      SUBROUTINE GSTART
C INITIALIZE GRAPHICS

      SUBROUTINE GDRAW(X1,Y1,X2,Y2)
C DRAW A LINE JOINING X1,Y1 TO X2,Y2

      SUBROUTINE GQUIT
C TERMINATE GRAPHICS
```

Here is a little program to draw a square using these library subroutines. I have set the size and corner of the square in a PARAMETER statement to make it easier for you to match it to whatever scale suits your computer.

```
C DRAW A LITTLE SQUARE - SCALING IS INSTALLATION DEPENDENT
      PARAMETER(CORNER=2.Ø, SIZE=1Ø.Ø)
      CALL GSTART
C MAKE THE SQUARE
      CALL GDRAW(CORNER,CORNER,CORNER+SIZE,CORNER)
      CALL GDRAW(CORNER+SIZE,CORNER,CORNER+SIZE,CORNER+SIZE)
      CALL GDRAW(CORNER+SIZE,CORNER+SIZE,CORNER,CORNER+SIZE)
      CALL GDRAW(CORNER,CORNER+SIZE,CORNER,CORNER)
C TERMINATE GRAPHICS
      CALL GQUIT
      END
```

On your computer the names of the drawing procedures are probably different, but you will have subroutines to do exactly the same things. The little programs that we develop here could be rewritten for your computer, or you could write an interface (sometimes called a binding or wrapping) between subroutines GSTART, GDRAW and GQUIT and your computer system.

Example This is an actual graphics interface which will make my graphics programs run on one machine that I know.

```
C AN INTERFACE TO A REAL GRAPHICS LIBRARY
      SUBROUTINE GSTART
C INITIALIZE GRAPHICS
      CALL START(2)
      END

      SUBROUTINE GDRAW(X1,Y1,X2,Y2)
C DRAW A LINE JOINING X1,Y1 TO X2,Y2
C MOVE TO X1,Y1 WITH PEN UP
      CALL PLOT(X1,Y1,3)
C DRAW TO X2,Y2 WITH PEN DOWN
      CALL PLOT(X2,Y2,2)
      END

      SUBROUTINE GQUIT
C TERMINATE GRAPHICS
      CALL ENPLOT
      END
```

Example This is a graphics interface for a computer with no graphics library!

```
C AN INTERFACE FOR A COMPUTER WITHOUT GRAPHICS
      SUBROUTINE GSTART
C INITIALIZE GRAPHICS
      PRINT*
      PRINT*,'GRAPHICS HAS BEEN INITIALIZED'
      PRINT*
      PRINT*,'YOUR COMPUTER HAS NO GRAPHICS. GET A PIECE OF '
      PRINT*,'GRAPH PAPER, AND FOLLOW THESE INSTRUCTIONS:'
      PRINT*
      END
```

```
      SUBROUTINE GDRAW(X1,Y1,X2,Y2)
C DRAW A LINE JOINING X1,Y1 TO X2,Y2
      PRINT 1Ø,X1,Y1,X2,Y2
   1Ø FORMAT('DRAW A LINE JOINING ',2F6.2,' TO ',2F6.2)
      END

      SUBROUTINE GQUIT
C TERMINATE GRAPHICS
      PRINT*
      PRINT*,'THAT IS THE END OF YOUR GRAPH'
      END
```

Exercise Make a graphics interface from GSTART, GDRAW and GQUIT to the actual graphics subroutines used by your computer. This could be useful.

Now I can present a subroutine for drawing a polygon. We specify its centre and radius. It is drawn so that the first line is at the bottom, and horizontal as in Fig. 11.2a. From the figure you

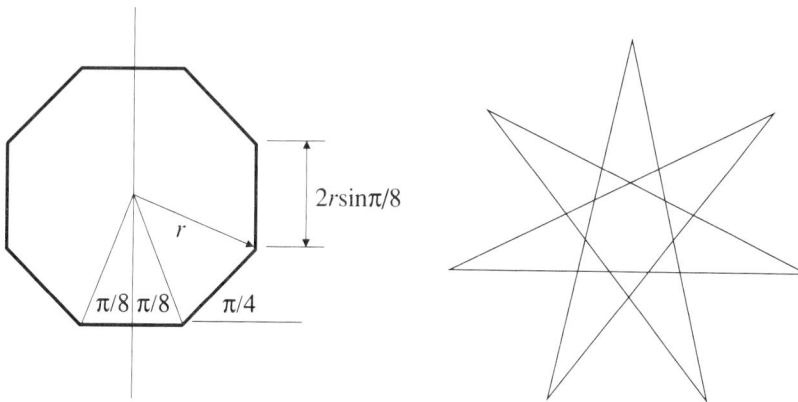

(a) The polygon $_8S_1$.   (b) The stargon $_7S_3$.

Fig. 11.2. Drawing polygons and stargons.

can see that the angle of the first vertex for a polygon with n sides is:

$$\theta = -\pi/2 \ - \pi/n$$

and we move around the outside by steps of $2\pi/n$ radians. Therefore I compute it in polar co-ordinates and draw it in Cartesian ones:

```
      SUBROUTINE POLYGN(XCENTR,YCENTR,RADIUS,NSIDES)
C A SUBROUTINE TO DRAW A POLYGON USING GRAPHICS INTERFACE
C INPUT PARAMETERS:
C    XCENTR, YCENTR - REAL VALUES, THE CENTRE OF THE POLYGON
C    RADIUS - REAL VALUE, THE RADIUS OF THE POLYGON
C    NSIDES - INTEGER VALUE, THE NUMBER OF SIDES
C OUTPUT PARAMETERS: NONE
C STATEMENT FUNCTIONS
      XCORD(RAD,ANG)=RAD*COS(ANG)
      YCORD(RAD,ANG)=RAD*SIN(ANG)
```

```
C MAKE THE POLYGON
      PIE=4.Ø*ATAN(1.Ø)
      THETA=2.Ø*PIE/REAL(NSIDES)
      OFFSET=PIE/REAL(NSIDES)
C FOLLOW THE POLYGON IN POLAR CO-ORDINATES, CONVERTING
C TO RECTANGULAR AS THE GRAPHICS CALLS ARE MADE
      DO 1Ø ISIDE = Ø, NSIDES-1
         THETA1=-PIE/2.Ø - THETA/2.Ø + THETA*REAL(ISIDE)
         THETA2=THETA1+THETA
         X1=XCENTR+XCORD(RADIUS,THETA1)
         Y1=YCENTR+YCORD(RADIUS,THETA1)
         X2=XCENTR+XCORD(RADIUS,THETA2)
         Y2=YCENTR+YCORD(RADIUS,THETA2)
         CALL GDRAW(X1,Y1,X2,Y2)
   1Ø CONTINUE
      END
```

Exercise The step from a polygon to a star is easy. Suppose we want a star of n points. A polygon is a sort of star, in which the vertices are joined in sequence. Suppose we skip over r vertices each time, and call it an $_nS_r$. The octagon of Fig. 11.2a is an $_8S_1$. If n is not a multiple of r, we get a beautiful star, like the $_7S_3$ in Fig. 11.2b. Write the subroutine to do it.

7 Documentation

Perhaps the most important part of the program development process is the final documenta-tion once the program has been developed and tested. The subprograms of FORTRAN are bril-liantly portable. You can easily introduce them into any program by getting the arguments right (and perhaps the COMMON area as we will see later). The documentation of a subroutine is particularly important in making this possible. I make here some suggestions about how documentation should be presented. A programmer who has any self-respect will have taken the trouble to write an efficient, well-structured and easily understood program. But FORTRAN does not always read like a natural language (nor do the other computing languages that are supposed to). Therefore the first requirement is a description of the program in words.

(i) A description of the program
Aim to describe fully the purpose of the program and all the methods used, explaining any theory beyond the most elementary algebraic facts. Most programs have limitations and these should be described. State what is required of the user in the way of input values, and what is returned in the way of results. Make it very clear which variables are modified by the program so that the user does not fall into the trap of using constants as actual arguments which are then destroyed by a subprogram.

(ii) A description of the program's interface
In the case of a main program give an explanation of the data input and output. For FUNC-TION or SUBROUTINE modules, make it absolutely clear which arguments are for input, which are for output, and which are for both. The type of each should be stated; it is suggested that the distinction should be made between arguments which must be variables only (because the subprogram replaces them), and those which can be any kind of value (variables, constants, or expressions).

(iii) A description of the structure of the program

Flowcharts are not as fashionable as they used to be, but in many cases they provide the quickest illustration of the structure of a program. Alternatively, use pseudocode to describe the structure. There are other methods which I have not discussed here.

(iv) A listing of the program itself with suitable comments.

It is a good idea to summarize (i) and (ii) in comments at the beginning of the program, as I have done in the examples. I have taken particular trouble to illustrate how you might describe a subroutine's interface in the section on differential equations earlier in this chapter.

(v) Use a helpful layout

There are many opinions about the layout of programs. I use an indentation scheme to identify the range of IF blocks and DO loops—begin each program unit with statements in column 7, but indent a further two spaces for each contained block. Where you are simulating a repeat or while structure with IF, you can indicate it with comments and indent the statements the simulated structure. You can see many examples of this in the text.

8 Problems

Problem 11.1 In Chapter 7 the method of successive approximation was introduced for finding the root of an equation. Write a subroutine for this. The function must be provided by the user, along with an indication of the accuracy expected. If you are looking for more work, try the Newton-Raphson iteration (Problem 7.2). Then you could tackle the method of False Position (Problem 7.1) with an option to switch on the Aitken acceleration (Problem 7.3).

Problem 11.2 Write a subroutine to find the roots of a cubic polynomial, covering all cases.

$$f(x) = ax^3 + bx^2 + cx + d = 0$$

Problem 11.3 A megapolygon is an interesting pattern. You join every vertex of a polygon to every other. Fig. 11.3a is a megaheptagon. Write a megapolygon subroutine.

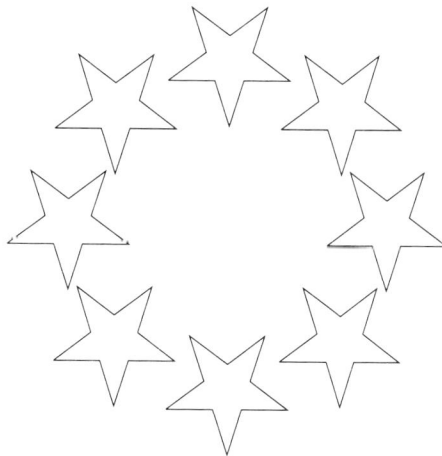

Problem 11.4. Write a subroutine to draw a circle of hollow stars, as in Fig. 11.3b.

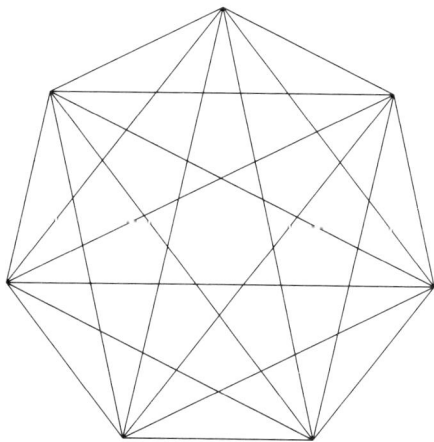

(a) A megaheptagon.   (b) A circle of stars.

Fig. 11.3. Some amazing graphics for you to draw.

Problem 11.5 The Runge-Kutta method also solves differential equations. It is more accurate than the Euler method given as an example in this chapter, but has an interesting ability to become wildly unstable if you pick too large a step size for it. If the equation is

$$dy(t)/dt = f(y)$$

then calculate the values of some variables k_1, k_2, k_3 and k_4 *in that order*:

$$k_0 = h\,f(y)$$
$$k_1 = h\,f(y+k_0/2)$$
$$k_2 = h\,f(y + k_1/2)$$
$$k_3 = h\,f(y + k_2)$$

and then find

$$y(t+h) = y(t) + 1/6 \{k_0 + 2k_1 + 2k_2 + k_3 \}$$

Write a subroutine to provide one step of this solution for a system in which there are two variables. There will be a set of ks to go with each variable. Do all the k_0s first, then all the k_1s and so on. Do not fall into the trap of using integer variable names for these things!

After you have used the subroutine to solve the same problem as presented with the Euler method, try the system of springs and masses shown in Fig. 11.4. for which

$$d^2x_1/dt^2 = - x_1 + (x_2 - x_1)$$
$$d^2x_2/dt^2 = - (x_2 - x_1)$$

Because there are two second derivatives here, you need to use four variables for x_1, x_2 and their derivatives. Solve this system by both the Euler and Runge-Kutta methods. Look at the effect of your choice of h on the accuracy and stability (if it is unstable, your errors will grow and grow). Use your graphics system to present the solutions.

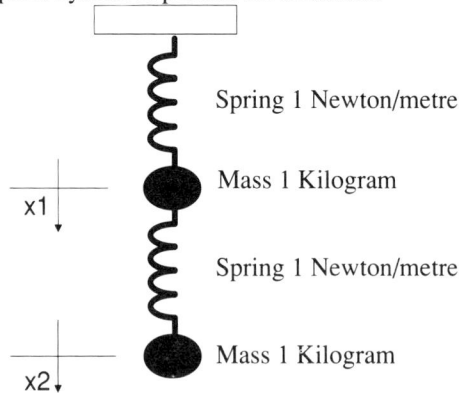

Spring 1 Newton/metre

Mass 1 Kilogram

x1

Spring 1 Newton/metre

Mass 1 Kilogram

x2

Fig. 11.4. A mechanical system.

Twelve

Arrays

1 The one and only data structure

A data structure brings together data objects so that we can manipulate them as a group. A FORTRAN array allows us to create a list or table of values of the same type. We can then refer to individual members of the array using subscripts, much as we would in mathematics. Some newer computer languages like Pascal have several other kinds of data structures. In Chapter 15 we will discuss how FORTRAN can achieve similar structures by simulating them.

In this simple FORTRAN program, we ask the user to enter a list of values, and then we find the average value. The DIMENSION statement creates the array called ULIST, which can have as many as 10 values. In manipulating the array the index I is used as the subscript which selects a value from the array. All these facilities are explained in this chapter:

```
      DIMENSION ULIST(1Ø)                            {Array created here}
      PRINT*,'A PROGRAM TO AVERAGE YOUR DATA'
   1Ø PRINT*,'YOU CAN ENTER FROM 1 TO 1Ø VALUES'
      PRINT*
      PRINT*,'HOW MANY VALUES WILL YOU ENTER?'
      READ*,NVALUE
      IF(NVALUE.LT.1. OR. NVALUE.GT.1Ø) GO TO 1Ø
      PRINT*
      PRINT*,'ENTER YOUR ',NVALUE,' REAL VALUES NOW '
      READ*,(ULIST(I),I=1,NVALUE)                    {Array defined here}
      SUM=Ø.Ø
      DO 2Ø I=1,NVALUE
         SUM = SUM+ULIST(I)                          {Array summed here}
   2Ø CONTINUE
      AVERG=SUM/NVALUE
      PRINT*
      PRINT*,'YOUR AVERAGE VALUE IS ',AVERG
      END
```

2 Declare an array

An array with one subscript is a list of values. The DIMENSION statement declares the size of an array, whose type is implied by the spelling of its name:

```
      DIMENSION name (limits) ,  name (limits)  ...
```

If you forget to declare an array, the computer will probably bombard you with misleading error messages about missing functions. This is because an array reference and a function reference look very similar. If you forget the array declaration, the computer will decide that you are trying to use a function which it cannot find.

The *limits* tell the computer the range of subscripts that you will use with that array. The limits take the form:

> *lower limit* : *upper limit*

In a main program, the limits must be expressions involving only integer constants. Later we will see that other forms allow us to pass limits to subprograms.

You can leave out the lower limit, in which case it is taken to be 1. For example

```
DIMENSION XRAY(1ØØØ)
```

declares that the real array XRAY will have subscripts varying from 1 to 1000. The size of an array is (*upper limit – lower limit* + 1). This statement

```
DIMENSION XREAL(Ø:63), IBIX(-5:5)
```

declares a real array XREAL of size 64, whose subscripts will lie in the range 0 to 63. The integer array IBIX has 11 members with subscripts from –5 to 5.

The DIMENSION statement must go near the beginning of the program unit. It may be mixed in with PARAMETER statements, so that the name of an integer constant can be used in forming the DIMENSION limits as long as the constant is declared first:

```
PARAMETER(LIMIT=1ØØ1, LENGTH=LIMIT/2)
DIMENSION IRAY(LENGTH)
```

We will see this combination in an example shortly. The required order of statements in programs is now:

Comments can go anywhere before END	Heading: PROGRAM (optional) or FUNCTION or SUBROUTINE (next chapter)		
	FORMAT statements can go after heading, before END	PARAMETER, DIMENSION or SAVE Statements	
		DATA statements	Statement functions
			Executable Statements
END is always the very end			

3 Use an array

Once an array has been declared in a DIMENSION statement, it is available to be used like any other variable, but with a subscript. A subscript used with an array must be an integer expression whose value lies within the limits for that array.

Now we can look at the sum again. To do a sum, we set aside an ordinary variable to accumulate the sum. In earlier chapters we summed values that we could compute according to mathematical rules. Now we can sum data held in an array:

```
      DIMENSION ULIST(1Ø)
         :
         :
      SUM=Ø.Ø
      DO 2Ø I=1,NVALUE
         SUM = SUM+ULIST(I)
   2Ø CONTINUE
      AVERG=SUM/NVALUE
```

4 A search, a shuffle and a sieve

The availability of arrays opens up a wide range of computational possibilities. Three examples presented here serve to illustrate the manipulation of subscripted data.

(i) Search for the largest value

Let us suppose we have a real array ULIST, which contains a number of values. We want to find the largest one which will be called XLARGE. This is a very common requirement, and the process is straightforward. I can assume that the largest value is the first one by writing

```
      XLARGE=ULIST(1)
```

This may be wrong, of course, but I now compare XLARGE to all the other values and put things right:

```
      DO 2Ø I=2,NVALUE
         IF(XLARGE.LT.ULIST(I)) XLARGE=ULIST(I)
   2Ø CONTINUE
```

When I have finished, the largest value has definitely been transferred to XLARGE.

Exercise Using the program given at the beginning of the chapter as a model, implement a program to find the largest and smallest values in an array whose values you enter as in the model. At the same time, find the subscript of the smallest and largest values. If the largest or smallest is a choice of several equal values, which do you find? If the test in the loop were .LE. what would you get?

(ii) A shuffle—reverse the values

In many applications, information has to be moved about within an array. Let us suppose that the values are to have their order reversed. To do this, we switch the first value with the last, the second with the second last and so on, stopping at the middle of the array. If the number of values is NVALUE, then we stop at NVALUE/2. If NVALUE is odd, does the value in the middle position in the array get switched with itself?

```
      DO 2Ø I=1,NVALUE/2
         SAVED=ULIST(I)
         ULIST(I)=ULIST(NVALUE-I+1)
         ULIST(NVALUE-I+1)=SAVED
   2Ø CONTINUE
```

Here is a complete program for trying out shuffles:

```
      DIMENSION ULIST(1Ø)
      PRINT*,'A PROGRAM TO REVERSE YOUR DATA'
   1Ø PRINT*,'YOU CAN ENTER FROM 1 TO 1Ø VALUES'
```

```
      PRINT*
      PRINT*,'HOW MANY VALUES WILL YOU ENTER?'
      READ*,NVALUE
      IF(NVALUE.LT.1. OR. NVALUE.GT.1Ø) GO TO 1Ø
      PRINT*
      PRINT*,'ENTER YOUR ',NVALUE,' REAL VALUES NOW '
      READ*,(ULIST(I),I=1,NVALUE)
C NOW REVERSE THEM
      DO 2Ø I=1,NVALUE/2
         SAVED=ULIST(I)
         ULIST(I)=ULIST(NVALUE-I+1)
         ULIST(NVALUE-I+1)=SAVED
   2Ø CONTINUE
C THIS IS HOW TO PRINT THEM
      PRINT*,'HERE IS YOUR ARRAY IN REVERSE ORDER'
      PRINT*,(ULIST(I),I=1,NVALUE)
      END
```

Exercise 'Rotate' the values in an array. You could do this to the left or to the right. A rotation to the left moves value 2 into value 1, value 3 into value 2 and so on. At the end you want to move the value that was originally value 1 into the final value, completing the rotation. But notice that the original value 1 is gone—unless you saved it:

	ULIST(1)	ULIST(2)	ULIST(3)	... ULIST(NVALUE-1)	ULIST(NVALUE)
Before	34.3	19.7	66.0	36.9	81.2
After	19.7	66.0	36.9	81.2	34.3

Do this. Then write a program to rotate to the right. That is a bit trickier.

(iii) Sieving for primes

Sieving is a quick method for finding prime numbers, which uses an array which will be quite large if many primes are to be found. Suppose we store every odd number from 3 up to some odd limit in an array. The length required is the integer part of limit/2. Since 3 is a prime number, we can set every multiple of 3 to 0, indicating that it is not prime. As you can see in Fig. 12.1, every third number is a multiple of 3. Then the next nonzero number is the prime 5, so we remove every fifth number after that to eliminate multiples of 5. We continue to print every nonzero number before removing its multiples. When we reach the square root of the upper limit, all the remaining nonzero numbers are primes which we also print.

In pseudocode, this is what I want to do:

```
create an array with length = limit/2 integer values
for i from 3 to limit stepping by 2 set array(i/2)=i
limitofsieve = sqrt(limit)/2
for i from 1 to limitofsieve then
    if array(i) .ne. 0 then
            print array(i)
            for j = i+array(i) to length stepping by array(i) set array(j) to zero
    end if
end for
for i from sievinglimit+1 to length if array(i) . ne. 0 print array(i)
```

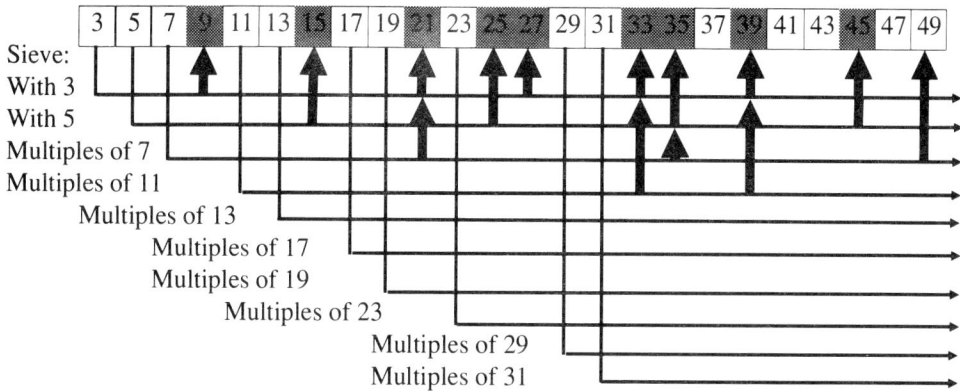

Fig.12.1. The sieve of Eratosthenes. The sieve to 49 is complete by the third prime found, 7. The ten primes to 31 will sieve all the way to 1023. The shaded numbers are not prime.

If you can spare the space for a big array, this is a wonderfully efficient method. For example, all the nonprime numbers less than 1001 have been sieved by the time the sieve reaches 31. It is called the sieve of Eratosthenes. Practise saying that. Here it is in FORTRAN:

```
C FIND PRIMES SIEVE OF ERASTOSTHENES
C LIMIT MUST BE ODD
      PARAMETER(LIMIT=1001, LENGTH=LIMIT/2)
      DIMENSION IRAY(LENGTH)
C SET UP THE ARRAY TO BE SIEVED
      DO 10 I=1,LIMIT,2
        IRAY(I/2)=I
   10 CONTINUE
C AND GO FOR IT
      PRINT*,'HERE ARE THE PRIMES FROM 3 TO',LIMIT
      PRINT*,'FOUND USING THE SIEVE OF ERATOSTHENES'
C FIRST THE ONES THAT NEED TO BE SIEVED
      LIMSIV=SQRT(REAL(LIMIT))/2
      DO 30 I=1,LIMSIV
        LOOKAT=IRAY(I)
        IF (LOOKAT.NE.0) THEN
          PRINT*,LOOKAT,' IS PRIME, SIEVING ITS MULTIPLES'
          DO 20 J=I+LOOKAT,LENGTH,LOOKAT
            IRAY(J)=0
   20     CONTINUE
        END IF
   30 CONTINUE
C NOW THE REMAINDER DO NOT NEED SIEVING
      DO 40 I=LIMSIV+1,LENGTH
        LOOKAT=IRAY(I)
        IF (LOOKAT.NE.0) PRINT*,LOOKAT,' IS PRIME'
   40 CONTINUE
      END
```

5 Reading and writing arrays

The most obvious way to display the contents of an array is to use constant subscripts. This will print three values on one line:

```
      DIMENSION XAMP(3)
      DO 1Ø K=1,3
         XAMP(K)=K
   1Ø CONTINUE
      PRINT 2Ø, XAMP(1), XAMP(2), XAMP(3)
   2Ø FORMAT(1X,3F1Ø.5)
      END
```

We can make it produce three lines by FORMAT repetition:

```
   2Ø FORMAT(1X,F1Ø.5)
```

If you were to put the PRINT in a loop you would get a new line for each value; probably you would not want that:

```
      DIMENSION IZMP(3)
      DO 1Ø K=1,3
         IZMP(K)=K
   1Ø CONTINUE
      DO 2Ø K=1,3
         PRINT*,IZMP(K)
   2Ø CONTINUE
      END
```

However here is a new way. Just name the array and all of it is printed, in this case on one line because the FORMAT permits it:

```
      DIMENSION IRAY(Ø:9)
      DO 1Ø K=Ø,9
         IRAY(K)=K
   1Ø CONTINUE
      PRINT'(1ØI4)',IRAY
      END
```

Exercise Try the above programs. Be sure you understand how new lines occur in the output. Make the second version double space. Can you make the final one use exactly two lines?

Example We can make the prime finding sieve of Eratosthenes print the entire array of zeros and primes by inserting

```
      PRINT 5Ø, IRAY
   5Ø FORMAT(1X,2ØI4)
```

after the statement labelled 40. The printout will take up 25 lines with 20 numbers on each if you leave the contsant LIMIT as it is.

How then can we print only part of an array without every value appearing on a new line? This certainly is not it:

```
DO 1Ø L=MIN,MAX
         PRINT*,ARRAY(L)
   1Ø CONTINUE
```

Our salvation is a facility called the implied DO-loop which allows us to print part of an array, and do a few other things besides. It appears only in input/output statements and in the DATA statement, introduced in the next section. To print part of an array, write something like this:

```
PRINT*, (ARRAY(L), L=MIN, MAX)
```

This statement will print the array elements from MIN to MAX. In general, in an input or output list, you can have an implied DO-loop as a member of the list:

(*list group*, *variable* = *min*, *max*, *inc*)

Brackets are always required to enclose an implied DO-loop.

The *list group* is a list of values to be printed or read. It can itself contain other implied DO-loops, themselves enclosed in additional pairs of brackets.

The *variable* is just like a DO-variable, and it takes all the values from *min* to *max*, by steps of *inc*. The loop behaves exactly like a DO loop and has the same rules, with one additional restriction. The *variable* can itself be part of an output (PRINT) list, but it cannot be a variable that is to be read in a READ list. Otherwise how is the computer to know what value to give it at the end of the READ operation?

Examples The variable appears in the output list:

```
      DIMENSION XSQ(1Ø)
      DO 1Ø K=1,1Ø
         XSQ(K)=K*K
 1Ø CONTINUE
      PRINT 2Ø, (K,XSQ(K),K=1,1Ø)
 2Ø FORMAT(1X,I4,'**2 =',F5.Ø)
      END
```

Look at this. The whole program in one PRINT statement:

```
      PRINT 2Ø, (K,K*K,K=1,1Ø)
 2Ø FORMAT(I5,' SQUARED IS',I5)
      END
```

At the other extreme, the variable may not be used in the list at all. This is a very pretty row of stars on your terminal:

```
      PRINT*, ('*',K=1,25)
```

If you use an implied DO loop for a list which refers to a FORMAT specification, you must always ensure that the list items match up with the types of the FORMAT specifiers as you run through the loop. Each individual item for printing must match the next FORMAT specifier. This is wrong:

```
      PRINT' (I5,F5.Ø)', (25, K=1,1Ø), (25.Ø, K=1,1Ø)
```

In the above statement, after printing the integer 25, you attempt to print another 25 when the FORMAT has moved on to the real specifier F5.0. Either of these is correct:

```
      PRINT' (I5,F5.Ø)', (25,25.Ø, K=1,1Ø)
```

```
      PRINT' (1ØI5,1ØF5.Ø)', (25, K=1,1Ø), (25.Ø, K=1,1Ø)
```

$$_0C_0$$
$$_0C_1 \qquad _1C_1$$
$$_0C_2 \qquad _1C_2 \qquad _2C_2$$
$$_0C_3 \qquad _1C_3 \qquad _2C_3 \qquad _3C_3$$
$$_0C_4 \qquad _1C_4 \qquad _2C_4 \qquad _3C_4 \qquad _4C_4$$
$$_0C_5 \qquad _1C_5 \qquad _2C_5 \qquad _3C_5 \qquad _4C_5 \qquad _5C_5$$
$$_0C_6 \qquad _1C_6 \qquad _2C_6 \qquad _3C_6 \qquad _4C_6 \qquad _5C_6 \qquad _6C_6$$

Fig.12.2. Pascal's Triangle of binomial coefficients.

Example It is desired to print Pascal's triangle, an array of binomial coefficients in the form of Fig. 12.2. Suppose the centre of the line is in column 35, and we want to print 10 lines of it. We will assume that the computer gives small integers 4 spaces, perhaps not correct. I should begin the first coefficient in column 34, and each one after that 2 columns earlier. This program assumes that I have a function called NCOMBS for the binomial coefficient, like the one in Chapter 10. Notice the use of the implied DO-loop to position the print mechanism (by printing the necessary number of spaces) and the implied DO-loop to acquire the required coefficient:

```
C A PROGRAM TO PRINT PASCAL'S TRIANGLE USING THE FUNCTION
C NCOMBS. MID IS THE COLUMN FOR STARTING THE FIRST LINE.
C MAD IS THE NUMBERT OF COLUMNS TO MOVE BACK FOR EACH LINE.
      PARAMETER(MID=34,MAD=2)
      DO 1Ø N=Ø,9
         IPLACE=MID-N*MAD
         PRINT*,(' ',K=1,IPLACE),(NCOMBS(N,IR),IR=Ø,N)
   1Ø CONTINUE
      END
```

Using an array, no function is required at all to compute $_nC_r$, because

$$_nC_r = {_{n-1}C_{r-1}} + {_{n-1}C_r}$$

This means that each coefficient is the sum of the two above it in the triangle. Therefore I can compute each row from the one above it. This is a nice recurrence, but you have to be careful about the order of the subscripts. Who needs an array of two dimensions for this calculation? Answer: A programmer like Winnie the Pooh, the bear of little brain:

```
C A PROGRAM TO PRINT PASCAL'S TRIANGLE USING RECURRENCE
C IN AN ARRAY. MID IS THE COLUMN FOR STARTING THE FIRST LINE.
C MAD IS THE NUMBERT OF COLUMNS TO MOVE BACK FOR EACH LINE.
C         PARAMETER(MID=34,MAD=2)
      DIMENSION ICF(Ø:1Ø)
C SET UP THE INITIAL CONDITIONS
      DO 1Ø K=1,9
         ICF(K)=Ø
   1Ø CONTINUE
      ICF(Ø)=1
C AND RUN THROUGH THE ROWS
```

```
        DO 3Ø N=Ø,9
C COMPUTE EACH ROW FROM ITS PREDECESSOR
          DO 2Ø IR=N,1,-1
            ICF(IR)=ICF(IR-1)+ICF(IR)
   2Ø CONTINUE
          IPLACE=MID-N*MAD
          PRINT*,(' ',K=1,IPLACE),(ICF(K),K=Ø,N)
   3Ø CONTINUE
        END
```

6 DATA statement considered useful

Until now, when you have run a FORTRAN program, its variables have been undefined at the beginning. To define them, we have used assignment, or perhaps we have read them in. Now we see that we can specify initial values for variables, a very useful thing particularly when we want to predefine an array. This is a concept sadly missed in standard Pascal.

Example This graphics program uses predefined arrays to make the outline of the bishop from a chess set. The outline is what graphics persons call a 'polyline'. As usual, I cannot resist a good recurrence. If you implemented our graphics interface in Chapter 11, you can run it:

```
C USE A PREDEFINED POLYLINE TO DRAW AN OBJECT
        DIMENSION BISHX(35),BISHY(35)
C THESE DATA STATEMENTS DEFINE THE OUTLINE OF A BISHOP
        DATA BISHX/Ø,Ø,1,3,2,2,3,4,3,3,4,4,3,3,4,5,5,
       +             6,6,7,6,8,8,7,7,8,8,7,8,9,9,8,1Ø,11,11/
        DATA BISHY/Ø,1,1,2,2,3,3,7,7,8,8,9,1Ø,12,13,13,14,
       +             14,13,13,11,12,1Ø,9,8,8,7,7,3,3,2,2,1,1,Ø/
C JOIN EACH POINT TO ITS NEIGHBOUR
C         CALL GSTART
        X1=BISHX(1)
        Y1=BISHY(1)
        DO 1Ø I=2,35
          X2=BISHX(I)
          Y2=BISHY(I)
          CALL GDRAW(X1,Y1, X2,Y2)
          X1=X2
          Y1=Y2
   1Ø CONTINUE
C AND CLOSE THE FIGURE
C         CALL GDRAW(X1,Y1, BISHX(1),BISHY(1))
        CALL GQUIT
        END
```

Exercise Now you do the rest: pawn, knight, rook, queen, king.

The DATA statement gives initial values to variables, and is defined as:

> **DATA** *variables* /*constants*/ , *variables* /*constants*/ . . .

Variables is a list of names separated by commas, and *constants* is a list of constants also separated by commas. There must be exactly the same number of variables asking for values as there are constants to be given to them. If necessary, conversion between real and integer will be carried out, as in the example above. If the name of an array is given, then the correct number of values must be given to fill the array.

Because only constants are permitted, any name appearing in the list of values must be the name of a constant defined in an earlier PARAMETER statement.

Examples   **DATA PIE/3.14159265/, E/2.71828182845/**

is the same as   **PARAMETER(APIE=3.14159265)**
        PARAMETER(AE=2.71828182845)
        DATA PIE,E/APIE,AE/

It can be convenient to assign the same value to several variables, so you can use a multiply-ing constant: **DATA I,J,K/3*Ø/**

but you cannot repeat a group—this is wrong: **DIMENSION ONETWO(1Ø)**
                DATA ONETWO/5*(1,2)/

In a FORTRAN program, the implied DO-loop can appear in two places, either in the list of an input or output statement, or in the list of variables in a DATA statement—nowhere else. The DO-variable is available within the list of variables (but not within the list of constants.) The DO-variable is also available to use as a subscript or as a DO-parameter for inner loops.

Example You can define part of an array: **DIMENSION ONETWO(1Ø)**
               DATA (ONETWO(K),K=1,9,2) /5*1/
               DATA (ONETWO(K),K=2,1Ø,2) /5*2/

which is what we were attempting earlier in the incorrect example.

7 Problems

Problem 12.1 Write a program to convert a number given as an array of values in any base, to an array of values in any other base. Without arrays, you would find it difficult to print the results in the correct order. Now it is easy.

Problem 12.2 Data in a real array can be 'smoothed' by applying to it an equation such as
$$s_n = 1/3 \{ 0.25\, r_{n-2} + 0.75\, r_{n-1} + r_n + 0.75\, r_{n+1} + 0.25\, r_{n+2} \}$$
where s_n is a smoothed value corresponding to the rough value r_n. Notice that if the rough values are in an array, some rough values are missing which you need for the first two and the last two results. You could make various assumptions about the missing r values. Do it. Smooth out the bishop in the graphics example, and try to find the best way to deal with the missing values.

Problem 12.3 For values of n in the previous problem which are not exact integers, we could compute additional smoothed values. If we did this, we would be 'interpolating' between the given rough values. Try this on the bishop.

Problem 12.4 Make a histogram of the occurrence of prime numbers over some divisions of a selected range. Using the graphics interface, draw the histogram. Now this could be useful.

Problem 12.5 The array which defines the bishop in the chess set assumes that the object is drawn by one continuous line. You could alter the co-ordinates to indicate when the 'pen' is up or down. One way would be to multiply each x co-ordinate by 2. Then you could make it odd if the pen is to be down, and even if the pen is up. This way you can define a complex figure made from many lines in a single array. Using this idea, make a drawing of your dwelling. Sketch it on squared paper before writing the DATA statements which define the picture.

Thirteen

Arrays as arguments

1 Pass it down

In FORTRAN many library FUNCTION or SUBROUTINE subprograms are available which take arrays of data and operate on them. To use them you write a main program which sets up the information for the subprogram, and then pass the array to the subprogram as a argument. With arrays as arguments, FORTRAN provides some powerful facilities but care is required so that you do not try to do crazy things.

First of all, if you are going to pass an array to a subprogram, the array must exist. Obvious as this may seem, it is easy to miss the point—your program must create an array before you can do anything with it. As you already know, this is done with the DIMENSION statement, which gives the computer information about the type and size of the array. We have so far used the DIMENSION statement with constant array bounds, which causes the computer to allocate space in its memory for the array.

If we now wish to tell a subprogram about the array, it is necessary to say where the array is to be found, and what it looks like. In FORTRAN we have great flexibility in what we can tell a subprogram, but we have also been given the power to get it wrong by mistake (or lie about it on purpose), with sometimes embarrassing results. The FORTRAN philosophy is that program units are independent of one another. The interface between subroutines, for example, is the CALL statement in one unit, and the SUBROUTINE statement in the unit being called. It is the responsibility of the programmer to make these match—the computer system will not check for us that our dummy arguments and our actual arguments match correctly.

2 Fixed size

The simplest and safest method for passing arrays between program units is to use a fixed size. Although this is inflexible, it is easy both to understand and to get right. Let us consider using a FUNCTION to find the largest value in an array of integers. Assume that there are exactly ten numbers. This subprogram does it:

```
FUNCTION MAXMUM(MYDEAR)
C FIND THE MAXIMUM VALUE IN THE INTEGER ARRAY MYDEAR
      DIMENSION MYDEAR(1Ø)
      MAX=MYDEAR(1)
      DO 1Ø K=2,1Ø
        IF(MAX.LT.MYDEAR(K)) MAX=MYDEAR(K)
   1Ø CONTINUE
      MAXMUM=MAX
      END
```

Here is a main program that could pass an array to the subprogram:

```
DIMENSION IRAY(1Ø)
DATA IRAY /3,2,5,1,6,3,4,2,5,3/
PRINT*,'THE LARGEST VALUE IS ',MAXMUM(IRAY)
END
```

Notice here that the array size is declared as 10 in both the main program and the subprogram. In the main program the actual space is allocated for the array and therefore it must be given constant array bounds. Because the array is a argument of the FUNCTION, no additional space is created; we are merely telling the subprogram where to find the array and how large it is.

Exercise Write a subprogram to find the minimum and maximum of an array of real values.

3 Adjustable dimensions and assumed size arrays

Passing array sizes as constant dimensions is inflexible. We would prefer to pass information about the size in the argument list. In FORTRAN you are required to declare the actual space used by an array, and you must tell every subprogram (FUNCTION or SUBROUTINE) about the size and type of every array it uses. Using fixed sizes, you have to set space aside for the largest possible array, and the subprogram has to be told what this size is. To change it, you would have to alter both the main program and the FUNCTION. But look at this instead:

```
      FUNCTION MAXMUM(MYDEAR,LENGTH)
C FIND THE MAXIMUM VALUE AMONG THE FIRST LENGTH
C VALUES IN THE INTEGER ARRAY MYDEAR
      DIMENSION MYDEAR(LENGTH)
      MAX=MYDEAR(1)
      DO 1Ø K=2,LENGTH
        IF(MAX.LT.MYDEAR(K)) MAX=MYDEAR(K)
   1Ø CONTINUE
      MAXMUM=MAX
      END
```

Notice the DIMENSION statement which gives a variable size:

```
DIMENSION MYDEAR(LENGTH)
```

This version of MAXMUM could be called from any program at all, provided the argument LENGTH is the actual length of the array as well as how much of it to search. This is called an *adjustable* dimension. It is available only in subprograms, and can be used only with arrays which are passed as arguments to the subprogram. This enforces the rule that an array must be given an actual constant size before it can be passed around. But in passing it around we can pass the size information along with it. With the adjustable dimension in MAXMUM we could use this main program, because 10 is both the actual length and the length to search:

```
DIMENSION IRAY(1Ø)
DATA IRAY /3,2,5,1,6,3,4,2,5,3/
PRINT*,'THE LARGEST VALUE IS ',MAXMUM(IRAY,1Ø)
END
```

If the length of the array is not the length we want to search, we can use another facility, the *assumed size* array. This allows a subprogram to know nothing about the size of an array except that its lower subscript bound is 1. In this version, the statement

```
        DIMENSION MYDEAR(*)
```
means that the actual size of the array is unknown:
```
        DIMENSION IRAY(100)
        PRINT*,'TO FIND THE MAXIMUM IN A LIST OF INTEGERS'
        PRINT*
    10 PRINT*,'ENTER LENGTH LESS THAN 101 FOR THE LIST:'
        READ*,LENGTH
        IF (LENGTH.GT.100) GO TO 10
        PRINT*
        PRINT*,'NOW ENTER THE LIST, ',LENGTH,' INTEGERS:'
        READ*,(IRAY(L),L=1,LENGTH)
        PRINT*,'THE LARGEST VALUE IS ',MAXMUM(IRAY,LENGTH)
        END

        FUNCTION MAXMUM(MYDEAR,LENGTH)
C FIND THE MAXIMUM VALUE AMONG THE FIRST LENGTH
C VALUES IN THE INTEGER ARRAY MYDEAR
C INPUT PARAMETERS
C  MYDEAR - INTEGER ARRAY DIMENSION UNKNOWN OF INTEGERS
C  LENGTH - THE NUMBER OF INTEGERS IN MYDEAR TO BE SCANNED
C             COMMENCING WITH MYDEAR(1)
C OUTPUT VALUE
C   THE FUNCTION RETURNS THE MAXIMUM VALUE FOUND
        DIMENSION MYDEAR(*)
        MAX=MYDEAR(1)
        DO 10 K=2,LENGTH
           IF(MAX.LT.MYDEAR(K)) MAX=MYDEAR(K)
    10 CONTINUE
        MAXMUM=MAX
        END
```

If a program using MAXMUM gives a value to LENGTH which is greater than the actual size of MYDEAR, the results will be wrong. The program would be accepted by the computer, and obeyed. When it searches beyond the actual array bounds it will find a silly answer.

Summary:

Main programs and other parts of programs which create arrays must use constant array bounds. Subprograms can either:

Use the correct constant bounds.

or

Form the bounds from arguments passed to the subprogram, but only with arrays that are also passed as arguments.

or

Use the assumed size *, but only with arrays that are passed as arguments. We will see later that the assumed size is only allowed for the final subscript if an array has several subscripts.

Exercise Write a subroutine which finds the mean μ and standard deviation σ^2 of a series of numbers. The mean of a series of n numbers x_i is

$$\mu = 1/n \sum_{i=1}^{n} x_i$$

and the standard deviation is

$$\sigma^2 = 1/n \sum_{i=1}^{n} (x_i - \mu)^2$$

You can form both of these sums in only one loop if you can find the trick.

4 A sorting subroutine with a finding function

Sorting is an important process which places a list of values or 'keys' in order. There are many sorting methods—a straightforward one is called the insertion sort. If the first $n-1$ keys in the array were already in order, we could select key n and scan the array for the correct place to insert it. Having found the correct place, we have to move part of the array along to make room, and then insert the test key. Now we have n values in order. Clearly there is nothing to do when $n=1$. So we start with $n=2$ and insert each key in turn up to the end of the array. You can see from Fig. 13.1 how the array becomes progressively more sorted.

Begin	86	82	54	2	32	76	94	29
Insert Key No. 2	82 → 86	54	2	32	76	94	29	
Insert Key No. 3	54 ⇄ 82 → 86	2	32	76	94	29		
Insert Key No. 4	2 → 54 → 82 → 86	32	76	94	29			
Insert Key No. 5	2	32 ⇄ 54 → 82 → 86	76	94	29			
Insert Key No. 6	2	32	54	76 ⇄ 82 → 86	94	29		
Insert Key No. 7	2	32	54	76	82	86	94	29
Insert Key No. 8	2	29 ⇄ 32 → 54 → 76 → 82 → 86 → 94						

Figure 13.1. Insertion Sort of 8 Random Numbers

Here is a subroutine to organize this. Note that the array of keys is an assumed size array:

```
      SUBROUTINE INSORT(IRAY, NSORT)
C INSERTION SORT OF THE INTEGER ARRAY IRAY
C INPUT PARAMETERS
C    IRAY - INTEGER ARRAY DIMENSION NSORT OR GREATER,
C             THE ARRAY TO BE SORTED
C    NSORT - INTEGER VALUE - THE NUMBER OF KEYS TO SORT
C OUTPUT PARAMETERS
C    IRAY - THE FIRST NSORT VALUES IN IRAY ARE SORTED
C             INTO ASCENDING ORDER
      DIMENSION IRAY(*)
      DO 20 K=2,NSORT
C SELECT A VALUE
         IVAL=IRAY(K)
```

```
          PRINT*,'NOW INSERT VALUE ',K,' WHICH IS ',IVAL
C FIND OUT WHERE IT BELONGS IN THE SORTED PART OF THE ARRAY
          LPLACE=LOCATE(IVAL, IRAY, K-1)
          PRINT*,'IT BELONGS IN POSITION ',LPLACE
C MOVE THE OTHERS ALONG AND PUT THIS VALUE IN THE RIGHT PLACE
          IF (LPLACE.LT.K) THEN
             DO 10 MOVE=K,LPLACE+1,-1
                IRAY(MOVE)=IRAY(MOVE-1)
   10        CONTINUE
             IRAY(LPLACE)=IVAL
          END IF
          PRINT*,'KEYS AFTER INSERTION ',(IRAY(L),L=1,NSORT)
   20 CONTINUE
      END
```

In this program, the function LOCATE is required to find the correct place to insert a key. There are a number of ways to do this. The most obvious is to search the array fragment from the beginning to locate the first value greater than the key. If none is found, the key is already in the correct place. This is the function LOCATE as a 'linear search':

```
      FUNCTION LOCATE(KEY, IRAY, NSCAN)
C SCAN THE FIRST NSCAN KEYS IN IRAY TO FIND THE CORRECT
C PLACE TO INSERT KEY IN INSERTION SORTING
C INPUT PARAMETERS
C   KEY - INTEGER VALUE WHOSE POSITION IS SOUGHT
C   IRAY - INTEGER ARRAY OF LENGTH AT LEAST NSCAN.
C          THE FIRST NSCAN VALUES MUST BE IN ASCENDING ORDER.
C   NSCAN - INTEGER VALUE - NUMBER OF SORTED VALUES TO SCAN
C OUTPUT PARAMETERS
C   THE VALUE OF FUNCTION LOCATE IS THE POSITION CHOSEN
C   FOR THE KEY, WHICH IS JUST BEFORE THE FIRST VALUE
C   WHICH IS GREATER THAN THE KEY. IF NO GREATER
C   VALUE IS FOUND, THE RESULT IS NSCAN+1.
      DIMENSION IRAY(*)
      LOCATE=NSCAN+1
      DO 10 L=1,NSCAN
        IF(KEY.LT.IRAY(L)) THEN
           LOCATE=L
           RETURN
        END IF
   10 CONTINUE
      END
```

Here is a main program which will both help you to try insertion sorting, and to do the exercise which follows:

```
C DO AN INSERTION SORT OF DATA ENTERED BY USER
C MAXIMUM OF 100 KEYS SET BY PARAMETER STATEMENT
      PARAMETER(MAXKEY=100)
      DIMENSION KEYS(MAXKEY)
```

```
      PRINT*,'A PROGRAM TO DEMONSTRATE INSERTION SORTING'
      PRINT*
      PRINT*,'ENTER NUMBER OF KEYS TO SORT, MAXIMUM ',MAXKEY
      READ*,NKEYS
      PRINT*
      PRINT*,'NOW ENTER THE ',NKEYS,' KEYS'
      READ*,(KEYS(L),L=1,NKEYS)
      PRINT*
      PRINT*,'BEFORE SORTING, KEYS ARE ',(KEYS(L),L=1,NKEYS)
      CALL INSORT(KEYS, NKEYS)
      PRINT*
      PRINT*,'AFTER SORTING KEYS ARE ',(KEYS(L),L=1,NKEYS)
      END
```

Exercise In the insertion sort, a linear search is used. We start at the beginning of the array and scan forward until the correct spot for insertion is located. A binary search is more efficient. In this, we check the middle value in the array as sorted so far, to find out in which half the new value belongs. Then we determine which quarter, eighth, and so on until the exact spot has been found. Write a version of the FUNCTION LOCATE which uses a binary search.

5 The sensational stacker

A stack is an array into which numbers are 'pushed' one at a time by a program. Another part of the program may come along and ask for one of these numbers. As illustrated in Fig. 13.2, you might want this to work in two ways. If you want the numbers to come out in the order they went in, like water from a pipe, this is a First In First Out (FIFO) or queue. Items on the shelf in a shop should be like a FIFO. If you want the last number that went in to come out first, this is a Last In First Out (LIFO) or stack—like taking the top piece of paper from your in-tray. The ones on the bottom can get very old. I have been avoiding some of mine for years.

Here are some procedures to help you organize a LIFO stack. You must set aside an array for each stack that you need. You start the stack up with SUBROUTINE STINIT, telling it which stack pointer you want to initialize. In this implementation, I use the first value in the array to say how many items have been pushed into the LIFO. STINIT is therefore very simple:

```
      SUBROUTINE STINIT(ISTACK)
C INITIALIZE THE INTEGER STACK ARRAY ISTACK
C ISTACK(1) IS THE NUMBER OF ITEMS IN THE STACK
      DIMENSION ISTACK(*)
      ISTACK(1)=Ø
      END
```

To place a new value in the stack, use PUSH. There is no safety check to prevent the stack from overflowing, because PUSH does not know the actual size of the array ISTACK:

```
      SUBROUTINE PUSH(LOB,ISTACK)
C PUSH THE INTEGER LOB INTO THE STACK ISTACK
      DIMENSION ISTACK(*)
      ISTACK(1)=ISTACK(1)+1
      ISTACK(ISTACK(1)+1)=LOB
      END
```

(a) The First-In-First-Out (FIFO) stack or queue behaves like a pipeline.

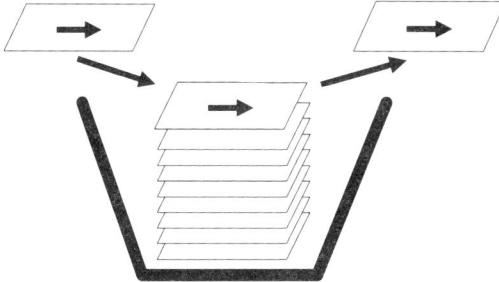

(b) The Last-In-First-Out stack behaves like my in-tray.

Figure 13.2. Illustrating the FIFO queue and LIFO stack.

The maximum number of values that can be pushed into the stack is one less than the array length, because the first value in the array is used to tell how many values are in the stack. This version of PUSH is told this maximum, MAX, and it can protect the stack provided the user tells the truth about MAX. Notice that the adjustable dimension of NDIGTS is MAX+1. If you lie, what you get is what you deserve (WYGIWYD):

```
      SUBROUTINE PUSH(LOB,ISTACK,MAX)
C PUSH THE INTEGER LOB INTO THE STACK ISTACK
C THIS VERSION CARRIES A SAFETY CHECK. IF THE
C NUMBER OF ITEMS IN THE STACK EXCEEDS MAX,
C NO ACTION IS TAKEN
      DIMENSION ISTACK(MAX+1)
      IF(ISTACK(1).LT.MAX) THEN
        ISTACK(1)=ISTACK(1)+1
        ISTACK(ISTACK(1)+1)=LOB
      END IF
      END
```

To get that latest value out of the stack, you use the FUNCTION POP, which has a safety net even with assumed size arrays:

```
      FUNCTION POP(ISTACK)
C RETURN THE TOP VALUE ON THE STACK
C IF THE STACK IS EMPTY YOU GET Ø
      DIMENSION ISTACK(*)
      POP=ISTACK(ISTACK(1)+1)
      IF (ISTACK(1).GT.Ø) ISTACK(1)=ISTACK(1)-1
      END
```

Here is a possible use of a stack. We read in a series of digits and push them into a LIFO as they are read. Then when we pop them out again we get them in reverse order. We use the safety version of PUSH. You can turn anything around this way:

```
C USE A STACK TO TURN SOME DIGITS AROUND
      DIMENSION NDIGTS(101)
      PRINT*,'A PROGRAM TO TURN YOUR DIGITS AROUND'
      PRINT*
   10 PRINT*,'ENTER NUMBER OF DIGITS TO REVERSE, MAX 100:'
      READ*,NUM
      IF (NUM.GT.100) GO TO 10
      CALL STINIT(NDIGTS)
      PRINT*,'NOW ENTER THE ',NUM,' DIGITS, ONE ON EACH LINE'
      DO 20 L=1,NUM
        READ*,MUM
        CALL PUSH(MUM,NDIGTS,100)
   20 CONTINUE
      PRINT*,'HERE THEY ARE BACKWARDS'
      PRINT*, (POP(NDIGTS),L=1,NUM)
      END
```

In the next Chapter we will see some really useful applications of stacks.

Exercise When converting numbers from one base to another, the answer comes out in the wrong order. A stack can solve this problem very neatly. Write a subroutine which is given an array of digits in one base, and returns the answer in the same array, but in another base.

6 Buffers and tables—DATA and SAVE in subprograms

We have used arrays which are defined in a main program and passed to a subprogram. However there are circumstances in which an array resides in a subprogram. Remember the rule: the space occupied by an array must be allocated somewhere with constant array bounds.

An important example of this is in 'buffering' data between an input or output device and a program. Often information has to be arranged into blocks of a particular length. You may prefer to pass values in smaller bunches, perhaps one at a time. Here is a subroutine for buffering. The length of the buffer is set by the PARAMETER statement, so it can be adapted to different applications. As shown it buffers single integers into groups of 8 before printing them:

```
      SUBROUTINE BUFOUT(IVALUE)
C A SUBROUTINE TO BUFFER PRINTED INTEGER VALUES
C INPUT PARAMETER
C  IVALUE = AN INTEGER VALUE WHICH IS PLACED IN THE BUFFER
C WHEN THE BUFFER IS FULL, IT WILL BE PRINTED AND RESTARTED
C THE BUFFER LENGTH IS SET IN THE PARAMETER STATEMENT
C NOTE THAT THERE IS NO MECHANISM FOR EMPTYING THE BUFFER
C WHEN IT IS PARTLY FULL - SEE EXERCISE AND ALSO CHAPTER 17
      PARAMETER (IBLOCK=8)
      SAVE
      DIMENSION IBUFFR(IBLOCK)
      DATA IPOINT /0/
C PLACE THE NEW VALUE IN THE BUFFER
      IPOINT=IPOINT+1
      IBUFFR(IPOINT)=IVALUE
C IF THE BUFFER IS FULL, EMPTY IT AND RESET IPOINT
```

```
      IF(IPOINT.EQ.8) THEN
        PRINT*,IBUFFR
        IPOINT=Ø
      END IF
      END
```

In this subroutine, initially there is no information in the buffer array IBUFFR. An integer IPOINT is used to point to the previous entry in the buffer, and is 0 when it is empty. The initial value 0 is assigned to IPOINT in a DATA statement. Each time the subroutine is used, information is left behind—integers which have been placed in the buffer, and the latest value of IPOINT. The SAVE statement ensures that this is possible.

Exercise Look back at the programs we used for finding prime numbers, either by brute force as in Chapter 8, or by sieving as in Chapter 12. Consider how you would alter these programs to print 8 primes on each line with and without a buffering subroutine.

Example It is often necessary to hide a table of values in a subprogram. Here we want to take a picture of some computer graphics with a camera whose exposure we can control. We pass the brightness of a spot on the screen to the function EXPOSE, to find out how many seconds of exposure are required to put that spot on film. The response of film is nonlinear—it is blind to low levels of light, responds well at medium intensities and then begins to respond less and less ('saturates') at high levels as most of the light sensitive substance has been used up.

We want to achieve a linear change in density of the film. To do this we do some experiments to find the desired exposure for a number of densities, and our exposure strategy is to join up the times by straight lines in between the observations. This is a 'piecewise linear' approximation to the ideal exposure times. Fig. 13.3 shows the curve for exposing an actual film.

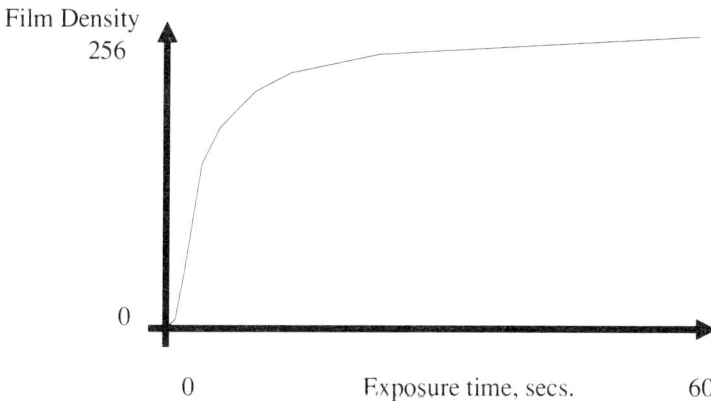

Fig.13.3. The exposure function of a black and white photographic film.

```
      FUNCTION EXPOSE(BRIGHT, ASA)
C CALCULATE AN EXPOSURE TIME FOR THE GIVEN REAL
C BRIGHTNESS BRIGHT ON A FILM OF THE GIVEN
C REAL ASA RATING, BY PIECEWISE LINEAR APPROXIMATION
C C EXPERIMENTAL BRIGHTNESSES FOR 8Ø ASA FILM ARE IN
C THE TABLE BRITES, WITH CORRESPONDING TIMES IN TIMES
C THE TIME WILL BE ZERO IF THE BRIGHTNESS IS OUT OF RANGE
      PARAMETER (NRANGE=16)
```

```
      DIMENSION BRITES(NRANGE+1), TIMES(NRANGE+1)
      DATA BRITES   /Ø.Ø, 16.Ø,   32.Ø,   48.Ø,   64.Ø,
     +                     8Ø.Ø,   96.Ø, 112.Ø, 128.Ø,
     +                    144.Ø, 16Ø.Ø, 176.Ø, 192.Ø,
     +                    2Ø8.Ø, 224.Ø, 24Ø.Ø, 256.Ø/
      DATA TIMES   /Ø.Ø,   1.8,   1.9,   2.1,   2.3,
     +                     2.5,   2.7,   3.1,   3.8,
     +                     4.2,   5.2,   6.Ø,   7.4,
     +                    1Ø.4,  13.Ø,  24.Ø,  6Ø.Ø/
C DETERMINE THE RANGE IF ANY OF THE BRIGHTNESS
      TIME=Ø.Ø
      B=BRIGHT
      DO 1Ø K=1,NRANGE
         BMIN=BRITES(K)
         BMAX=BRITES(K+1)
         IF(B.GE.BMIN. AND. B.LT.BMAX) THEN
C FOUND THE RANGE, DO THE LINEAR APPROXIMATION AND EXIT
            TMIN=TIMES(K)
            TMAX=TIMES(K+1)
            TIME=TMIN + (B-BMIN)*(TMAX-TMIN)/(BMAX-BMIN)
            GO TO 2Ø
         END IF
   1Ø CONTINUE
C WHEN WE ARRIVE HERE, THE TIME IS KNOWN FOR ASA 8Ø
   2Ø EXPOSE=TIME*8Ø.Ø/ASA
      END
```

In the function EXPOSE, we save the exposure values at the 'breakpoints' of the curve in the array TIMES, which is defined in the DATA statement. (As nothing is ever altered, there is no need for SAVE.) In EXPOSE the intensity is used to work out which straight line piece to use, and the exposure is calculated by the necessary approximation.

7 How to cheat

When you pass an array to a subprogram, you inform the FUNCTION or SUBROUTINE about the location, size and type of the array. Because FORTRAN modules are independent, there is no way that the computer can check that you are telling the truth. You can force the subprogram to accept a convenient lie, but you must be careful that you really know what you are doing.

A subprogram believes that the array begins where the actual argument is, which becomes 'associated' with the dummy array. This is so useful and common that it is not considered cheating at all. (In Pascal it is against the rules.).

A subprogram knows the length of an array from the information you give in the DIMENSION statement. One way of ducking this is to use an assumed size array. Another is to lie about the bounds altogether. FORTRAN cannot check on you. However it is your responsibility to keep subscripts within the actual array bounds.

Example Here is a program which filters or 'smooths' an array of data. It uses a formula:

$$Y_n = 1/3 \, (0.25 \, X_{n-2} + 0.75 \, X_{n-1} + X_n + 0.75 \, X_{n+1} + 0.25 \, X_{n+2})$$

The subroutine SMUTH is passed an entire array. Since the formula extends both ways around X_n, we cannot apply it to the first two or the last two values. There we apply a modified version. In between, the function FLIT gives the result. The actual argument of FLIT is a subscripted value. The function believes it is dealing with an array whose bounds are 0 to 2. Actually we have associated XIN(K) with FRAG(0). We then proceed *apparently* to exceed the array bounds of FRAG. As long as we never exceed the *actual* array bounds of XIN, this is safe:

```
      SUBROUTINE SMUTH(XIN, XOUT, LEN)
C INPUT PARAMETERS
C   XIN - REAL ARRAY DIMENSION(LEN) OF DATA FOR SMOOTHING
C   LEN - THE INTEGER LENGTH OF DATA, MUST BE AT LEAST 5
C OUTPUT PARAMETERS
C   XOUT - REAL ARRAY DIMENSION(LEN) OF SMOOTHED DATA
C NOTE THAT XIN AND XOUT MUST BE DIFFERENT ARRAYS
      DIMENSION XIN(LEN), XOUT(LEN)
C DO THE ENDS USING VARIATIONS ON THE FORMULA
      XOUT(1)=(XIN(1)+1.5*XIN(2)+Ø.5*XIN(3))/3.Ø
      XOUT(2)=(XIN(2)+Ø.75*XIN(1)+Ø.75*XIN(3)+Ø.5*XIN(4))/3.Ø
      XOUT(LEN-1)=(XIN(LEN-1)+Ø.75*XIN(LEN)
     +    +Ø.75*XIN(LEN-2)+Ø.5*XIN(LEN-3))/3.Ø
      XOUT(LEN)=(XIN(LEN)+1.5*XIN(LEN-1)+Ø.5*XIN(LEN-2))/3.Ø
C NOW THE POINTS IN BETWEEN
      DO 1Ø K=3,LEN-2
         XOUT(K)=FLIT(XIN(K))
   1Ø CONTINUE
      END

      FUNCTION FLIT(FRAG)
C COMPUTES A SMOOTHED VALUE AT MIDPOINT OF ARRAY FRAG
C INPUT PARAMETER
C   FRAG - REAL ARRAY OF LENGTH AT LEAST 5
C OUTPUT VALUE
C   THE FUNCTION RETURNS A SMOOTHED VALUE FOR
C   FRAG(Ø) BASED ON A 5 POINT FILTERING FORMULA
C   YOU CAN SET THE COEFFICIENTS AND GAIN YOURSELF
      DIMENSION FRAG(Ø:2), COEFFS(-2:2)
      DATA COEFFS/Ø.25,Ø.75,1.Ø,Ø.75,Ø.25/
      DATA GAIN /Ø.33333333333333333/
      SUM=Ø.Ø
      DO 1Ø K=-2,2
         SUM=SUM+COEFFS(K)*FRAG(K)
   1Ø CONTINUE
      FLIT=SUM*GAIN
      END
```

Exercise Just to whet your appetite for really dangerous living, you could have given the array bounds of FRAG as *. This would result in the actual argument XIN(K) in SMUTH being associated with FRAG(1) in FLIT. A simple change or two to FLIT would then make this work. There are several alternatives, some nastier than others. Do it.

8 Some things to remember

In passing an array to a FUNCTION or SUBROUTINE, certain information must be given:

(i) Where is the array?

An array must originate with constant subscript bounds, often in the main program. A subprogram knows only the starting position of its actual arguments.

(ii) How large is the array?

The size is established with constant array bounds, as detailed in Chapter 12. In passing an array to a subprogram, subscript bounds are given in one of three ways:

(a) Constant bounds, just as in the calling program. If the array is a dummy argument, no new space is allocated to it. You cannot change the size of an array this way.

(b) Variable bounds. The integer expressions for the bounds can include constants and dummy arguments of the subprogram. You cannot alter the size of an array this way.

(c) Assumed size bounds. You give the subprogram no information about the bounds, by stating them as *. The bounds are assumed to be from 1 to an unknown limit.

(iii) What type is the array?

The subprogram knows this from the dummy arguments and declarations you may make about them. Do not mismatch types when using a subprogram.

(iv) What is the shape of the array?

This is an important question for multidimensional arrays, discussed in Chapter 15, where you will discover a rich new vein of possibilities for getting into trouble.

9 Problems

Problem 13.1 The smoothing filter discussed above can also be used to compute additional values of a function in between the ones given (see also Problems 12.2 and 12.3). Write a subroutine which is given an array of values, and interpolates to give more values. If the number of new values is an exact multiple of the number of old ones, it is easier. What if it is not?

Problem 13.2 Write really useful subroutines for making a histogram. The range of values to be histogrammed and the number of categories or 'bins' in the histogram should be adjustable.

Problem 13.3 Write a subroutine (or several) for finding the area under a tabulated function. You will have to do some research to find suitable methods.

Problem 13.4 An efficient method of sorting uses two arrays. You merge adjacent fragments of an array *A* of length 1 into fragments of an array *B* of length 2. You can then merge these back into groups of 4, and so on. Make a subroutine which merges two fragments of one array which are already in order into a larger fragment of another array. (If I told you exactly how to do this it would spoil all the fun.) Control the merging subroutine with a master sorting routine. It is easy if the array length is a power of 2—otherwise be careful at the end.

Begin:		86	82	54	2	32	76	94	29
Two-merged:		82	86	2	54	32	76	29	94
Four-merged:		2	54	82	86	29	32	76	94
Result: Eight-merged	2	29	32	54	76	82	86	94

Fourteen

Recursion is possible

1 You can't do this

As you know, in recurrence a process is repeated using modified values each time. Recursion is one way of doing this by having the process, a SUBROUTINE or FUNCTION, call itself. Do not confuse recurrence, the technique, with recursion, a means of implementation.

As a simple example of both, suppose you wish to print all the numbers from 1 to 10. You could do this by printing 10 after you have printed 1 to 9. That can be done by printing 9 after printing 1 to 8, and so on. You may think this is obvious, but you could express the process as a pseudocode procedure to print all the numbers from 1 to n:

```
procedure print_from_one_to_limit (limit)
  if limit>1 print_from_1_to_limit (limit-1)
  print limit
end
```

This is a silly way to print 10 numbers, but it expresses the idea of recursion. In FORTRAN you might be tempted to try this:

```
      SUBROUTINE RECURN(LIMIT)
C SORRY YOU CANNOT DO THIS MUCH AS WE WOULD LIKE YOU TO
      IF(LIMIT.GT.1) CALL RECURN(LIMIT-1)
      PRINT*,LIMIT
      END
```

But you can't. In FORTRAN a subprogram may not call itself, either directly as above, or indirectly. The computer has exactly one copy of each subprogram and variable—they are static. If a subprogram calls itself, it loses the values it had before the call. It also can no longer find its way back to the place which first called it—a more subtle point but just as devastating.

In languages which allow recursion, such as Pascal, the arguments and private variables are created when a procedure is activated, and pushed onto a stack. When the procedure is finished, the computer returns to the state before it was activated by popping things back from the stack. Recursion chews up memory and is slow, but it is very fashionable in Computer Science.

2 But you can do this

You can always implement a recursive procedure by creating your own stack. You simulate the creation of new variables by the recursive call, and the recovery of the old ones after the completion of the recursive call by managing the stack yourself. It is straightforward.

To make a process call itself, save all the values you need later in stacks, set the arguments for the recursive call, and jump to the beginning of the process. This simulates a recursive call.

To simulate the return from the recursive call, you must restore the program to the state it should be in after the most recent recursive call has been completed. Usually this is just a case of recovering the variables from the stack, but sometimes there are complications.

When you reach the end of the process, you can tell if there have been additional recursive calls, because there will be information in the stack. If so, pop what is needed from the stack, and jump back to the point after the recursive call.

Here is the counting process implemented that way, using the stacking subprograms developed in Chapter 13. There are lots of comments to help you create your own recursions:

```
      SUBROUTINE RECURN(LIMIT)
C HOW TO DO A RECURSION IN FORTRAN 77
C SET ASIDE AND INITIALIZE A STACK OF THE REQUIRED DEPTH
      PARAMETER (IDEEP=25)
      DIMENSION LIMSTK(IDEEP)
      CALL STINIT(LIMSTK)
C BEGINNING OF RECURSIVE PART
   1Ø IF(LIMIT.GT.1) THEN
C         HERE YOU WANT TO SAY
C         CALL RECURN(LIMIT-1)
C WHENEVER YOU NEED A RECURSIVE 'CALL', PUSH ANY VARIABLES
C YOU NEED LATER ONTO STACKS (INCLUDING ARGUMENTS IF YOU
C WILL NEED THEM), SET THE ARGUMENTS OF THE RECURSIVE CALL,
C AND JUMP TO THE BEGINNING OF THE RECURSIVE PART.
         CALL PUSH(LIMIT,LIMSTK)
         LIMIT=LIMIT-1
         GO TO 1Ø
      END IF
C THIS IS THE POINT OF RETURN FROM THE RECURSIVE CALL
C ENSURE THAT THE PROGRAM IS IN THE CORRECT STATE,
C THEN CARRY ON WITH THE REST OF THE PROCESS
   2Ø PRINT*,LIMIT
C THIS IS THE END OF THE RECURSIVE PROCEDURE
C IF THE STACK IS NOT EMPTY, POP THE VARIABLES BACK FROM
C THE STACK AND GO BACK TO THE POINT OF THE RECURSIVE RETURN
      IF(LIMSTK(1).GT.Ø) THEN
         LIMIT=POP(LIMSTK)
         GO TO 2Ø
      END IF
      END
```

Exercise Look at this recursion. Can you predict what it would print? Do it in FORTRAN.

```
process zowie (limit)
    for i from 1 to limit call zowie (limit)
    print limit
end
```

Exercise The following illegal FORTRAN subroutine is different from the previous example. You have to do something to restore the state of the program after the recursive calls. Do it.

```
SUBROUTINE CRENUR(LIMIT)
IF(LIMIT.GT.1) THEN
   CALL CRENUR(LIMIT-1)
   PRINT*,LIMIT
END IF
END
```

3 The amazing Quicksort

True recursion is impossible in FORTRAN, and it is often inefficient. So why do we care about it? Because some algorithms express themselves most naturally as recursive procedures.

One of the most important recursive algorithms is 'Quicksort'. Although it has a bad worst case, on average Quicksort is the fastest known sorting procedure which does not require a full size working array. It does require some space for its stack, but usually not much.

If we have an array of keys to be placed in ascending order, as in Fig. 14.1, we can select any key and divide the array into two parts. One contains all the keys that are not greater than our selection, and the other contains all those that are greater. If we do that, we also know exactly where our selected key goes. We have partitioned the array into two parts which are separated by our chosen key, which may as well be the first value in the array. If we are lucky the partitions are of roughly equal size. The partitioning procedure tells us where the chosen key has been put, and next we sort the two partitions. In doing that we will get new partitions, and so on. In other words, we recursively do the partitioning of the partitioning of the partitioning. . .

Start	69	32	94	97	22	84	40	79	35	71
Partition by 69	35	32	40	22	**69**	84	97	79	94	71
Partition by 35	22	32	**35**	40	**69**	84	97	79	94	71
Partition by 84	22	32	**35**	40	**69**	71	79	**84**	94	97

Fig. 14.1. Quicksort recursively partitions an array.

Here it is in pseudocode:

```
process quicksort (keyarray, start, finish)
   { Sort the keyarray from start to finish }
   if length>1 then
      partition(keyarray, start, finish, where)
      quicksort(keyarray, start, where-1)
      quicksort(keyarray, where+1, length)
   end if
end
```

Now if you understand this, recursion holds no terror for you. It is easy. Make sure you see what is happening. The whole process of sorting 10 keys is presented in Figure 14.1.

To put quicksort into FORTRAN, we need an explicit stack for the boundaries of the partitions. The recursion proceeds until the stack is empty:

```
      SUBROUTINE QUICK(KEYS, ISTRT, IFNSH)
C QUICKSORT OF KEYS FROM ISTRT TO IFNSH
C INPUT PARAMETERS:
C   KEYS - INTEGER ARRAY DIMENSION(1: AT LEAST IFNSH)
C           OF VALUES TO BE SORTED INTO ASCENDING ORDER
C   ISTRT, IFNSH - INTEGER VALUES GIVING LIMITS OF
C           THE PARTITION TO BE SORTED
C OUTPUT PARAMETERS
C   KEYS(ISTRT) TO KEYS(IFNSH) ARE REPLACED BY THE
C           REORDERED VALUES
C THE SUBROUTINE CONTAINS AN INTERNAL STACK. AN ERROR MESSAGE
C IS GIVEN AND THE DATA WILL BE INCOMPLETELY SORTED IF THE
C SIZE ALLOCATED TO THE STACK IS INSUFFICIENT
      PARAMETER (IDEPTH=64)
      DIMENSION LESTAK(IDEPTH+1), KEYS(*)
      CALL STINIT(LESTAK)
C USE LOCAL VARIABLES SO THAT ISTRT AND IFNSH ARE NOT ALTERED
      IS=ISTRT
      IF=IFNSH
   1Ø IF (IF.GT.IS) THEN
          CALL PARTIT(KEYS, IS, IF, IWHERE)
C SAVE ARGUMENTS FOR SECOND RECURSIVE CALL IF POSSIBLE
          IF (LESTAK(1).LT.IDEPTH-1) THEN
             CALL PUSH(IWHERE+1, LESTAK)
             CALL PUSH(IF, LESTAK)
          ELSE
             PRINT*,'INSUFFICIENT STACK DEPTH FOR QUICKSORT'
          END IF
C MAKE THE ACTUAL FIRST RECURSIVE CALL
          IF=IWHERE-1
          GO TO 1Ø
      END IF
C ALL THE SECOND RECURSIVE CALLS ARE LURKING IN THE STACK
      IF (LESTAK(1).GT.Ø) THEN
         IF=POP(LESTAK)
         IS=POP(LESTAK)
         GO TO 1Ø
      END IF
      END
```

All we need now is a method of partitioning the array each time. There is no point in expressing it as a recursion. Consider this array, and set two indices called *less* and *more* initially at the ends of the array to be partitioned:

less									*more*
69	32	94	97	22	84	40	79	35	71

We use *less* to point at a place that is either to the left of the correct position, or at it. Similarly *more* is either to the right or in the correct place. At first, *less* is pointing at the test value. Move *more* to the left until it points at a value which is less than the test value. (This could happen at the beginning.) Everything to the right of *more* belongs there, but the value *more* is now pointing at belongs to the left of *less*. So switch the values pointed at by *more* and *less*:

less   *more*

| 35 | 32 | 94 | 97 | 22 | 84 | 40 | 79 | 69 | 71 |

Now the roles are reversed. The test value is pointed at by *more*, and *less* is moved to the right until it finds a value which is greater than the test value. Switching again, we have everything to the left of *less* and to the right of *more* on the correct side of the test value:

            less   *more*

| 35 | 32 | 69 | 97 | 22 | 84 | 40 | 79 | 94 | 71 |

Keep moving *more* and *less* in turn until *less* =*more*. Then the value 69 is in the right place, and both *less* and *more* are pointing at it. Magic!

                        less more

| 35 | 32 | 40 | 22 | 69 | 84 | 97 | 79 | 94 | 71 |

In FORTRAN:

```
      SUBROUTINE PARTIT(KEYS, ISTART, IFINAL, MORE)
C PARTITION STAGE OF QUICKSORT
C PLACE KEYS(ISTART) IN THE CORRECT POSITION KEYS(IWHERE) SO
C THAT ALL KEYS(I).LE.KEYS(IWHERE) FOR I.LT.IWHERE, AND
C ALL KEYS(I).GT.KEYS(IWHERE) FOR I.GT.IWHERE.
C INPUT PARAMETERS
C   KEYS - INTEGER ARRAY DIMENSION (1: AT LEAST IFINAL)
C   ISTART - INTEGER SUBSCRIPT OF START OF RANGE TO PARTITION
C   IFINAL - INTEGER SUBSCRIPT OF END OF RANGE TO  PARTITION
C OUTPUT PARAMETERS
C   KEYS HAS BEEN REORDERED FROM ISTART TO IFINAL
C   MORE - INTEGER VARIABLE, THE SUBSCRIPT OF THE PARTITION
      DIMENSION KEYS(*)
      LESS=ISTART
      MORE=IFINAL
C KEYS(LESS) IS THE TEST VALUE. SEARCH DOWN FROM MORE
C UNTIL A SMALLER KEYS(MORE) IS FOUND
   10 DO 20 KMORE=MORE,LESS+1,-1
         IF(KEYS(MORE).LT.KEYS(LESS)) GO TO 30
         MORE=MORE-1
   20 CONTINUE
   30 IF(MORE.EQ.LESS) RETURN
      CALL SWITCH(KEYS(MORE), KEYS(LESS))
C NOW KEYS(MORE) IS THE TEST VALUE. SEARCH UP FROM LESS
C UNTIL A LARGER KEYS(LESS) IS FOUND
      DO 40 KLESS=LESS,MORE-1
         IF(KEYS(LESS).GT.KEYS(MORE)) GO TO 50
```

```
           LESS=LESS+1
    4Ø CONTINUE
    5Ø IF (MORE.EQ.LESS) RETURN
       CALL SWITCH(KEYS(MORE),KEYS(LESS))
       GO TO 1Ø
       END

       SUBROUTINE SWITCH(I,J)
C SWITCH THE INTEGER VARIABLES I AND J
       IT=I
       I=J
       J=IT
       END
```

Exercise Quicksort is an important algorithm because it is the fastest known way of sorting randomly ordered data which does not require a spare array. This assumes that you do not count the stack, which is usually quite small anyway. For n disordered keys, the number of comparisons is some multiple of $n \log_2 n$. Here are are two ways of improving Quicksort:

(i) The worst case for Quicksort is when the data is already sorted! This is because you will have to search the whole array in vain to find that the correct place to insert the first key is precisely where it is. You then proceed to do the same for the second, and so on. For an array of n keys, how many comparisons do you make in this worst case? How can it be avoided? What is the worst case for the depth of the stack, and how can it be avoided?

(ii) As Quicksort proceeds, lots of small partitions occur and it is inefficient to sort these with quicksort because it has relatively high 'overheads' for small partitions. The obvious improvement is to sort a partition of length 2 by a direct comparison. Not so obvious is what to do for partitions a bit larger that that. Use an alternative sort for partitions whose size is from 3 to LIMBUB, some upper limit. Do the necessary research to discover the best choice for LIMBUB. A random number generator, such as the one suggested in Problem 10.3 is a good way of generating arrays of disordered values for sorting.

4 Tail recursion

Tail recursion is the term given to a special case of recursion which is particularly easy to deal with. If the recursive call is the last step in the process, then you must be finished with all the variables of the process. You can simply assign new values to the arguments of the recursion, and jump to the beginning of the process. No stack is required. Most FORTRAN programmers would probably not visualize a process like this recursively in the first place.

Example To count forwards we wanted a recursion like this:

```
       SUBROUTINE RECURN(LIMIT)
C SORRY YOU CANNOT DO THIS MUCH AS WE WOULD LIKE YOU TO
       IF(LIMIT.GT.1) CALL RECURN(LIMIT-1)
       PRINT*,LIMIT
       END
```

Now consider this, which may look similar but there is an important difference. It would count backwards. Can you see why?

```
      SUBROUTINE UNCURN(LIMIT)
C SORRY YOU CANNOT DO THIS EITHER BUT IS IS TAIL RECURSIVE
      PRINT*,LIMIT
      IF(LIMIT.GT.1) CALL UNCURN(LIMIT-1)
      END
```

The backwards count is a tail recursion. You can implement it without a stack like this:

```
      SUBROUTINE UNCURN(LIMIT)
C AN IMPLEMENTATION OF A COUNTDOWN TAIL RECURSION
   1Ø PRINT*,LIMIT
      IF(LIMIT.GT.Ø) THEN
         LIMIT=LIMIT-1
         GO TO 1Ø
      END IF
      END
```

There is no comparable scheme for the forward count because the value of LIMIT is required after the recursive call.

Exercise Implement the function ISUMTO(LIMIT) discussed at the end of Chapter 10. Can you make it tail recursive?

5 FORTRAN language considered useful

I would like this opportunity to reply to the misguided person who says that the lack of recursion in FORTRAN is sufficient reason for calling it useless. That of course is a pretty wild statement, even for a Pascal freak. I would guess that about 5 million people know how to write FORTRAN, and between them they have probably written a billion programs. A million of these programs are probably useful.

Recursion is almost always inefficient in its use of memory and its speed of execution. Therefore in real programs it is usually better to avoid recursion or to simulate it using an explicit stack. Your Pascal programmer writes recursively and then has to undo it into an explicit stack anyway. Your FORTRAN programmer simulates recursion in the first place using a stack. Sounds pretty useful to me.

6 Problems

Problem 14.1 This is a recursive scheme for making the sum

$$x + x/2 + x/4 + \ldots$$

```
      FUNCTION ADDUP(X)
      PARAMETER (SMALL=1E-6)
         IF XSMALL ADDUP = X + ADDUP(X/2)
      END
```

Implement it in FORTRAN.

Problem 14.2 Express the computation of the binomial coefficient $_nC_r$ as a recursion (See Chapter 10, Section 3.) Then implement it in FORTRAN.

Problem 14.3 Write a subroutine to find all the prime factors of a number using recursion—no loops. Make it print the primes in order from largest to smallest. Then make it print from smallest to largest. Does either let you use a tail recursion?

Problem 14.4 Mutual recursion occurs when two subprograms call one another. This recursive scheme would carry out one side of a most interesting conversation:

```
      SUBROUTINE SAYNO(LIMIT)
      DO 10 K=1,LIMIT
         CALL SAYJOE(K)
  10  CONTINUE
      PRINT*,('NO. ',K=1,LIMIT)
      PRINT*
      END

      SUBROUTINE SAYJOE(LIMIT)
      DO 10 K=1,LIMIT
         CALL SAYNO(K)
  10  CONTINUE
      PRINT*,('JOE! ',K=1,LIMIT)
      PRINT*
      END
```

It would be accepted by your FORTRAN compiler but then fail disasterously when you run it. Why? Implement the intended conversation. Hint: make it into a single subprogram.

Problem 14.5 These problems are getting more and more recursive! The Towers of Hanoi is an entertainment used to illustrate the process of recursion. There are three (or more) poles. On one sits a tower of *n* rings, which are all of different sizes, and arranged with the largest at the base and the smallest at the top, as in Fig. 14.2. Write a program which shows all the steps in moving the tower from one pole to another without ever placing a larger ring on top of a smaller one. The answer can be found in lots of places. Try to do it without looking it up.

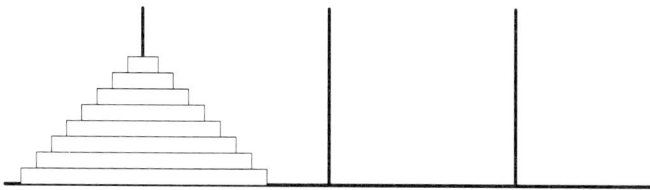

Fig. 14.2. The towers of Hanoi

Problem 14.6 . Ackerman's function is perhaps the ultimate useless equation. What an honour it must be to have such a thing named after you! All it does is recurse:

$A(m,n) = A(m-1, A(m,n-1))$

which is stopped by the cases

$A(0,n) = n+1$

$A(m,0) = A(m-1,1)$

So write a pointless program to do it. (Give up if your eyesight starts to weaken.)

Fifteen

About data structures

1 Not very rich

Data in a computer can be represented in various forms. We have used variables to represent real and integer values, and we have seen arrays of values. In FORTRAN the only composite data structure is the array. Compared with newer computer languages, FORTRAN is not rich in built-in data structures. However any data structure can be simulated—it is just sometimes more difficult. Pascal for example has a set type, which we will implement here in FORTRAN. There are many other important data structures which do not occur in either FORTRAN or Pascal, such as 'stacks' and 'trees'. These have to be simulated in either language.

We use an approach to data structuring which is easy and convenient. The method is to define the basic functions and subroutines that are required to manipulate a data structure before attempting to do anything with it. With these *access procedures* organized in advance, using the data structure in real programs becomes easier (and safer). A program does not manipulate a data structure directly, but instead uses the predefined access procedures as an interface.

An example of this approach has already been presented. The stack, introduced in Chapter 13, is an important data structure. The access procedures STINIT, PUSH and POP were defined. Then when we implemented recursion in Chapter 14, we could concentrate on the important concepts rather than get confused by details of stack manipulation. Indeed there is no need for a stack user to have any knowledge of the exact details of the data structure, just a description of the access procedures. The stack as we implemented it is an *abstract data structure*, for which we have created *access procedures* to perform all the necessary manipulations.

2 'Pointers'

A pointer is used to indicate the position of data in a data structure; it literally points at data. This means that every subscript used with an array is a kind of pointer. If we consider the stack manipulation subprograms from Chapter 13, we see that the variable called ISTACK(1) is a kind of pointer in effect it indicates the status of the stack. If ISTACK(1) is zero the stack is empty, and we call this the null pointer. Otherwise it tells the PUSH routine that there is data in the stack, and points at the last occupied member of the stack. The stack is a data structure using pointers which holds a simple list of information:

```
      SUBROUTINE PUSH(LOB,ISTACK)
C PUSH THE INTEGER LOB INTO THE STACK ISTACK
      DIMENSION ISTACK(*)
      ISTACK(1)=ISTACK(1)+1
      ISTACK(ISTACK(1)+1)=LOB
      END
```

3 Trees

The tree is a very special data structure of nodes linked with pointers. Each node contains data, and also several pointers to other nodes. In a binary tree, there are two pointers, one to the 'left' and the other to the 'right'. This of course means that some ordering is implied, often simply a case of putting data values in order, as in sorting. Here is a simple tree:

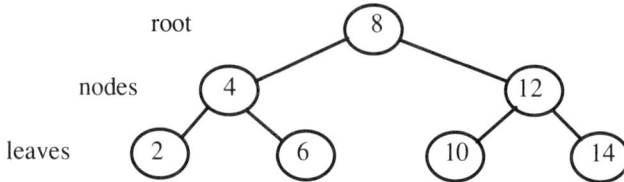

There are 7 nodes in this tree. The one at the apex is called the root, and the ones with no further connections are called leaves.

Among other things, a tree is particularly efficient for searching. If there are 2^{n-1} items in a perfectly 'balanced' tree, then a pointer can search from the root of the tree to any node in at most $n-1$ moves, just two moves in the simple tree above. A tree with 1023 nodes can be searched in 9 moves!

A number of access procedures might be used with trees. We might create a tree, add data to it, delete a node from it, and retrieve information from it in various ways. Again access procedures are useful because they have only to be written once, and then the fine detail can be forgotten, allowing the tree to be used without fussing over internal details of its structure.

Let us implement a tree which stores one integer value in each node. The tree will be an integer array. The first value in the array will point at the last occupied position in the data structure, and if it is zero we know that the tree is empty. This subroutine initializes a tree:

```
      SUBROUTINE INTREE(ITREE, MXTREE)
C INITIALIZE THE TREE DATA STRUCTURE.
C INPUT PARAMETERS
C    ITREE - INTEGER ARRAY DIMENSION MXTREE OR GREATER,
C                THE TREE DATA STRUCTURE
C OUTPUT PARAMETERS
C    ITREE - EVERY ELEMENT OF ITREE IS SET TO NULL
         PARAMETER(NULL=0)
         DIMENSION ITREE(MXTREE)
         DO 10 K=1,MXTREE
            ITREE(K)=NULL
   10 CONTINUE
         END
```

Each node contains a value and two pointers to further nodes. The data shown in the simple tree above could be arranged this way:

Right Pointers

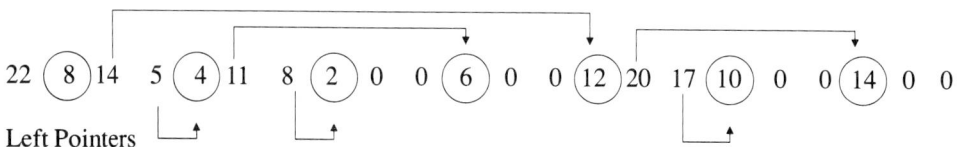

Left Pointers

The key to the tree is that the data is ordered. Suppose the order is from left to right. When we want to insert a new value in the tree, we search down the tree, moving left or right until we reach the bottom. If we do it correctly, we are then able to insert the new data. Automatically the new value will be less than everything to its right.

Suppose we now want to add 7 to the above tree. We begin by comparing 7 with the root of the tree, and find that it should go to the left. We find there is a node to the left of the root, containing 4, so the 7 belongs to the right of that. Then we encounter 6, so that the 7 now goes to the right again. But here we find the tree points to nothing at all, so we can add a new leaf:

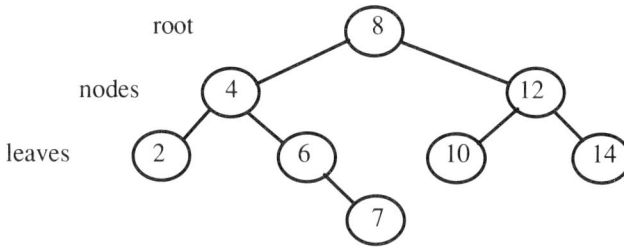

This is straightforward to implement. At each node, we compare the new data with the value stored at the node. If it is less than the new data, we want to move right, otherwise left:

```
C NOT AN EMPTY TREE, FOLLOW IT TO CORRECT NODE
      NODPTR=2
   1Ø NODE=ITREE(NODPTR)
      IF (NEWVAL.GT.NODE) THEN
C MOVE TO THE RIGHT AND GO BACKTO 1Ø
      ELSE
C MOVE TO THE LEFT AND GO BACK TO 1Ø
      END IF
```

However when we try to move left or right, we may find that there is nothing to move to. This will be when the pointer out of the node is null. When that happens it is time to insert the new data and alter the null pointer to point at it. For a right move, then, this is what to do:

```
      NODPTR=2
   1Ø NODE=ITREE(NODPTR)
      IF (NEWVAL.GT.NODE) THEN
C MOVE TO THE RIGHT
C    EITHER TO A FURTHER NODE AND GO BACK TO 1Ø
C    OR ADD A NEW LEAF WHEN A NULL POINTER FOUND
      ELSE
C MOVE TO THE LEFT
C    EITHER TO A FURTHER NODE AND GO BACK TO 1Ø
C    OR ADD A NEW LEAF WHEN A NULL POINTER FOUND
      END IF
```

In FORTRAN, this is a subroutine which adds a new value to a tree. It calls a further subroutine to add the new leaf when the time comes. Easy, really when you think about it:

```
      SUBRØUTINE ADTREE(NEWVAL, ITREE, MXTREE)
C A SUBPROGRAM FOR TREE BUILDING BY SEARCHING THE TREE
C DATA STRUCTURE ITREE AND ADDING A NEW NODE TO IT
C INPUT PARAMETERS
C   NEWVAL - INTEGER VALUE TO BE ADDED TO THE TREE IN
C            LEFT TO RIGHT ORDER
C   ITREE  - INTEGER ARRAY DIMENSION MXTREE OR GREATER
C            WHICH HAS BEEN INITIALIZED PREVIOUSLY BY
C            SUBROUTINE INTREE, AND MAY HAVE BE USED
C            ON PREVIOUS CALLS TO ADTREE
C OUTPUT PARAMETERS
C   ITREE  - INTEGER ARRAY DIMENSION MXTREE OR GREATER
C            TO WHICH THE NEW NODE IS ADDED
C THE TREE DATA STRUCTURE IS AS FOLLOWS:
C   ITREE(1) IS THE INDEX OF THE LAST OCCUPIED POSITION
C   IN THE TREE ARRAY. IF ZERO, THE TREE IS EMPTY.
C   ITREE(2) AND EVERY THIRD ELEMENT THEREAFTER CONTAINS
C   A DATA VALUE ENTERED INTO THE TREE.
C   ITREE(3) AND EVERY THIRD ELEMENT THEREAFTER CONTAINS
C   A POINTER TO A NODE ON THE 'RIGHT', OR NULL IF NONE.
C   ITREE(4) AND EVERY THIRD ELEMENT FOLLOWING CONTAINS
C   A POINTER TO A NODE ON THE 'LEFT', OR NULL IF NONE.
      PARAMETER(NULL=Ø)
      DIMENSION ITREE(MXTREE)
C CHECK FOR EMPTY TREE, AND CREATE ROOT IF NECESSARY
      IF(ITREE(1).EQ.NULL) THEN
         ITREE(1)=1
         CALL ADLEAF(NEWVAL, 1, ITREE, MXTREE)
         RETURN
      END IF
C NOT AN EMPTY TREE, FOLLOW IT TO CORRECT NODE
      NODPTR=2
   1Ø NODE=ITREE(NODPTR)
C MOVE TO THE RIGHT
C   EITHER TO A FURTHER NODE AND GO BACK TO 1Ø
C   OR ADD A NEW LEAF WHEN A NULL POINTER FOUND
      IF(NEWVAL.GT.NODE) THEN
         IF(ITREE(NODPTR+1).NE.NULL) THEN
           NODPTR=ITREE(NODPTR+1)
           GO TO 1Ø
         ELSE
           CALL ADLEAF(NEWVAL, NODPTR+1, ITREE, MXTREE)
         END IF
      ELSE
C MOVE TO THE LEFT
C   EITHER TO A FURTHER NODE AND GO BACK TO 1Ø
C   OR ADD A NEW LEAF WHEN A NULL POINTER FOUND
```

```
          IF(ITREE(NODPTR+2).NE.NULL)  THEN
             NODPTR=ITREE(NODPTR+2)
             GO TO 1Ø
          ELSE
             CALL ADLEAF(NEWVAL, NODPTR+2, ITREE, MXTREE)
          END IF
       END IF
       END

       SUBROUTINE ADLEAF(NEW, IFROM, ITREE, MXTREE)
C ADD A NEW LEAF TO THE TREE DATA STRUCTURE ITREE
C INPUT PARAMETERS
C    NEW     - INTEGER VALUE OF THE DATA FOR THE NEW LEAF
C    IFROM   - INTEGER INDEX OF THE POINTER TO THE NEW
C               LEAF FROM THE PREVIOUS NODE
C    ITREE   - INTEGER ARRAY DIMENSION MXTREE OR GREATER
C               CONTAINING THE TREE DATA STRUCTURE AS DESCRIBED
C               FOR SUBROUTINE ADTREE
C OUTPUT PARAMETERS
C    ITREE -  ON OUTPUT A NEW NODE HAS BEEN ADDED TO THE
C               TREE, POINTED AT FROM ITS PREDECESSOR
       PARAMETER(NULL=Ø)
       DIMENSION ITREE(MXTREE)
C PREVENT THE TREE FROM EXCEEDING THE AVAILABLE SPACE
C OBTAIN A POINTER TO THE NEW NODE
       IPOINT=ITREE(1)
       IF(IPOINT+3.GT.MXTREE) THEN
          PRINT*,'SORRY THERE IS NO MORE ROOM IN THE TREE'
          RETURN
       END IF
       IPOINT=IPOINT+1
C SET UP POINTER FROM PREVIOUS NODE
       ITREE(IFROM)=IPOINT
C PUT NEW VALUE IN THE NODE
       ITREE(IPOINT)=NEW
C SET UP NULL POINTERS FROM NEW NODE
       ITREE(IPOINT+1)=NULL
       ITREE(IPOINT+2)=NULL
C UPDATE THE POINTER TO END OF STRUCTURE
       ITREE(1)=IPOINT+2
       END
```

Many operations with trees express themselves recursively. Indeed you might well consider the building process as a recursion. Here is a nice example of the recursive approach to describe a process, even though we cannot implement it recursively. This is a description of the method of printing the contents of a tree in left to right order. If IPOINT is initially a pointer to the root of a tree, then we wish to achieve this recursive scheme:

```
      SUBROUTINE PRTREE(IPOINT, ITREE, MXTREE)
      PARAMETER(NULL=Ø)
      DIMENSION ITREE(MXTREE)
      IF(IPOINT.NE.NULL) THEN
C GO LEFT
         CALL PRTREE(ITREE(IPOINT+2), ITREE, MXTREE)
C THEN PRINT THIS NODE
         PRINT*,ITREE(IPOINT)
C THEN GO RIGHT
         CALL PRTREE(ITREE(IPOINT+1), ITREE, MXTREE)
      END IF
      END
```

Of course the subroutine cannot call itself in FORTRAN. Here is an implementation that will work, using an explicit stack:

```
      SUBROUTINE PRTREE(ITREE, MXTREE)
C A SUBPROGRAM TO PRINT A TREE IN LEFT TO RIGHT ORDER
C    ITREE - INTEGER ARRAY DIMENSION MXTREE OR GREATER
C            WHICH CONTAINS THE TREE DATA STRUCTURE AS
C            DESCRIBED FOR SUBROUTINE ADTREE
      PARAMETER(NULL=Ø)
      DIMENSION ITREE(MXTREE),ISTACK(16)
      CALL STINIT(ISTACK)
C IF TREE IS EMPTY, THERE IS NOTHING TO PRINT
      IF(ITREE(1).EQ.NULL) THEN
        PRINT*,'TREE IS EMPTY'
        RETURN
      END IF
C TREE IS NOT EMPTY, COMMENCE SCANNING
      IPOINT=2
   1Ø CONTINUE
      IF(IPOINT.NE.NULL) THEN
        CALL PUSH(IPOINT, ISTACK)
C GO LEFT, A RECURSIVE CALL
        IPOINT=ITREE(IPOINT+2)
        GO TO 1Ø
      END IF
C RE-ESTABLISH CONDITIONS BEFORE LAST RECURSIVE CALL
   2Ø IPOINT=POP(ISTACK)
      IF(IPOINT.NE.NULL) THEN
        PRINT*,ITREE(IPOINT)
C GO RIGHT, A TAIL RECURSIVE CALL
        IPOINT=ITREE(IPOINT+1)
        GO TO 1Ø
      END IF
C IS THERE ANYTHING IN THE STACK TO PRINT
      IF(ISTACK(1).NE.NULL) GO TO 2Ø
      END
```

Exercise Write a program which will build you a tree, and print a diagram of the tree showing the root on one line followed on another line by the nodes it points at, and so on.

4 'Sets'

A *set* is a collection of objects. In a computer, if we can assign a unique tag to each kind of object that might occur, then we can perform some useful manipulations. For example, here are some flowers which might be present in our garden. We define an index for each as follows:

1 Rose	3 Tulip	5 Iris	7 Daisy
2 Peony	4 Daffodil	6 Petunia	8 Zinnia

Let us create a garden. An empty garden would be a null set, that is a garden containing no flowers at all. We need a procedure to make a null set—which is also useful for initializing a set before we put anything into it. We will use an integer to tell us exactly what is in the set. The value 0 will be an empty or null set:

```
      SUBROUTINE NULSET(MYSET)
C INITIALIZE THE SET MYSET TO THE NULL SET
      MYSET=Ø
      END
```

Then we need a procedure which enables us to introduce a flower. We do not count how many there are, we only say that a particular flower is there—that is the key to understanding sets.

We will let 1 be the code for roses, as it is anyway, and 2 the code of the peony. So far this is obvious. If a garden set has value 1 we know there is at least one rose there, if 2 there is a peony, and if 3 both (rose + peony). So far so good. But how do we handle a tulip—we cannot make it 3? If we code a tulip as 4, any number from 0 to 7 tells us which of the first three flowers is in the garden. Then a daffodil can be 8, and so on. We find that the code of flower number n has to be 2^n. As long as that code is not already in the set, we can add its code to the set.

To examine a code for a particular member of a set, we need to divide the set value by 2^{n-1} and see if that is odd. For example if the set contains tulips and daffodils, its value will be 12. To check on the tulip, we divide by $2^{(3-1)}$ and get 3. Since that is odd, we know the tulip is present. Here then is how to add a member to a set:

```
      SUBROUTINE ADDSET(MYSET, IVAL)
C ADD THE INTEGER VALUE IVAL TO THE SET VARIABLE MYSET
C THE MAXIMUM SIZE IS SET BY THIS PARAMETER STATEMENT
      PARAMETER (MAX=15)
      IF (IVAL.GT.Ø.AND.IVAL.LE.MAX) THEN
         ICODE=2**(IVAL-1)
         IF(MOD(MYSET/ICODE,2).NE.1) THEN
           MYSET=MYSET+ICODE
         END IF
      END IF
      END
```

We also might want to remove a member of a set:

```
      SUBROUTINE DELSET(MYSET, IVAL)
C DELETE THE INTEGER VALUE IVAL FROM THE SET VARIABLE MYSET
C THE MAXIMUM VALUE IS SET BY THIS PARAMETER STATEMENT
```

```
      PARAMETER (MAX=15)
      IF (IVAL.GT.Ø.AND.IVAL.LE.MAX) THEN
         ICODE=2**(IVAL-1)
         IF (MOD(MYSET/ICODE,2).EQ.1) THEN
            MYSET=MYSET-ICODE
         END IF
      END IF
      END
```

A function INSET allows you to extract information about a particular member of the set:

```
      FUNCTION INSET(MYSET, IVAL)
C DISCOVER IF THE VALUE IVAL IS IN THE SET MYSET
C RETURNS Ø IF NOT PRESENT, 1 IF PRESENT
C THE MAXIMUM SIZE IS SET BY THIS PARAMETER STATEMENT
      PARAMETER (MAX=15)
      IF(IVAL.GT.Ø.AND.IVAL.LE.MAX) THEN
         ICODE=2**(IVAL-1)
         INSET=MOD(MYSET/ICODE,2)
      ELSE
         INSET=Ø
      END IF
      END
```

It is also quite easy to print the whole set—notice the use of INSET:

```
      SUBROUTINE PRTSET(MYSET)
C PRINT THE STATUS OF THE SET VALUE MYSET
C THE MAXIMUM SIZE IS SET BY THIS PARAMETER STATEMENT
      PARAMETER(MAX=15)
         PRINT*, (INSET(MYSET,K),K=1,MAX)
      END
```

A set implemented in this way uses an integer as the set variable. Because the range of an integer is limited, the number of different objects that can make up the set is limited. The access procedures given above assume that this limit is 15, the maximum you could get in most small computers. This is because the value 2^{15} (32768) is just too large for a 16 bit signed integer. It is possible that you could extend this limit.

Exercise Find out the maximum size of set that can be implemented in your computer using the access procedures given above. To extend this even further, use an array. It will be necessary to work out the subscript as well as the code of each member of a set. Write access procedures which do this, and be sure to prevent illegal manipulations of the set.

5 High rollers

Here is an example of the usefulness of the abstract data structure that we have developed for sets. The game of *Craps* is played with two dice, which the player rolls together. The sum of the two dice is used to decide whether the player wins, loses or rolls again. On the first roll, you could win or lose immediately, or you could establish a target for later rolls:

First roll: Sum   Result
                2 or 3   You lose immediately (crap out)
                7 or 11   You win immediately
                anything else   You roll again for your *point*
                                        which is the same as this roll.

After that, you keep rolling until you win by rolling your point, or you lose by rolling a 7.

Let us suppose we have a function IROLL which gives us a random number from 1 to 6. (I told you how to do that in Problem 10.3.) The sum of two of these simulates the roll of the dice. (This is not the same as a random number from 1 to 11. Why?)

You could quite easily write a program full of IF statements which played dice. However using the set type defined in the previous section we get a much neater program. We define the winners as a set IWINRS, and the losers as a set LOSERS. How convenient the set type is!

```
C A PROGRAM TO PLAY CRAPS WITH YOU
C        PRINT*,'WELCOME TO THE GAME OF DICE'
C SET UP THE WINNING AND LOSING SETS FOR THE FIRST ROLL
   1Ø CALL NULSET(IWINR1)
      CALL ADDSET(IWINR1,7)
      CALL ADDSET(IWINR1,11)
C SET UP THE LOSING SET
      CALL NULSET(LOSERS)
      CALL ADDSET(LOSERS,2)
      CALL ADDSET(LOSERS,3)
C COMMENCE A PLAYER'S NEXT TURN
      PRINT*,
      PRINT*,'------------------------------------'
      PRINT*,'OKAY HIGH ROLLERS, WHOSE TURN IS NEXT'
      PRINT*,
      IWINRS=IWINR1
      DO 2Ø K=1,9999
C COMMENCE A ROLL
        PRINT*,'ENTER 1 TO ROLL, ANYTHING ELSE TO QUIT'
        READ*,IPLAY
        IF(IPLAY.NE.1) STOP
        IROLL=(IRAND(6)+IRAND(6))
        PRINT*
        PRINT*,'YOUR NEXT ROLL IS ',IROLL
        PRINT*
        IF(INSET(LOSERS,IROLL).EQ.1) THEN
          PRINT*,'SORRY BUDDY, YOU LOSE'
          GO TO 1Ø
        ELSE IF(INSET(IWINRS,IROLL).EQ.1) THEN
          PRINT*,'*******************************'
          PRINT*,'YOU ARE A WINNER, CONGRATULATIONS'
          PRINT*,'*******************************'
          GO TO 1Ø
        ELSE
```

```
              PRINT*,'KEEP ROLLING, OLD BUDDY'
              IF(K.EQ.1) THEN
C AFTER THE FIRST ROLL, SET NEW WINNERS AND LOSERS
                 CALL NULSET(IWINRS)
                 CALL ADDSET(IWINRS,IROLL)
                 CALL NULSET(LOSERS)
                 CALL ADDSET(LOSERS,7)
              END IF
           END IF
     2Ø CONTINUE
        END
```

6 Problems

Problem 15.1 Write a subroutine to delete a value from a tree. In ADTREE, what happens if you try to add a duplicate data value? So how will you handle this in deleting a node?

Problem 15.2 The order of building a tree affects its structure dramatically. For example if you add values in ascending order, the tree is all linked to the right, and searching becomes inefficient. A balanced tree has the minimum depth of linking by having every node pointing both ways as far as possible. Write a subroutine which, given any tree, balances it.

Problem 15.3 Using sets you can sieve for many more primes than with integers. You will have to implement a very large set as suggested in the exercise at the end of Section 4 of this chapter. You begin by considering that all numbers are in the set, then remove all multiples of each prime in succession. This was done as an example in Chapter 12. Now use sets to achieve a very large sieve. Can you make it continue beyond the largest set you can create?

Problem 15.4 Three particularly important operations on sets are the union, intersection and difference of two sets. The union of two sets collects the objects which are in either set together into one set. The intersection is a set containing only objects that are in both sets. The difference is the first set with everything in the second set removed from it:

Garden 1	Garden 2	Union	Intersection	Difference
Rose		Rose		Rose
Peony	Peony	Peony	Peony	
	Tulip	Tulip		
	Iris	Iris		
Petunia		Petunia		Petunia

Implement these operations with the subroutines UNISET, INTSET and DIFSET:

```
        SUBROUTINE UNISET(ISET1, ISET2, ISET3)
C RETURNS VARIABLE ISET3 AS UNION OF ISET1 AND ISET2
        SUBROUTINE INTSET(ISET1, ISET2, ISET3)
C RETURNS VARIABLE ISET3 AS INTERSECTION OF ISET1 AND ISET2
        SUBROUTINE DIFSET(ISET1, ISET2, ISET3)
C RETURNS VARIABLE ISET3 AS DIFFERENCE SET1 - SET2
```

Sixteen

Multidimensional arrays

1 In the main program

For the previous four chapters we have applied arrays of one dimension, which have one subscript. Now we will see how to use arrays with up to seven subscripts. Arrays of one dimension have space assigned to them by the DIMENSION statement:

DIMENSION *name* **(***bounds***)** , *name* **(***bounds***)** , . . .

A multidimensional array is declared in a similar way, by specifying bounds for up to seven subscripts, but applications of more than three are somewhat rare. The DIMENSION statement in its most general form is then

DIMENSION *name* **(***bounds, bounds* . . . **)** , *name* **(***bounds, bounds* . . . **)** . . .

where up to seven *sets of bounds* can be given for each *name*. An array of two dimensions has two sets of bounds, one of three dimensions has three sets and so on.

The following statements define multidimensional arrays:

```
DIMENSION TWODEE(5,5), THIN(Ø:9,4)
DIMENSION RAVER(2,3,2,3,2,3,2)
```

Once any array is declared, it must always be used with the correct number of subscripts, separated by commas. The array TWODEE defined above is an array of two dimensions, and both subscripts can run from 1 to 5. The size of the array is therefore 25 elements. In general the size of a multidimensional array is the product of the sizes of its individual subscript bounds. RAVER is therefore a seven dimensional array which has 432 members, despite the modest looking size of its individual bounds. Multidimensional arrays can get very big!

As we know, there are special facilities for passing array bounds to subprograms. We will discuss how these work with multidimensional arrays in the next section.

Example Over a five year period, the four cities of Grotsylvania have kept records of the occurrence of parking meter vandalism, with the following results:

| | Parking Meters Vandalized | | | |
Year	Northminster	Southleigh	Eastchester	Westhampton
1	35	226	191	121
2	163	45	338	335
3	228	281	42	187
4	121	264	109	143
5	182	370	16	17

We can represent this data by an integer array of two dimensions:

```
DIMENSION KVANDL(5,4)
```

The first subscript is the row number in the table, while the second subscript is the column number. We want to compute some sums using this data, and FORTRAN conveniently allows us to set the data up in a DATA statement. For now we use an implied DO-loop to match the data list to positions in the table. The mysteries of the arrangement of data in the memory of the computer are left until later in this chapter:

```
DATA (KVANDL(1,L), L=1,4) /  35, 226, 191, 121 /
DATA (KVANDL(2,L), L=1,4) / 163,  45, 338, 335 /
DATA (KVANDL(3,L), L=1,4) / 228, 281,  42, 187 /
DATA (KVANDL(4,L), L=1,4) / 121, 264, 1Ø9, 143 /
DATA (KVANDL(5,L), L=1,4) / 182, 37Ø,  16,  17 /
```

Here is a little program which prints the table, does the row and column sums, and tells us all about it. Notice that we use the subscripts in an obvious way in computing the sums and printing the results, although to get a nice layout there are some tricky FORMAT specifications. If you do not understand them, refer to Chapter 6. Why have I used an array for the city sums? Well then, why can I compute the yearly sums 'on the fly' instead of using another array?

```
      DIMENSION KVANDL(5,4), LSUM(4)
      DATA (KVANDL(1,L), L=1,4) /  35, 226, 191, 121 /
      DATA (KVANDL(2,L), L=1,4) / 163,  45, 338, 335 /
      DATA (KVANDL(3,L), L=1,4) / 228, 281,  42, 187 /
      DATA (KVANDL(4,L), L=1,4) / 121, 264, 1Ø9, 143 /
      DATA (KVANDL(5,L), L=1,4) / 182, 37Ø,  16,  17 /
C PRINT SOME HEADINGS
      PRINT*
      PRINT*,'   PARKING METER VANDALISM RECORDS'
      PRINT*
      PRINT*,'YEAR   NORTH   SOUTH    EAST    WEST   TOTAL'
      PRINT*
C PRINT TABLE ALONG WITH ROW SUMS
      DO 3Ø KYEAR=1,5
        KSUM=Ø
        DO 2Ø LCITY=1,4
          KSUM=KSUM+KVANDL(KYEAR,LCITY)
  2Ø    CONTINUE
        PRINT '(6(I5,2X))',KYEAR,(KVANDL(KYEAR,L),L=1,4),KSUM
  3Ø  CONTINUE
C COMPUTE THE CITY SUMS IN AN ARRAY
      DO 4Ø LCITY=1,4
        LSUM(LCITY)=Ø
        DO 4Ø KYEAR=1,5
          LSUM(LCITY)=LSUM(LCITY)+KVANDL(KYEAR,LCITY)
  4Ø  CONTINUE
C FINALLY SHOW THE CITY SUMS
      PRINT*
      PRINT '(''TOTALS '',4(I5,2X))', LSUM
      END
```

Exercise Add to this program a search to find the worst city for each year, and the worst year for each city. As you do not yet know how to create an array of messages, it is sufficient to call the worst city by its number.

Exercise How would you define the unit matrix in a DATA statement?

2 Subprograms

As we have seen, there are special ways of passing information about array bounds to subprograms. Remember that an array must originate somewhere, with constant, truthful subscript bounds. It is always possible to use an array of fixed size which is local to the subroutine or function, and it is also possible to state the size of the array explicitly.

As we know, adjustable dimensions can be passed to a subprogram. There is no difference using several subscripts. Any or all subscripts can be adjustable. Truthful information about the array bounds should be given when the subprogram is used.

Example Here is the subroutine TRANSP to transpose the square array IRAY which is variable in size. To transpose a square array, the element IRAY(I,J) is switched with IRAY(J,I) over the whole array. It is not necessary to do the diagonal members:

```
      SUBROUTINE TRANSP(IRAY, ISIZE)
C TRANSPOSE A SQUARE INTEGER ARRAY IRAY, WHOSE
C DIMENSIONS ARE (ISIZE, ISIZE)
      DIMENSION IRAY(ISIZE, ISIZE)
      DO 1 I=1, ISIZE-1
        DO 1 J=I+1, ISIZE
          IHOLD=IRAY(I,J)
          IRAY(I,J)=IRAY(J,I)
          IRAY(J,I)=IHOLD
    1 CONTINUE
      END
```

This is another example of using two subscripts to run through an organized set of operations. Why is the variable IHOLD used?

An assumed size can be used with arrays of higher dimension, but only for the final subscript. It is possible to write

```
      SUBROUTINE MAD(WILD, N)
      DIMENSION WILD(3*N, *)
```

or

```
      SUBROUTINE CRAZED(LOCO, INUM, JNUM)
      DIMENSION LOCO(INUM, INUM+JNUM, *)
```

but in both of these cases, only the final dimension is assumed.

3 Reading and writing

We have seen that it is easy to use arrays in the input and output statements of FORTRAN. To obtain the entire array, the name was given in an input/output list. A single element was printed if a subscript was used, and a range of subscripts could be covered by an implied DO-loop. If a FORMAT was used, the correct number and type of FORMAT specifications had to be given.

The situation with multidimensional arrays is similar, apart from an unfortunate piece of bad design when using arrays of two dimensions. This causes a lot of confusion among programmers, usually novices, but it can also affect some surprisingly experienced people. The usual mathematical shorthand for a 3x3 array is

$$A = \begin{pmatrix} A(1,1) & A(1,2) & A(1,3) \\ A(2,1) & A(2,2) & A(2,3) \\ A(3,1) & A(3,2) & A(3,3) \end{pmatrix}$$

For consistency a programmer should remember that A(I,J) refers to row I and column J. So what do you expect the following program to print?

```
DIMENSION IAMBIG(3,3)
DATA ((IAMBIG(K,L),L=1,3),K=1,3) /1,2,3,4,5,6,7,8,9/
PRINT '(3I3)', IAMBIG
END
```

Unfortunately FORTRAN was designed to read and write arrays of two dimensions in *column major* order, by running the first subscript most rapidly. The program just given would print

$$\begin{pmatrix} 1 & 4 & 7 \\ 2 & 5 & 8 \\ 3 & 6 & 9 \end{pmatrix}$$

which is not what is wanted.

This is the transposition problem. It is easy for a novice to get FORTRAN confused with mathematics and make a lot of errors. The best way around this problem is to adopt the mathematical notation, and develop the habit of always writing input and output statements using implied DO-loops (and also in DATA statements). It is best to write

```
DIMENSION IAMBIG(3,3)
DATA ((IAMBIG(K,L),L=1,3),K=1,3) /1,2,3,4,5,6,7,8,9/
PRINT '(3I3)', ((IAMBIG(K,L),L=1,3),K=1,3)
END
```

which will give you what you want:

$$\begin{pmatrix} 1 & 2 & 3 \\ 4 & 5 & 6 \\ 7 & 8 & 9 \end{pmatrix}$$

The (very important) rule is:

The first subscript varies most rapidly

unless over-ruled by the use of implied DO-loops.

Exercise In the X,Y plane, a lump whose height is

$$h_1 = 25\,(9 - x^2 - y^2)^{1/2}$$

sticks up through the surface whose height is

$$h_2 = (x - 1)^2 + (y - 1)^2$$

Looking down from above, the higher of these two surfaces would be seen. Write a program to calculate and print the height seen from above for x from –5 to 5 and y from –5 to 5. Where h_1 includes a negative square root, take it as zero. Obtain the result from this program as a nice square printout, and draw on it by hand lines of equal height in the manner of a topographical map. Is the lump in the correct place? If not, you have transposed it.

4 Arrays and memory—how to cheat

The memory of the computer holds the program along with all its variables and constants. Array variables occupy the space set aside by the DIMENSION statement. An array of one dimension is stored in consecutive spaces. For multidimensional arrays, memory is also consecutive. In general the first subscript varies most rapidly. With several subscripts, the second subscript varies the second most rapidly, and so on. An array of two dimensions is stored in 'column major' order. This explains the peculiarities of the DATA and input/output statements.

Value	Array IQ	Array IQQ
100	IQ(1,1)	IQQ(1)
130	IQ(2,1)	IQQ(2)
160	IQ(3,1)	IQQ(3)
110	IQ(1,2)	IQQ(4)
140	IQ(2,2)	IQQ(5)
170	IQ(3,2)	IQQ(6)
120	IQ(1,3)	IQQ(7)
150	IQ(2,3)	IQQ(8)
180	IQ(3,3)	IQQ(9)

Fig. 16.1. Equivalent memory storage for the arrays IQ and IQQ.

For example, the array VANDALS used earlier in this chapter was defined by a series of DATA statements. It could be done with just one statement, and without any implied DO-loops. The data would have to be given in column order. This is less clear and not as easy to modify:

```
DATA KVANDL/35,163,228,121,182,226,45,281,264,370,191,338,
+42,109,16,121,335,187,143,17 /
```

Now for the cheating. FORTRAN does not actually check the number of subscripts or their bounds when we pass arrays to subprograms. Therefore as long as we respect the boundaries of the actual array in memory, we can do amazing things. For example, if the array is:

```
DIMENSION IQ(3,3)
DATA IQ/100,130,160,110,140,170,120,150,180/
```

its arrangement in memory is shown in Fig. 16.1. A value IQ(I,J) is found at the equivalent single subscript IQQ(I+(J−1)*3).

```
      CALL SUBONE (IQ)                    CALL SUBTWO(IQ)

      SUBROUTINE SUBONE(IRAY)             SUBROUTINE SUBTWO(IQQ)
C USE A CONVENTIONAL APPROACH     C CHEAT LIKE CRAZY TO SHOW HOW
      DIMENSION IRAY(3,3)                 DIMENSION IQQ(9)
      IVAL=100                            IVAL=100
      DO 10 I=1,3                         DO 10 I=1,3
        DO 10 J=1,3                         DO 10 J=1,3
          IRAY(I,J)=IVAL                      IQQ(I+(J-1)*3)=IVAL
          IVAL=IVAL+10                        IVAL=IVAL+10
   10 CONTINUE                          10 CONTINUE
      END                                 END
```

This is important—for every array of two dimensions there is an equivalent array of one dimension which could be used in its place. We can change its shape from an array with bounds (3,3) to an array with a single subscript in the range 1 to 9! In practice, all arrays are really one dimensional arrangements of data in the computer's memory. We can use a different number of subscripts, or the same number with different bounds as long as we know what we are doing. Usually, but not always, this is applied in allowing a subprogram to pretend that an array has only one subscript, when it may have originally been defined with several.

Consider a more general case:

```
SUBROUTINE EXAMPL(ARAY, IDIM1, IDIM2)
DIMENSION ARAY(IDIM1, IDIM2)
```

For simplicity, the lower subscript bounds are both 1. This array, whose dimensions are IDIM1 by IDIM2, would be equivalent to an array of one dimension IDIM1*IDIM2, so that it would always be possible to refer to it by an equivalent scheme like:

```
SUBROUTINE EXAMPL(ARAY, IDIM1, IDIM2)
DIMENSION ARAY(IDIM1*IDIM2)
```

In this case every subscript (I,J) would be replaced by I+(J–1)*IDIM1.

ARAY(I,J) corresponds to **ARAY(I + (J-1)*IDIM1)**

We can draw two important and practical conclusions from this:

First, the final dimension, IDIM2, is not used to work out the address, I+(J–1)*IDIM1. This is why FORTRAN allows this size to be assumed, but not IDIM1. It is possible to write:

```
SUBROUTINE EXAMPL(ARAY, IDIM1)
DIMENSION ARAY(IDIM1, *)
```

Second, it should now be clear why the true value of IDIM1 must be given to a subprogram. If the first dimension is not actuallyf IDIM1, the addresses will be calculated incorrectly. Extending this argument to all arrays, the importance of this rule can now be appreciated.

(i) Only the final dimension can be assumed.
(ii) All the others must be given truthfully.

For convenience, the address calculation for arrays is summarized in Table 16.1, in the general case where the lower bounds on the multidimensional subscripts may not be 1.

Table 16.1. Computing the equivalent addresses for arrays in FORTRAN 77. The subscript in one dimension has a lower bound of 1, as does an assumed size array with a bound of (*).

Dimension bounds	Subscript	Equivalent subscript in one dimension
(ILO:IHI)	(I)	1 + (I-ILO)
(ILO:IHI, JLO:JHI)	(I,J)	1 + (I-ILO) + (J-JLO)*(IHI-ILO+1)
(ILO:IHI, JLO:JHI, KLO:KHI)	(I,J,K)	1 + (I-ILO) + (J-JLO)*(IHI-ILO+1) + (K-KLO)*(JHI-JLO+1)*(IHI-ILO+1)

and so on for up to 7 subscripts.

5 Equations and matrices

Using two subscripts, arrays can represent either systems of linear equations or matrices. A series of equations like this:

$$a + b + c = 12$$

$$a + 2b + 1.5c = 18.5$$

$$2a + 1.5b + 3c = 27$$

is often represented in an array such as A:

$$A = \begin{pmatrix} 1 & 1 & 1 \\ 1 & 2 & 1.5 \\ 2 & 1.5 & 3 \end{pmatrix} = \begin{pmatrix} a_{11} & a_{12} & a_{13} \\ a_{21} & a_{22} & a_{23} \\ a_{31} & a_{32} & a_{33} \end{pmatrix}$$

A holds the coefficients of the equation. Another array y represents the right hand side:

$$y = \begin{pmatrix} 12 \\ 18.5 \\ 27 \end{pmatrix} = \begin{pmatrix} y_1 \\ y_2 \\ y_3 \end{pmatrix}$$

The whole system of equations is then written by the matrix equation

$$Ax = y$$

Here, x is the array of unknowns:

$$x = \begin{pmatrix} x_1 \\ x_2 \\ x_3 \end{pmatrix} = \begin{pmatrix} a \\ b \\ c \end{pmatrix} \qquad \text{The solution of these is} \qquad \begin{pmatrix} 1 \\ 2 \\ 3 \end{pmatrix}$$

When equations are solved by hand, variables are eliminated in turn to give smaller sets of equations. This can be done systematically. If the equations are

$$a_{11} x_1 + a_{12} x_2 + a_{13} x_3 = y_1 \quad (1)$$
$$a_{21} x_1 + a_{22} x_2 + a_{23} x_3 = y_2 \quad (2)$$
$$a_{31} x_1 + a_{32} x_2 + a_{33} x_3 = y_3 \quad (3)$$

then the variable x_1 can be eliminated from equation (2) by subtracting equation (1) times a_{21}/a_{11} from equation (2). Similarly subtracting a_{31}/a_{11} times (1) from (2) removes x_1 from equation (3). This gives a new set of equations:

$$a_{11} x_1 + a_{12} x_2 + a_{13} x_3 = y_1 \quad \text{(1) (unchanged)}$$
$$b_{22} x_2 + b_{23} x_3 = y_2' \quad \text{(4) } (x_1 \text{ gone, two new coefficients, new } y_2')$$
$$b_{32} x_2 + b_{33} x_3 = y_3' \quad \text{(5) } (x_1 \text{ gone, two new coefficients, new } y_3')$$

Now we can remove x_2 from equation (5) by subtracting b_{32}/b_{22} times equation (4) from it:

$$a_{11} x_1 + a_{12} x_2 + a_{13} x_3 = y_1 \quad \text{(1) (unchanged)}$$
$$b_{22} x_2 + b_{23} x_3 = y_2' \quad \text{(4) (unchanged)}$$
$$c_{33} x_3 = y_3'' \quad \text{(6) } (x_2 \text{ gone, new coefficient, new } y_3'')$$

To program this in FORTRAN, consider that the original array of coefficients and the right hand side are operated on to eliminate x_1; this gives a replacement set of coefficients and a new right hand side. A further operation eliminates x_2, and the result is an array in 'upper triangular form'. If we choose some suitable indices then the procedure can be described in pseudocode for an array A of N equations:

For each column K from 1 to N–1
   For each row I from K+1 to N
      Operate on Y(I) by letting
         $Y(I) = Y(I)–Y(K)*A(I,K)/A(K,K)$
      And also along the row for J from K to N
         Operate on A(I,J) by letting
           $A(I,J) = A(I,J)–A(K,J)*A(I,K)/A(K,K)$
   End of I loop
End of K loop

There is a subtle problem in translating this directly into FORTRAN; it will not work exactly as stated because the procedure obliterates A(I,K) while it is still needed. This is fairly easy to see once it is pointed out. The first thing to be computed in row I is a new A(I,K) (when J = K in the recipe above). Unfortunately the previous value of A(I,K) is still needed to complete row I. It is necessary to preserve the value A(I,K) somehow. This is quite simple. Before operating on the row for J from K to N, compute and save the value Z = A(I,K)/A(K,K) which is then available for the whole of the row.

Here is a FORTRAN subroutine for the elimination task just described:

```
            SUBROUTINE GLIM(A,Y,N)
C GAUSS ELIMINATION - CONVERT A TO UPPER
C TRIANGULAR FORM AND ALSO ALTER Y
            DIMENSION A(N,N), Y(N)
C OUTER LOOP - ELIMINATE COLUMN
            DO 3Ø K=1,N-1
C INNER LOOP - ROW TO OPERATE ON
               DO 2Ø I=K+1,N
C THIS LOOP ACTUALLY DOES IT
                  Z=A(I,K)/A(K,K)
                  DO 1Ø J=K,N
                     A(I,J)=A(I,J)-A(K,J)*Z
   1Ø           CONTINUE
C OPERATE ALSO ON Y
                  Y(I)=Y(I)-Y(K)*Z
   2Ø        CONTINUE
   3Ø CONTINUE
            END
```

This has not yet solved our equations. However with the coefficient array transformed into an upper triangle, we can find the solution x by back substitution:

$$x_3 = y''_3 / c_{33}$$
$$x_2 = (y'_2 – b_{23} x_3) / b_{22}$$
$$x_3 = (y_1 – a_{12} x_2 – a_{13} x_3) / a_{11}$$

which can be described in the general case of N equations as first:

$X(N) = Y(N)/A(N,N)$ and then for each row K from N – 1 to 1:

$$X(K) = \left\{ Y(K) - \sum_{J=K+1}^{N} A(K,J)*X(J) \right\} / A(K,K)$$

To prove that the program is not so difficult, here is a general purpose subroutine to solve N equations in N unknowns, whose coefficents are given in the N by N real array A. The right hand side is given in Y and the answer is also returned in Y. A and Y are, of course, modified in the course of the procedure:

```
      SUBROUTINE GAUSS(A,Y,N)
C SOLVE AX = Y BY GAUSSIAN ELIMINATION
C A = INPUT REAL ARRAY OF COEFFICIENTS
C     DIMENSION (N,N). IT IS DESTROYED.
C Y = INPUT REAL ARRAY OF RIGHT HAND SIDES
C      DIMENSION (N). IT IS REPLACED BY
C     THE SOLUTION X.
C N = INPUT INTEGER VALUE, NUMBER OF EQUATIONS
      DIMENSION A(N,N), Y(N)
C CALL GLIM TO DO THE ELIMINATION STEP
      CALL GLIM(A,Y,N)
C CALL BSUB FOR BACK SUBSTITUTION
      CALL BSUB(A,Y,N)
      END
```

Exercise I have not given you the subroutine BSUB required to do back substitution. You write it. Test it with the set of equations given at the beginning of this section.

6 Matrices and equations

An array of one dimension can be considered to be a vector. Whether it is interpreted as a row or a column vector depends on the programmer.

Example It is easy to write a function for the inner product of two vectors x and y each of length n. By definition the inner product p is

$$p = \sum_{k=1}^{n} x_k \, y_k$$

which could be interpreted as the product of the lengths of the vectors times the cosine between them. Here it is:

```
      FUNCTION PRODIN(X,Y,N)
C FIND INNER PRODUCT OF REAL VECTORS
C X AND Y, BOTH DIMENSION (N)
      DIMENSION X(N), Y(N)
      PRODIN=0.0
      DO 10 K=1,N
         PRODIN=PRODIN+X(K)*Y(K)
   10 CONTINUE
      END
```

Exercise The norm of a vector is its inner product with itself, and is the square of its length. You could of course accomplish this with

```
      CALL PRODIN(X,X,N)
```

However it is better to write a special function VNORM(X,N). Do it.

An array of two dimensions could be regarded as a matrix. For example, the statement

DIMENSION A(3,4)

could define the matrix

$$\begin{pmatrix} a_{11} & a_{12} & a_{13} & a_{14} \\ a_{21} & a_{22} & a_{23} & a_{24} \\ a_{31} & a_{32} & a_{33} & a_{34} \end{pmatrix}$$

and when you use subscripts like A(I,J), you are referring to row I and column J of the matrix. This is the standard notation used by everyone for matrices. (Because of the way FORTRAN stores arrays in column major order in memory, the unwary programmer is sometimes tricked into unintentional transposition of matrices.)

Example Here is a subroutine to multiply a column vector by a matrix. To work, the sizes of the input and output arrays have to conform.

$$\begin{array}{ccccc} y & = & A & x \\ \text{result} & & \text{matrix} & \text{column vector} \\ \text{size} & & \text{size} & \text{size} \\ m & & m \times n & n \end{array}$$

```
      SUBROUTINE MBYVEC(A,X,Y,M,N)
C
C MULTIPLY MATRIX BY VECTOR Y = A*X
C
C A = INPUT REAL MATRIX DIMENSIONS (M,N)
C X = INPUT REAL VECTOR DIMENSION (N)
C Y = OUTPUT REAL VECTOR DIMENSION (M)
C M,N = INPUT INTEGER ARRAY SIZES. NOTE
C         THAT TO CONFORM X IS N, Y IS M
C
      DIMENSION A(M,N), X(N), Y(M)
      DO 20 I=1,M
        SUM = 0.0
        DO 10 K=1,N
          SUM = SUM + A(I,K)*X(K)
   10   CONTINUE
        Y(I) = SUM
   20 CONTINUE
      END
```

Exercise Two matrices which conform can be multiplied. The product

$$C = AB$$

is possible if the second dimension of A and the first of B are the same. The definition of the multiplication is:

$$c_{ij} = \sum_{k=1}^{r} a_{ik} b_{kj}$$

where *r* is the common size of *A* and *B*. The product *C* has the first dimension of *A* and the second of *B*. Write a subroutine for matrix multiplication.

7 Problems

Many problems involving arrays of two dimensions actually present themselves in the form of equations or matrices. The first two problems given here do not involve the concept of an array as a matrix.

Problem 16.1 Calculate a table of loan repayments.

Theory: whenever regular payments are made, whether it is savings or loan repayments, a geometric series is formed. If you borrow an amount XLOAN, at an interest rate of INT % per period, and make a repayment at the end of the first period, called PMT, then after that first payment you owe

XLOAN*FACTOR – PMT

where

FACTOR = 1.0 + FLOAT(INT)/100.0

is the magnification of your loan by the interest charged in each period. During every addition-al period, what you owe is magnified again and you make another repayment. You will find that after N periods you owe

XLOAN*FACTOR**N
– PMT* { (FACTOR**(N–1) + FACTOR**(N–2) + . . . + FACTOR + 1.0 }

which sums to XLOAN*FACTOR**N – PMT*(1.0 – FACTOR**N)/(1.0 – FACTOR)

The loan is repaid when this falls to zero. The part

XLOAN*FACTOR**N

represents how much you would owe if you made no repayments, and the part

PMT*(1.0 – FACTOR**N)/(1.0 – FACTOR)

represents the accumulated value of your payments. This could be used on its own to calculate how much can be saved by regular investment.

The reader will probably agree that this is complicated enough to be worth presenting as a table. Print a table of loan repayments for a loan of 100 units at rates of 4%, 8%, 12% and 16%, and to cover loans lasting for between 1 and 25 periods. Use pretty FORMAT arrangements.

Problem 16.2 Using the same approach, work out how to calculate the amount still owing after each repayment on a loan of 1000 units over N periods at *i* %. Write a program to produce a set of tables. Do this in an array of three dimensions.

Problem 16.3 The Gaussian elimination procedure can give poor results if the equations are numerically difficult. Notice that the value of Z = A(I,K)/A(K,K) is used in computing new coefficients for the whole array below and to the right of A(K,K), which is called the *pivot ele-ment*. If some pivot is very small, all the new coefficients using it will be very large. The next pivot will then be large and produce very small coefficients. The method can start to oscillate and as a result of limits on the precision of the computer it can give answers which are inac-curate, or even wrong. What can be done?

It is possible to exchange rows of a system of equations without changing the result. It is also possible to exchange columns, but this changes the order of the results. Therefore you can search all rows and columns beyond the pivot element A(K,K) to find the largest coefficient. Switch the largest coefficient into the pivot position. Then divide row K by the new A(K,K) to make the pivot A(K,K) always 1.0. At the end the order of the result has to be restored. Do it.

Problem 16.4 In graphics it is often desired to paint in or 'fill' an area whose outline has been described. The screen is represented by a two dimensional array of 'pixels' in which each integer value represents a colour. If the outline and fill colour are the same, ICOLR, the recursive seed fill algorithm starts at a given place (I,J) and does this:

```
      SUBROUTINE SEEDER(IPIX,M,N,I,J,ICOLR)
C SEED FILL THE INTEGER ARRAY IPIX OF DIMENSIONS (M,N)
C STARTING AT (I,J) WITH FILL AND STOP COLOUR ICOLR
      DIMENSION IPIX(M,N)
C PROTECT IT FROM GOING OUTSIDE
      IF(I.GE.1 .AND. I.LE.M .AND. J.GE.1 .AND. J.LE.N) THEN
        IF(IPIX(I,J).NE.ICOLR) THEN
C COLOUR THIS PIXEL AND THEN DO THE SAME TO ITS NEIGHBOURS
          IPIX(I,J)=ICOLR
          CALL SEEDER(IPIX,M,N,I,J+1,ICOLR)
          CALL SEEDER(IPIX,M,N,I+1,J,ICOLR)
          CALL SEEDER(IPIX,M,N,I,J-1,ICOLR)
          CALL SEEDER(IPIX,M,N,I-1,J,ICOLR)
        END IF
      END IF
      END
```

As it stands, it is impossible because it calls itself. Implement this in FORTRAN 77 by simulating the recursive calls. It is very inefficient since it visits each pixel many times. Make it more efficient. You could spend a lot of time on this!

Problem 16.5 Write a subprogram to transpose a two dimensional array so that the values in position (I , J) of a M by N array are exchanged with the values in position (J , I) of an N by M array. This is easy enough if the arrays are different, but what if you want them to use the same space in memory? Very tricky indeed.

Seventeen

Sharing variables

1 Now this is useful

In FORTRAN it has always been easy to build libraries of subprograms and combine them in packages or applications programs. This is one of its traditional strengths, based on the independence of program units. We have seen how programs can share information through the argument lists of SUBROUTINE and FUNCTION statements. The programmer must ensure that the interface between programs is used correctly—there is no automatic checking that arguments are correctly matched.

Now we will see another way of passing values between subprograms by sharing common areas of memory in the computer. These values are visible only to the program units which need them. Also, by careful planning, different parts of a program can save memory by using COMMON temporarily. This is useful, but again the programmer must ensure that it is done correctly.

2 Memory and blank COMMON

Variables and constants in FORTRAN are 'static'. They are given space when a program is first placed in the computer, and this space persists until the program terminates. Every variable is part of the program unit that uses it, and can be shared through subprogram argument lists. Values which are not arguments are private to the program unit which uses them.

However if you want program units to share space in memory, COMMON will allow it. The COMMON statement creates space in a main program which subprograms can share:

      COMMON *variables*

This will reserve memory for the named *variables*. With arrays, the subscript bounds can be stated in the COMMON statement, or a DIMENSION statement (but not both). For example the COMMON area illustrated by Fig. 17.1 can be defined by:

```
DIMENSION A(5,5)
      COMMON X,Y,Z,A
```
or
```
      COMMON X,Y,Z,A(5,5)
```

These have the same effect. Space is created in COMMON for the ordinary variables X, Y, and Z and the array A.

There are two basic reasons for using blank COMMON. First, the argument lists of subprograms can be shortened or eliminated, which may improve readability. You can also reduce the amount of space taken by a program by sharing working space

X
Y
Z
A(1,1)
A(2,1)
A(3,1)
A(4,1)
A(5,1)
A(1,2)
A(2,2)
etc.

Fig. 17.1. Illustrating variables in a COMMON area.

in different parts of the program which may be used in totally different ways.

When you have made a COMMON area in a main program, you can use it in any subroutines or functions which have their own COMMON statements. In a subprogram, the COMMON statement tells where the variables are to be found. For example, with the COMMON area of Fig. 17.1, a subroutine INVENT could be used to define A(I,J) as X + Y**I + Z**J.

```
      SUBROUTINE INVENT
      PARAMETER (ISZ=5)
      COMMON P, Q, R, S(ISZ,ISZ)
      DO 20 I=1,ISZ
        DO 10 J=1,ISZ
          S(I,J)=P+Q**I+R**J
10    CONTINUE
20  CONTINUE
      END
```

INVENT refers to values in COMMON by different names from the main program. You must be careful that the values match exactly by type and position. If they do not, you are on your own in dangerous territory. However, it is not necessary for the COMMON blocks to be the same size. A subprogram can use less than the full COMMON area, but not more.

There are, naturally, some restrictions, as follow:

1. In subprograms, an array in COMMON cannot have an adjustable or assumed size dimension. This is wrong:

```
SUBROUTINE WRONG(M)
      COMMON SUMRAY(M)
```

2. A variable in COMMON can be passed as an argument to a subroutine if the subroutine doesn't know it is in COMMON. However, it is forbidden to have a variable named both in COMMON and as the dummy argument in the same subroutine, because terrible conflicts would be possible. This we forbid:

```
      SUBROUTINE FORBID(CRAZY)
      COMMON CRAZY
```

3. A DATA statement cannot define values in COMMON. This prevents conflicts between main programs and subroutines. Who would win here?

```
      COMMON MANIAC              SUBROUTINE FIGHT
      DATA MANIAC/0/            COMMON IDIOT
      CALL FIGHT                 DATA IDIOT/999/
      END                        END
```

It will be seen later that there is a special facility for assigning predefined values to "named" COMMON.

The COMMON statement is another statement whose position in a program is constrained. It must be placed with the DIMENSION statements and can be mixed with them. Indeed, both COMMON and DIMENSION are examples of 'specification statements'. More of these will be introduced in the next few chapters, and they can be mixed together. In section 8 of this chapter the rules of statement ordering will be summarized again.

3 Named COMMON—a superior concept

Named COMMON allows several different areas of memory to be created, so that you can control which subprograms share which areas. This is very helpful in creating 'packages', whose internal data is private. For example a graphics library, an applications package and a user's program could all have different named COMMONs yet work together. This is a great aid in making programs transportable.

The good news is that named COMMON need not be defined in the main program, and initial values can be assigned to it using DATA statements in a special program unit known as the BLOCK DATA subprogram. A restriction is that a particular named COMMON has to be exactly the same size in all program units which use it.

The *name* of a COMMON area is defined between slashes in a COMMON statement. It must not be the same as any subprogram name (including standard functions such as ATAN).

COMMON /*name*/ *variables*, /*name*/ ...

If the name is blank, //, you are creating space in the normal 'blank' COMMON.

Example Let us reconsider the use of a stack. In Chapter 13 we defined an array to be used as a stack, and passed it to the stack manipulation routines. To avoid having to pass too many things, I put the stack pointer in the array. Instead, we can have a separate pointer and the stack in a private COMMON:

```
      PARAMETER (MAX=1ØØ)
      COMMON /STACK/ IPOINT, ISTACK(MAX)
```

To initialize the stack, call STINIT as before but with no arguments:

```
      SUBROUTINE STINIT
C INITIALIZE THE INTEGER STACK ARRAY ISTACK. THE STACK
C IS IN THE NAMED COMMON /STACK/. THE POINTER IS IPOINT,
C THE NUMBER OF ITEMS ALREADY IN THE STACK. THE ACTUAL
C STACK IS ISTACK. SET THE DEPTH WITH MAX.
      PARAMETER (MAX=1ØØ)
      COMMON /STACK/ IPOINT, ISTACK(MAX)
      IPOINT=Ø
      END
```

The procedures PUSH and POP are now:

```
      SUBROUTINE PUSH(LOB)
C PUSH THE INTEGER LOB INTO THE STACK ISTACK
C IF THE STACK IS FULL, LOB REPLACES THE TOP
      PARAMETER (MAX=1ØØ)
      COMMON /STACK/ IPOINT, ISTACK(MAX)
      IF (IPOINT.LT.MAX) IPOINT=IPOINT+1
      ISTACK(IPOINT)=LOB
      END

      FUNCTION POP()
C RETURN THE TOP VALUE ON THE STACK
C IF THE STACK IS EMPTY YOU GET Ø
      PARAMETER (MAX=1ØØ)
```

```
COMMON /STACK/ IPOINT, ISTACK(MAX)
IF(IPOINT.GT.Ø) THEN
  POP=ISTACK(IPOINT)
  IPOINT=IPOINT-1
ELSE
  POP=Ø
END IF
END
```

This is an important example. You may recall in Chapter 15 some emphasis on abstract data types which used access procedures to hide the implementation details. Unfortunately we had to pass around arrays and pointers. No longer! Now we can hide it all away.

Exercise Reconsider the simulation of sets presented in Chapter 15, and hide it all away in a named COMMON area. Also refer to Problem 15.4 if you want to make it really useful.

4 Block DATA—turtle graphics

A variable which resides in blank COMMON cannot be given an initial value by a DATA statement. However this can be done if the data is in named COMMON, another of its advantages. BLOCK DATA is a special kind of subprogram whose sole purpose is to assign initial values to variables in named COMMON.

A BLOCK DATA subprogram begins with a BLOCK DATA statement, and ends with an END statement. It contains only a definition of the named COMMON (or COMMONs) using the necessary named COMMON, DIMENSION or type statements. After those you put the DATA statements which can initialize variables in named COMMON.

Example The array NUMBRS in the COMMON area COUNT is to be defined. Other variables in the same named COMMON are not initialized. The entire subprogram is

```
BLOCK DATA
DIMENSION A(4), B(4)
DIMENSION NUMBRS(1Ø), ARAY(5,5)
COMMON /COUNT/ A,B,C,I,J,K
COMMON /COUNT/ NUMBRS, IRAY
DATA NUMBRS /1,2,3,4,5,6,7,8,9,Ø/
END
```

Several named COMMON blocks can be set up in this way. A program can have more than one BLOCK DATA subprogram, but if all or part of an area is redefined then the last BLOCK DATA subprogram is used for the initial value.

Example Now we can define a really useful graphics package. The basic subroutines GSTART, GDRAW and GQUIT from Chapter 11 have no memory of the position of the graphics pen. Often graphics commands are described in terms of a 'turtle', (a small friendly reptile) which moves about on your graphics screen carrying a pen, which might be up or down, as

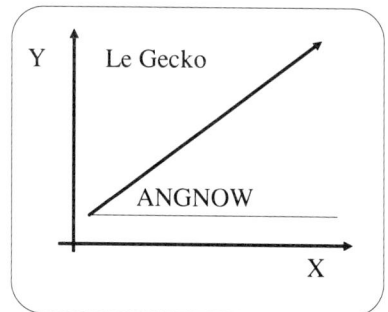

Fig. 17.2. Gecko Graphics (joke).

Useful Statements of FORTRAN 77 (Items in square brackets are optional parts.)

Executable statements

CALL *name* (*actual arguments*) Chapter 11
CONTINUE Chapters 8, 9
DO *label variable* = *start, finish, step* Chapters 8, 9
END Chapter 2
GO TO *statement number* Chapters 4, 7, 9
IF (*logical expression*) *statement* Chapters 4, 7, 9
the block IF Chapters 4, 7, 9
   IF (*logical expression*) THEN
   ELSE IF (*logical expression*) THEN
   ELSE
   END IF
RETURN Chapter 11
STOP Chapter 7

Input-Output statements

BACKSPACE *control list* Chapter 20
CLOSE *control list* Chapter 20
END FILE *control list* Chapter 20
INQUIRE *control list* Chapter 20
OPEN *control list* Chapter 20
PRINT *format, values* Chapters 2, 3, 6, 20
READ (*control list*) *variables* Chapter 20
READ *format* , *variables* Chapters 4, 6, 20
REWIND *control list* Chapter 20
WRITE (*control list*) *values* Chapter 20

Non-executable statements

Specification statements
DIMENSION *name* (*bounds*) [, *name* (*bounds*) . . .] Chapter 12
COMMON [/ *name* /] *name* [(*bounds*)] [, . . .] Chapter 17
Type *name* [(*bounds*) , *name* (*bounds*) . . .] Chapter 19
IMPLICIT *type* (*ranges*) [, *type* (*ranges*) . . .] Chapter 19
PARAMETER (*name* = *constant*) [, (*name* = *constant*) . . .] Chapter 10
EXTERNAL *names* Chapter 19
INTRINSIC *names* Chapter 19
SAVE [*names*] Chapters 10, 17

Other non-executable statements
Statement function definitions:
  name (*dummy arguments*) = *expression* Chapter 10
BLOCK DATA Chapter 17
DATA *variables* / *constants* / [, *variables* / *constants* / . . .] Chapter 10
FORMAT (*Specification*) Chapter 6
FUNCTION Chapter 10
  also *type* FUNCTION(*dummy arguments*) Chapters 18, 19
PROGRAM *name* (*machine-dependent options*) Chapter 2
SUBROUTINE *name* (*dummy arguments*) Chapter 11

Types of FORTRAN 77 are the implicit types REAL and INTEGER, and the explicit types
CHARACTER, COMPLEX, LOGICAL and DOUBLE PRECISION.

FORMAT descriptions Chapters 6 (integers and reals), 18 (characters) and 19 (others)

w = field width n = no.of similar items d = no.of digits e = no. of digits in exponent k = scale factor

[n]Iw[.d] integer [n]Fw.d real without exponent [n]Ew.d[Ee] real with exponent [n]Dw.d real without
exponent [n]Gw.d[Ee] real with exponent if necessary [n]Lw logical [n]Aw characters nX blanks
kP set scale factor SP print all signs SS print minus signs only S print signs optionally BN ignore
blanks BZ blanks are zero '*character constant*' / new line n(*repeated group*)

in Fig. 17.2. The system remembers the position of the turtle and also which way it is facing. By telling it to turn and move you can make drawings.

Here is a main program which would draw a square using turtle graphics:

```
        PROGRAM SQUARE                      DO 1Ø K=1,4
        CALL GSTART                            CALL MOVEBY(1.Ø)
C GO TO THE STARTING POINT                     CALL TURNBY(9Ø.Ø)
        CALL MOVETO(1.Ø, 1.Ø)          1Ø CONTINUE
        CALL PENDWN                        CALL GQUIT
                                           END
```

The memory of the turtle is defined in a named COMMON called /TURTLE/, with the present pen position being (XNOW, YNOW), the angle the turtle is facing called ANGNOW, and the pen status IPEN, where 0 means up and 1 means down. The initial values are set by this BLOCK DATA subprogram:

```
C DEFINE INITIAL STATE OF THE TURTLE
        BLOCK DATA
        COMMON/TURTLE/ XNOW, YNOW, ANGNOW, IPEN
        DATA XNOW, YNOW /2*Ø.Ø/
        DATA ANGNOW /Ø.Ø/, IPEN /Ø/
        END
```

These are the subroutines that make up the turtle system. We can turn the turtle to face a particular direction with TURNTO, or rotate it a particular amount with TURNBY. Similarly we can move to a particular place with MOVETO, or by a particular amount in the direction the turtle is facing using MOVEBY.

```
        SUBROUTINE TURNTO (ANG)
C POINT THE TURTLE IN THE DIRECTION ANG DEGREES
        COMMON/TURTLE/ X, Y, ANGNOW, I
        ANGNOW=ANG
        END

        SUBROUTINE TURNBY (ANG)
C TUEN THE TURTLE BY ANG DEGREES ANTICLOCKWISE
        COMMON/TURTLE/ X, Y, ANGNOW, I
        ANGNOW=ANGNOW+ANG
        END

        SUBROUTINE MOVETO(X,Y)
C MOVE THE TURTLE TO THE CO-ORDINATE (X,Y)
        COMMON/TURTLE/ XNOW, YNOW, Z, IPEN
C IF THE PEN IS DOWN YOU DRAW
        IF (IPEN.EQ.1) CALL GDRAW(XNOW, YNOW, X, Y)
C UPDATE THE PEN POSITION
        XNOW=X
        YNOW=Y
        END
```

```
      SUBROUTINE MOVEBY(DIST)
C MOVE THE TURTLE DIST UNITS THE WAY IT IS FACING
      COMMON /TURTLE/ XNOW, YNOW, ANGNOW, I
C GET THE ANGLE IN RADIANS
      RADS=ANGNOW*ATAN(1.Ø)/45.Ø
C COMPUTE THE DESTINATION
      XNEXT=XNOW+DIST*COS(RADS)
      YNEXT=YNOW+DIST*SIN(RADS)
      CALL MOVETO(XNEXT,YNEXT)
      END
```

The pen is up to begin with, and is controlled by the subroutines PENUP and PENDWN. All they do is save the new pen position which is needed whenever a move is made. Notice that the three real values in COMMON /TURTLE/ are taken care of by a real array—IPEN will be in the correct memory location. As far as memory space is concerned, one real is as good as another. Although an integer ought to take the same space as a real, only experts should fool around with mixed types.

```
      SUBROUTINE PENUP              SUBROUTINE PENDWN
      COMMON/TURTLE/ X(3), IPEN     COMMON/TURTLE/ X(3), IPEN
      IPEN=Ø                        IPEN=1
      END                           END
```

Exercise Add line dashing facilities to the turtle package. Initially the lines will be solid ones, but in this exercise you will provide a mechanism for making optional dashed ones. When dashing, whenever the pen goes from up to down, the dash pattern should restart. If the pen stays down, the pattern continues smoothly on successive calls to moveto or moveby. Hold the details of the pattern in named COMMON and provide access subroutines to alter it.

5 EQUIVALENCE

COMMON can be used to make variables in different program units share the same memory. By using an EQUIVALENCE statement you can force variables or arrays in the same program unit to occupy the same space. You would only do this as a means of saving memory in a program which is getting too big for your computer. This was important when computer memories were generally small and expensive, but is less necessary now. Clearly it has to be used carefully to avoid destroying data. The EQUIVALENCE facility will be eliminated from future versions of FORTRAN, so do not use it unless it is really necessary.

The EQUIVALENCE statement associates a number of variables with each other, meaning that they share the same space.

Example Three arrays can be made to share the same space by these statements:

```
      DIMENSION ICOEFF(Ø:1Ø), IQ(3,3)
      DIMENSION XRAY(2,3,4)
      EQUIVALENCE (ICOEFF, IQ, XRAY)
```

Fig. 17.3 shows how the arrays are arranged in memory, assuming that real and integer variables use the same space. This ought to be true for standard FORTRAN 77.

ICOEFF(0)	IQ(1,1)	XRAY(1,1,1)
ICOEFF(1)	IQ(2,1)	XRAY(2,1,1)
ICOEFF(2)	IQ(3,1)	XRAY(1,2,1)
ICOEFF(3)	IQ(1,2)	XRAY(2,2,1)
ICOEFF(4)	IQ(2,2)	XRAY(1,3,1)
ICOEFF(5)	IQ(3,2)	XRAY(2,3,1)
ICOEFF(6)	IQ(1,3)	XRAY(1,1,2)
ICOEFF(7)	IQ(2,3)	XRAY(2,1,2)
ICOEFF(8)	IQ(3,3)	XRAY(1,2,2)
ICOEFF(9)		XRAY(2,2,2)
ICOEFF(10)		XRAY(1,3,2)
		XRAY(2,3,2)
		XRAY(1,1,3)
		etc.

Fig. 17.3. Alignment of arrays in memory using EQUIVALENCE.

You are able to use any of these arrays at any time by their separate names, using the correct number of subscripts. Because these arrays share the same physical memory space, be sure that their different uses do not interfere. If you change XRAY(2,2,1), for example, you are destroying IQ(1,2) and ICOEFF(3). They are destroyed, and not merely redefined, because a real value is placed there which has no meaning if referred to as an integer.

The general form of the EQUIVALENCE statement is

      EQUIVALENCE *(variable list)* , *(variable list) ,* . . .

The lists of variables are separated by commas and enclosed within brackets. The variables can be ordinary ones, or array names with or without subscripts. Without subscripts the first member of the array is intended. The EQUIVALENCE statement forces all the named variables to occupy the same memory location, and the remainder of any arrays line up accordingly. You may find it helps to draw a sketch of the memory layout to understand it. Indeed where either COMMON or EQUIVALENCE (or both) are concerned a memory map is a valuable part of the documentation.

If you specify an impossible arrangement you will get caught, as in this example:

```
DIMENSION X(9), INCA(2,2)
EQUIVALENCE (X(2), INCA)
EQUIVALENCE (X(7), INCA(1,2))
```

In the above statement you cannot align X(2) with INCA(1,1) at the same time as X(7) with INCA(1,2) Arrays cannot be broken into pieces.

There are a few things which cannot be done with EQUIVALENCE:

(i) Although an ordinary variable is allowed to have the same name as a function, it may not then be used in an EQUIVALENCE statement.

(ii) A subprogram cannot refer in an EQUIVALENCE statement to one of its dummy arguments.

EQUIVALENCE is a specification statement, like DIMENSION or COMMON, and like them its position in the program is constrained. COMMON, DIMENSION, and EQUIVALENCE statements can be mixed together at the beginning of the program unit. The rules for ordering statements are summarized again at the end of this chapter.

6 COMMON and EQUIVALENCE

You can use the EQUIVALENCE statement to associate some variables with others which are declared to be in COMMON. If this is done they all wind up in COMMON. To organize such an arrangement, remember that that the COMMON statements dictate the layout of the COMMON area. EQUIVALENCE will simply align other variables with COMMON. Consider the statements

```
COMMON X, Y, Z
DIMENSION X(2), Y(2), Z(2)
COMMON INDEX(3)
DIMENSION ZIPPY(4), NUTTY(3)
EQUIVALENCE (ZIPPY, X), (NUTTY, Z(2))
```

Here the DIMENSION and EQUIVALENCE statements have not influenced the layout of COMMON, as shown by Fig. 17.4.

An EQUIVALENCE statement is allowed to make blank COMMON longer, as in

```
DIMENSION MORE(1Ø)
COMMON I,J,IRAY(5)
EQUIVALENCE (J,MORE)
```

However you cannot extend blank COMMON backwards. This is wrong:

```
EQUIVALENCE (I,MORE(3))
```

A named COMMON cannot be extended in either direction by the use of EQUIVALENCE. Two different named COMMONs cannot be associated by EQUIVALENCE.

X(1)	ZIPPY(1)
X(2)	ZIPPY(2)
Y(1)	ZIPPY(3)
Y(2)	ZIPPY(4)
Z(1)	
Z(2)	NUTTY(1)
INDEX(1)	NUTTY(2)
INDEX(2)	NUTTY(3)
INDEX(3)	

Fig. 17.4. Using COMMON and EQUIVALENCE together.

7 COMMON and SAVE

In Chapter 10, the SAVE statement forced a subprogram to preserve the status of all or some of its variables between one CALL and the next. COMMON blocks provide a useful way of making this happen without SAVE. Once they have been defined in the first place, all variables in blank COMMON remain defined through all the units that make up a program.

This is not quite true of a named COMMON block. If it appears in a main program, then it remains defined provided that more than one subprogram uses it. If it appears in only one subprogram, then it is treated like a local variable, and becomes undefined when the subprogram is finished. In that situation a SAVE statement will be necessary if you want to keep values defined. A special feature of SAVE is that the name of a COMMON block can be given with slashes around it to preserve the entire block:

```
SAVE / name /
```

8 The order of statements—yet again

In this chapter several new statements have been introduced which belong at the beginning of program units. Here the rules regarding ordering are summarized, not quite in their final form. The specification statements used so far are COMMON, DIMENSION, EQUIVALENCE, PARAMETER and SAVE, but more are to follow.

Comments can go anywhere before END	Heading: PROGRAM (optional) or FUNCTION or SUBROUTINE or BLOCK DATA		
	FORMAT statements can go after heading, before END	Specification Statements	
		DATA statements	Statement functions
			Executable Statements
END is always the very end			

9 Problems

Problem 17.1 Write subroutines which use the turtle graphics package to draw polygons and stargons, as were described in Chapter 11, and illustrated in Fig. 11.2.

Problem 17.2 If you enjoy both recreational graphics and recursion, find out what is meant by a Sierpinski curve, and draw one of them.

Problem 17.3 The basic graphics package, GSTART, GDRAW and GQUIT can be improved by defining some graphical attributes in a special COMMON. Introduce a transformation into the basic graphics routine GDRAW so that the position of the pen behaves like:

$$\begin{pmatrix} \text{XPAPER} \\ \text{YPAPER} \end{pmatrix} = \begin{pmatrix} a & b \\ c & d \end{pmatrix} \begin{pmatrix} \text{XUSER} \\ \text{YUSER} \end{pmatrix} + \begin{pmatrix} \text{XSHIFT} \\ \text{YSHIFT} \end{pmatrix}$$

(XUSER ,YUSER) is a user co-ordinate which the graphics system translates into a paper or screen co ordinate (XPAPER, YPAPER). The transformation provides shifting, rotation and magnification. If initially you define

   $a = d = 1$ and $b = c = \text{XSHIFT} = 0$

the transformation has no effect. This should be set up in a labelled COMMON using BLOCK DATA. The user can then apply successive magnification, rotation and shifting by calling suitable subroutines, or restore the original transformation. You work out the mathematics.

Problem 17.4 Introduce a rectangular 'window' into the graphics system so that lines which cross the window edge are 'clipped', with only the visible parts drawn. An initial window is defined in named COMMON, Provide facilities for changing its position and size.

Problem 17.5 Using COMMON the tree data structure can be manipulated more easily. Reconsider the access procedures for trees introduced in Chapter 15.

Problem 17.6 A polyline is a fundamental graphical data structure. It is a list of the vertices which define the outline of an object. For example, instead of drawing stars one line at a time, you could first define a polyline and then draw the same star any number of times. By manipulating the transforms of Problem 10.3, the same object can be drawn in any place with any magnification at any angle (possibly clipped by a window). Consider the creation of an abstract polyline data type. Design access procedures for building polylines. Develop a subroutine for drawing them. Build a five pointed hollow star. Then draw the polyline in a circle of stars like Fig. 11.3b, by manipulating the transformation you defined in Problem 17.3. If you have done all this, you have created the complete Bloggs Kernel System (BKS).

Eighteen

About characters

1 Characters and lengths

To use a name to represent a character item, declare it in a CHARACTER statement:

    CHARACTER *names*

This is a *type statement*. Items which are not reals or integers must be declared by a type statement. The CHARACTER statement goes near the beginning of a program unit, and follows the rules for ordering statements given at the end of the previous chapter.

A character item has a length. This is the number of characters it can hold—not the same as the size of an array. Length is controlled by the CHARACTER statement, as in these examples:

`CHARACTER ALPHA`	ALPHA is a character item of length 1.
`CHARACTER*4 ITEM`	ITEM is a character item of length 4.
`CHARACTER JAZZ*4`	JAZZ is a character item of length 4.
`CHARACTER*6 SIXES, TWOS*2`	SIXES has length 6. TWOS has length 2.

The length can be attached to the keyword CHARACTER by a *, and then it takes effect for the whole statement. If no length is given, it is 1. A length attached to an item applies only to that item. An item could be the name of a variable, a constant defined later in a PARAMETER statement, or a character function that you are going to use.

The length specification can be an unsigned integer constant greater than zero, as above, or it can be an integer constant expression in brackets which gives a positive length, for example

    `PARAMETER (MORE=1)`
    `CHARACTER*(3*4+MORE) BLOB`

2 Constants and variables

We have seen character string constants many times. They are enclosed by apostrophes, and to put apostrophes inside you have to double them. You get the length by counting the characters, allowing for the special nature of apostrophes:

    `'CONSTANT'` is a character string constant of length 8.

    `'ISN''T'`   is a character string constant of length 5.

Exercise What on earth does this print? Work it out and then try it.

    `PRINT '(''TO GET '''' YOU MUST PUT '''''''''')'`
    `END`

You can give a name to a string constant in a PARAMETER statement. To do this, you have to declare items to be of type character before any PARAMETER statement that gives them a value. However if you use an integer constant to define a length, that has to come first. This is why you are allowed to mix type and PARAMETER statements. Define each constant before you use it:

```
PARAMETER (LA=5, LB=4, LC=9)
CHARACTER*(LA) ITEMA, ITEMB*(LB), ITEMC*(LC)
PARAMETER (ITEMA='WATER' , ITEMB='GATE')
PARAMETER (ITEMC=ITEMA//ITEMB)
PRINT*,ITEMC
END
```

I hope you have mastered the difference between constants given names by PARAMETER and variables given initial values by DATA:

```
CHARACTER MESAGE*4Ø
DATA MESSAGE /' THIS GIVES A MESSAGE AN INITIAL VALUE'/
```

3 Expressions, assignment and more about length

The only character operation is 'concatenation' which joins strings together. The new length is the sum of the lengths joined. You write it as two slashes:

  character value **//** *character value*

Character values can be used in assignment statements,

  variable = expression

With a character *variable*, *expression* must be a character value—there is no conversion:

```
CHARACTER*6 HOME
HOME='LON'//'DON'
PRINT*, HOME            prints LONDON
```

To use character items, you must know what happens when the lengths of items do not match. Pascal is very rude to you about things like that. FORTRAN is more helpful. To make the assignment the right hand end of the expression is either chopped off or filled with spaces:

```
CHARACTER*6 HOME

HOME='BRONX'
PRINT*, HOME                 prints BRONX   (a space at the end).

HOME='ALBEQUERQUE'
PRINT*, HOME                 prints ALBEQU
```

We will see later that a length of (*****) can be used for the dummy arguments of subprograms.

4 Comparisons, codes and functions

The normal relational operators can be used between character items:

```
CHARACTER TEXT

IF(TEXT.LT.'M') PRINT*, TEXT, ' IS BEFORE M'
```

You can usually rely on the capital letters A to Z being in order. The lengths need not match:

'ABC' is less than 'ABCD'	'ZZZ' is less than 'ZZZA'
'MONEY' is less than 'NOTHING'	'LONGER' is less than 'SHORT'

You can safely use .EQ. or .NE. to check for equality. However there are several different character codes used on different computers. In these, the numbers might come before or after the letters. There may be other characters in between letters of the alphabet, and the capital letters might come before or after the small ones. The most important character sequence is the ASCII code, listed in Table 18.1.

Table 18.1 Printable characters of the ASCII code

Symbol	Decimal Code	Symbol	Decimal Code	Symbol	Decimal Code	Symbol	Decimal Code
Space	32	8	56	P	80	h	104
!	33	9	57	Q	81	i	105
"	34	:	58	R	82	j	106
#	35	;	59	S	83	k	107
$	36	<	60	T	84	l	108
%	37	=	61	U	85	m	109
&	38	>	62	V	86	n	110
'	39	?	63	W	87	o	111
(	40	@	64	X	88	p	112
)	41	A	65	Y	89	q	113
*	42	B	66	Z	90	r	114
+	43	C	67	[	91	s	115
,	44	D	68	\	92	t	116
–	45	E	69	]	93	u	117
.	46	F	70	^	94	v	118
/	47	G	71	_	95	w	119
Ø	48	H	72	`	96	x	120
1	49	I	73	a	97	y	121
2	50	J	74	b	98	z	122
3	51	K	75	c	99	{	123
4	52	L	76	d	100			124
5	53	M	77	e	101	}	125
6	54	N	78	f	102	~	126
7	55	O	79	g	103	Delete	127

FORTRAN 77 provides some functions for ASCII comparisons, called 'lexical functions':

LGE(a,b) .TRUE. if character value a is the same or later than character value b in the ASCII code.

LLE(a,b) .TRUE. if a is the same or earlier than b in the ASCII code.

LGT(a,b) .TRUE. if a is later than b in the ASCII code.

LLT(a,b) .TRUE. if a is earlier than b in the ASCII code.

The lexical functions can be used directly in IF statements:

```
IF(' '.LT.'A') THEN
  PRINT*,'BLANK IS LESS THAN A'
ELSE
  PRINT*,'BLANK IS NOT LESS THAT A'
END IF
```

```
      IF (LLT(' ','A')) THEN
        PRINT*,'BLANK IS LEXICALLY LESS THAN A'
      ELSE
        PRINT*,'BLANK IS LEXICALLY NOT LESS THAN A'
      END IF
      END
```

There are a few other intrinsic functions for dealing with characters:

LEN(a)   Integer result, the length of the character string a.

ICHAR(a)   Integer result, the numerical value of the first character in the string a, according to the machine dependent sequence.

CHAR(I)   Character result length 1. The character whose numerical position is I in the machine dependent sequence. We expect that if a = CHAR(I), then I = ICHAR(a) (and vice versa if a has length 1).

INDEX(a,b)   Integer result, the starting position within string a of the first appearance of the shorter string b, or zero if b does not occur.

Exercise To place items in alphabetical order, we would require the blank to be less than 'A'. Check this out using the relational operators and the lexical functions. Now look at what CHAR and ICHAR tell you. What will happen about alphabetical ordering if you have a mixture of upper and lower case letters? What about numbers?

5 In and out—plot a graph

With list-directed PRINT, character values are displayed according to their actual length as we have seen. To use list-directed input, you have to enclose your input data in apostrophes:

```
      CHARACTER ALPHA*4
      READ*, X, ALPHA, I
```

When the program is run, you could provide this input:

```
      3.14, 'IT''S', 73
```

Double apostrophes are needed, just as in string constants. As you might expect, if the length of the input string is not exactly right, the leftmost characters are taken and either truncated or blank filled to give the correct length.

To avoid having to give apostrophes, you can use formatted input and output, but then your data must be exactly the length expected. The special FORMAT description for characters is

  n **A** w

which specifies n fields of width w characters. Both n and w are optional, and we need to know what happens about lengths. First of all, if w is not given, the length used is that of the variable being read or printed.

This prints four characters: This requires exactly (yes!) six characters as input:

```
      CHARACTER THING*4                 CHARACTER ENTITY*6
      PARAMETER(THING='FOURTEEN')         READ 20, ENTITY
      PRINT '(1X,A)', THING            20 FORMAT(A)
```

If the width w of the A description is given then it will be obeyed exactly. On output w characters will be printed, and on input exactly w characters are required.

If *w* is given and is less than the length of the item in the READ or PRINT list, the usual thing happens. On output the leftmost characters are printed, while on input the length of the data must be exactly what the FORMAT says, which is be ranged left and filled with blanks.

We have a new situation if the width given in the FORMAT is greater than the width of the list item. For printed output, the result is ranged right, preceded by blanks. On input the rightmost characters are taken.

This prints five blanks before HELLO:

```
      PRINT 1Ø, 'HELLO'
 1Ø FORMAT(1X, A1Ø)
```

This requires you to give six characters even though CORNER wants only four of them:

```
      CHARACTER CORNER*4
      READ '(A6)', CORNER
```

The A specification makes it easy to plot graphs, down the page rather than across. Note the use of blanks:

```
C PROGRAM TO MAKE A HOLLOW PYRAMID
      CHARACTER BLANK, STAR
      PARAMETER (BLANK=' ', STAR='*')
 1Ø FORMAT(12ØA)
      DO 2Ø K=1,5Ø
         PRINT 1Ø, (BLANK,L=1,K-1), STAR
 2Ø CONTINUE
      DO 3Ø K=49,1,-1
         PRINT 1Ø, (BLANK,L=1,K-1), STAR
 3Ø CONTINUE
      END
```

Exercise The above examples illustrate all you need to plot a graph of a single function. Plot a graph of the function

$$f(x) = e^{(-x^2/2)}$$

Now try to put sin *x* and cos *x* on the same graph without using a character array, since official-ly you do not know about them yet.

6 Substrings and arrays

A substring is a piece of a character variable. Anywhere you can use a character variable, you can ask for a fragment of it instead by writing:

variable (*start* : *finish*)

Start and *finish* are integer expressions to select the substring. Clearly it only makes sense if

$1 \leq start \leq finish$

A substring gives a character value of length *finish* – *start* + 1 taken from inside the original string. *Start* and *finish* are both optional. If *start* is not given, it is 1. If *finish* is omitted, it is the end of the original string. Substrings are a useful facility not duplicated in other languages, notably Pascal.

Example We can take a positive integer value and turn it into a string. FORTRAN does this when we PRINT an integer, but let us try it for ourselves. Assuming the numbers from 0 to 9 are represented by sequential codes in the machine, we can get the codes of each digit and put them in the string. This program restricts us to 4 digits, finding them in reverse order using the MOD function. Notice the expression which converts an integer digit into a character code:

```
C CONVERT AN INTEGER TO A STRING
      PARAMETER (LENGTH=4)
      CHARACTER ANSWER* (LENGTH)
      IRANGE=1Ø**LENGTH-1
C GET A SUITABLE INTEGER FOR CONVERSION
   1Ø PRINT*,'ENTER AN INTEGER IN THE RANGE Ø TO ',IRANGE
      READ*, INT
      IF ((INT.LT.Ø).OR.(INT.GT.IRANGE)) GO TO 1Ø
C INITIALLY THE ANSWER IS BLANK
      DO 2Ø LOC=1,LENGTH
         ANSWER(LOC:LOC)=' '
   2Ø CONTINUE
C CONVERT DIGITS UNTIL THE NUMBER IS ZERO.
      LOC=LENGTH
   3Ø ANSWER(LOC:LOC)=CHAR(ICHAR('Ø')+MOD(INT,1Ø))
      INT=INT/1Ø
      LOC=LOC-1
      IF(INT.GT.Ø) GO TO 3Ø
      PRINT*,ANSWER
      END
```

Exercise Will it work on your computer? Alter the maximum number of digits to cover the range of integers on your machine. Then make it deal with negative integers. Finally, write the opposite program—accept a string, check that it represents an integer, and convert it to one.

We must not confuse arrays with substrings. The substring selects bits from a string. An array of strings is also possible. We can declare a character array in a DIMENSION statement provided its type and length are declared in a CHARACTER statement. Alternatively we can declare the array bounds in the CHARACTER statement itself, much as we could with arrays in COMMON. These are equivalent:

```
CHARACTER*4 GONK       DIMENSION GONK(1Ø)   CHARACTER*4 GONK(1Ø)
DIMENSION GONK(1Ø)     CHARACTER GONK*4
```

Example Arrays can help us to plot graphs. By using an array of mostly blanks, we can arrange for several curves and an axis to be displayed together. This program makes the graph shown in Fig. 18.1:

```
C USES A CHARACTER ARRAY TO PLOT A GRAPH
      CHARACTER CHBLNK, CHAXIS, CHCOS, CHSIN
      PARAMETER (CHBLNK=' ', CHAXIS='I')
      PARAMETER (CHSIN='S', CHCOS='C')
      PARAMETER (MAXLIN=7Ø, NLINES=24)
      PARAMETER (YMID=26.5, YSCALE=25.Ø)
      CHARACTER LINE(MAXLIN)
```

```
C SET THE RANGE AND RESOLUTION OF THE GRAPH
        XTOP=8.Ø*ATAN(1.Ø)
        DX=XTOP/NLINES
C NOW PLOT THE GRAPH
        DO 2Ø X=Ø.Ø,XTOP,DX
C FIRST CLEAR THE LINE
          DO 1Ø L=1,MAXLIN
            LINE(L)=CHBLNK
     1Ø    CONTINUE
C COMPUTE THE PRINT POSITIONS FOR SIN AND COS
          ICOLS=YMID+YSCALE*SIN(X)
          ICOLC=YMID+YSCALE*COS(X)
C PUT THE SYMBOLS IN THE ARRAY - NOTE PRIORITY
          LINE(26)=CHAXIS
          LINE(ICOLS)=CHSIN
          LINE(ICOLC)=CHCOS
          PRINT '(12ØA)', LINE
     2Ø CONTINUE
        END
```

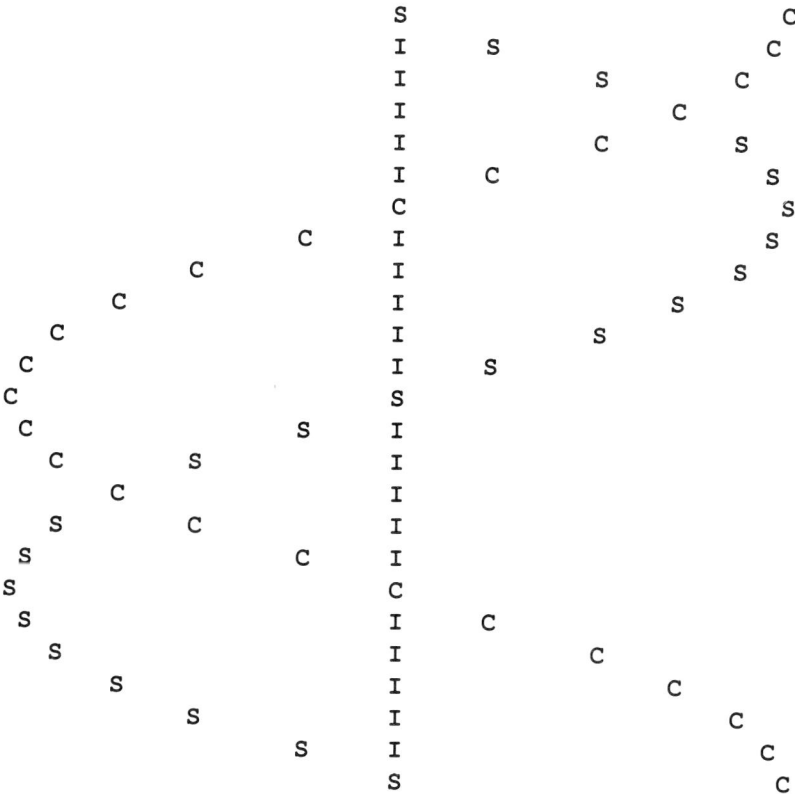

```
                                 S                              C
                                 I       S                        C
                                 I               S           C
                                 I                     C
                                 I                 C       S
                                 I       C                  S
                                 C                            S
                     C           I                            S
                  C              I
                C                I                        S
              C                  I                    S
            C                    I                S
           C                     I          S
          C                      S
           C            S         I
             C       S           I
               C     C           I
            S        C           I
          S            C         I
         S                       C
        S                        I       C
          S                      I         C
            S                    I            C
               S                 I              C
                    S            I                C
                         S       I                 C
                                 S                   C
```

Fig. 18.1. You can do this with a character array

Exercise The graph of Fig. 18.1 runs down the paper. Make it run across.

7 Functions and subprograms

You can create a character statement function. You first declare the name and length in a CHARACTER statement, and also declare any character dummy arguments of the function.

Example This statement function appends character number I to its argument. Here it is used with the ASCII code for an exclamation mark.

```
CHARACTER ZAP*6, WHAM*4
ZAP(WHAM,I)=WHAM // ' ' // CHAR(I)
PRINT*, ZAP('BANG',33)
END
```

The statement function

name (*arguments*) = *expression*

must have an expression of type character if the function is of type character. Since the only character operation is concatenation, the number of things you can do with a character statement function is limited.

The function subprogram of type character is a separate program unit beginning with

CHARACTER*length* **FUNCTION** *name* (*arguments*)

The integer constant *length* is optional, and is taken to be 1 if not given. In the program that will use a character function, you must state its length in a CHARACTER statement.

Example The function SQUOZE removes all double spaces from a line of text. The argument is a string OLD of length 120, and characters are copied to SQUOZE, skipping repeated blanks. The result is then blank filled:

```
      CHARACTER*12Ø FUNCTION SQUOZE (OLD)
C A CHARACTER FUNCTION TO REMOVE MULTIPLE BLANKS FROM THE
C INPUT STRING OLD, A CHARACTER VALUE OF LENGTH 12Ø
      CHARACTER*12Ø OLD
      ITO=1
      LIMIT=12Ø
C COPY CHARACTER ITO TO IFROM, BUT DO NOT
C ADVANCE ITO WHENEVER THERE ARE TWO BLANKS
      DO 1Ø L=1,LIMIT-1
        SQUOZE(ITO:ITO)=OLD(L:L)
        IF(OLD(L:L).NE.' ') THEN
          ITO=ITO+1
        ELSE IF(OLD(L+1:L+1).NE.' ')THEN
          ITO=ITO+1
        END IF
  1Ø CONTINUE
      SQUOZE(ITO:ITO)=OLD(LIMIT:LIMIT)
C BLANK FILL THE RESULT
      DO 2Ø L=ITO+1,LIMIT
        ITO=ITO+1
        SQUOZE(ITO:ITO)=' '
  2Ø CONTINUE
      END
```

As with all character facilities, the behaviour of the lengths of character items is important. When you use a character value as an actual argument, it has a length of its own. This value will be either chopped or blank filled to match the length of the dummy argument. The result of a function also has a particular length which may again be altered by the program using it.

A very special length facility makes it easier to create portable subprograms. You can give an assumed length of (*) for the function itself or its dummy arguments. The actual length is then worked out when the program is used. The first few lines of SQUOZE could be:

```
      CHARACTER*(*) FUNCTION SQUOZE (OLD)
C A CHARACTER FUNCTION TO REMOVE MULTIPLE BLANKS FROM THE
C INPUT STRING OLD, A CHARACTER VALUE OF LENGTH 12Ø
      CHARACTER*(*) OLD
      ITO=1
      LIMIT=LEN(OLD)
```

Exercise Write a function to scan an input value TEXT and replace every occurrence of the string OLD by a string NEW. Be sure it works correctly for all combinations of lengths.

There are no further surprises with the use of characters in subroutines. Character values or variables can be used as arguments of subroutines, with the lengths of the dummy arguments either given explicitly or assumed.

Example Here we do all anagrams of a four letter word. We get these by rotating the four letter word to give us the four possible first letters, following each by all the anagrams of the remaining three found the same way. Sounds recursive? See Problem 18.5.

```
C DEMONSTRATE SUBROUTINE WITH CHARACTER ARGUMENT
      CHARACTER*4 WORD
      PRINT*,'TYPE IN A FOUR LETTER WORD FOR ALL ITS ANAGRAMS
      READ '(A)',WORD
      CALL ANAGRM(WORD)
      END

      SUBROUTINE ANAGRM(STRING)
C MAKE ALL THE ANAGRAMS OF THE GIVEN STRING LENGTH 4
      CHARACTER*4 STRING
      DO 1Ø K=1,4
        CALL ROTATE(STRING(1:4))
        DO 1Ø L=1,3
          CALL ROTATE(STRING(2:4))
          DO 1Ø M-1,2
            CALL ROTATE(STRING(3:4))
            PRINT*,STRING
  1Ø CONTINUE
      END
```

Exercise Deliberately I have not given you the subroutine ROTATE which is vital for the above program. Here are the first few lines. Finish it.

```
      SUBROUTINE ROTATE(THING)
C ROTATE LEFT THE CHARACTER VALUE THING WHOSE LENGTH
C IS NOT KNOWN UNTIL THE SUBROUTINE IS CALLED
```

8 A dynamic FORMAT

We have seen many times a character constant used as a format specifier when reading or printing formatted data. A recent example was:

```
READ '(A)', WORD
```

Can a character variable or even a substring be a format specifier? Yes! A program can read in a format specification as character data, or alter it when the program is running.

Example

```
CHARACTER FROTHY*24
PRINT*,'ENTER YOUR FORMAT NOW'
READ*, FROTHY
PRINT FROTHY,'CLEVER ISN''T IT ?'
END
```

You could give this program some valid format specification, such as

```
'(8X,A17)'
```

9 Problems

Problem 18.1 Write a character function which, given an integer value in a suitable range, provides the equivalent hexadecimal string (base 16), as given as in Table 18.2.

Table 18.2. Hexadecimal symbols for the numerical values shown.

Digit	Symbol	Digit	Symbol	Digit	Symbol	Digit	Symbol
Ø	Ø	5	4	8	8	12	C
1	1	5	5	9	9	13	D
2	2	6	6	1Ø	A	14	E
3	3	7	7	11	B	15	F

Problem 18.2 Write a program to read a hexadecimal string and convert it to an integer. Make the input length variable—for example you may prefer to enter F for 15 rather than 000F.

Problem 18.3 Write a subroutine to edit a line of text interactively. Make it print the given line of text, and then accept the changes typed underneath. Alter only characters which have non-blank changes entered. Finally make it able to insert or delete characters (including blanks).

Problem 18.4 Write a subroutine to sort an array of strings into alphabetical order. Using this, create a program which will assist an author to make an index. The writer enters keywords and page numbers into your program until a particular string tells you that it is finished. You then sort, remembering to keep the page numbers with the strings, and print the result. To make it really helpful you should enable the user to build the index in several sessions, by adding new entries to a file of old ones. To do this, you need to refer to Chapter 20.

Problem 18.5 The anagram program would appear to require the correct number of loops to achieve anagrams of a particular length. There are a number of ways of making it general. This may involve recursion. Do it.

Nineteen

Types and Typing

1 Implicit typing

This informative chapter discusses all the data types available in FORTRAN 77. First we learn how to extend implicit typing beyond reals and integers, and that we can use explicit typing with reals and integers. Then we study some new types: double precision, complex and logical. We will also see that we can use variables to represent the names of external or intrinsic subprograms. After that is a summary of the rules for combining, comparing and converting types. Finally the statements of FORTRAN 77 are classified and the rules for statement ordering are given in their complete form.

The most commonly used types are the basic real and integer types which we have used extensively. Names referring to these types are recognized by their spelling—this is called implicit typing. Real names begin with the letters A to H or O to Z. Integer names begin with I, J, K, L, M or N. If we were restricted to this, it would be impossible to have any other type of data. However there is also explicit typing, in which the type of individual data items is declared. The character type was introduced in Chapter 18, where we always declared character items explicitly in the CHARACTER statement.

The IMPLICIT statement can alter or confirm the spelling rules for real and integer data, and also create implicit spelling of other types:

> **IMPLICIT** *typename* (*letters or range*) , . . .

Here, *typename* is the name of a FORTRAN 77 type: REAL, INTEGER, CHARACTER, DOUBLE PRECISION, COMPLEX or LOGICAL. The *letters* are a list of single letters such as (A,C,H), or a range of letters of the alphabet like (I–N) which we wish to associate with a particular type. However IMPLICIT does not alter the type of any of the intrinsic functions.

Examples The default implicit typing of FORTRAN is the same as:

> **IMPLICIT REAL(A-H), INTEGER(I-N), REAL(O-Z)**

With the character type, you can also alter the default length of a character item (which is 1). Here is a scheme with implied typing for all data types:

```
IMPLICIT COMPLEX (C)
IMPLICIT DOUBLE PRECISION(D, P)
IMPLICIT LOGICAL(L)
IMPLICIT CHARACTER*4(H)
```

Exercise IMPLICIT alters or confirms the spelling conventions for types. If a letter is not mentioned, its typing is not altered. After the statements in the above example, what are the default spellings for real and integer names? What is the type of the intrinsic function CHAR?

IMPLICIT is a specification statement which belongs at the beginning of the program unit to which it refers. At the end of this chapter you will find the final word on statement ordering. In mixing IMPLICIT and PARAMETER, you must be sure that the type of a name is established before you associate a constant value with it:

```
IMPLICIT CHARACTER*4 (F)
PARAMETER (FIRST4='ABCD')
```

It is illegal to write conflicting ranges for implicit typing. This is wrong:

```
IMPLICIT REAL(A-H), COMPLEX(C)
```

2 Explicit typing

A type statement will override any implicit scheme that might be in force. The CHARACTER statement was a type statement, as are REAL, INTEGER, DOUBLE PRECISION, COMPLEX and LOGICAL.

Example In the statements

```
IMPLICIT REAL (I)
INTEGER ICICLE, COOL
REAL MOTHER
```

the IMPLICIT scheme makes most quantities beginning with I into reals, but the INTEGER statement has changed this to make ICICLE and COOL into integer variables. The REAL statement forces MOTHER to be a real name.

You could make very confusing programs if you use IMPLICIT to modify the normal scheme for real and integer names, and then override your own implied spellings. Although these facilities can be very convenient, the best programmers do not mess about with the names of real and integer quantities.

Type statements can be used to define the type of variable names, the names of symbolic constants, array names, function names, or the names of external programs. They cannot modify the type of an intrinsic function of FORTRAN 77. It is meaningless to attempt to assign a type to the name of a main program, a SUBROUTINE subprogram, a named COMMON, or a BLOCK DATA subprogram. In fact it would not be allowed.

Type statements can also be used to define the the dimension bounds of arrays:

```
REAL KWOTA(8), QUOTA(8)
INTEGER YES(10), NO(10)
```

The above statements not only state the dimension bounds of four arrays but also force two changes of type. KWOTA becomes a real array and YES an integer one. The type statements and the DIMENSION statement can be used in many combinations. However, the declaration of the dimension bounds of an array can only occur once.

The COMMON, REAL, INTEGER, DIMENSION, and EQUIVALENCE statements can be mixed together in any order. This could provide some messy and confusing results. I recommend that you should adopt your own standards for declaring types, such as this:

(i) First give your REAL, INTEGER or other type statements. Specify the dimensions in these statements unless the arrays are named in a COMMON statement.

(ii) Then put DIMENSION if necessary, but why not give all dimension bounds either in a type statement or in a COMMON statement? If you did that, there would be no DIMENSION statements, and the types of all arrays would be stated explicitly.

(iii) Then put your COMMON statements. For arrays in COMMON specify the dimension bounds in the COMMON statement.

(iv) Finally your EQUIVALENCE scheme. It is better not to have one.

The ability to change the type of a name also extends to statement functions and external functions. Suppose that an arithmetic statement function which is real is to be created, which converts any angle in degrees to the equivalent in the range 0°–360° (called the principal angle). For private reasons, you want to call the function MINE. Use either one of these:

```
IMPLICIT REAL MINE                      REAL MINE
MINE(THETA)=MOD(THETA,36Ø.Ø)    MINE(THETA)=MOD(THETA,36Ø.Ø)
```

The type of a function subprogram can also be controlled. A function for shifting the binary digits of an integer to the left might be called SHIFT. You must write

```
        INTEGER SHIFT
```

in any program that refers to SHIFT. The integer function SHIFT can be created using the INTEGER FUNCTION statement, which declares the type of the function explicitly:

```
        INTEGER FUNCTION SHIFT(I,ISHF)
C SHIFT I LEFT BY ISHF PLACES,  (NEGATIVE MEANS RIGHT)
C IS CORRECT FOR TWOS COMPLEMENT INTEGERS
        IF(ISHF.LT.Ø) THEN
          SHIFT=(I-1)/2**(-ISHF)
        ELSE
           SHIFT=I*2**ISHF
        END IF
        END
```

3 DOUBLE PRECISION

Sometimes you need more digits of precision than are standard for real values on your computer. The DOUBLE PRECISION statement declares names to be of type double precision:

> **DOUBLE PRECISION** *list of names*

In general, double precision will give twice as many significant digits as real values. Double precision names can refer to arrays, and so the information about the dimension bounds can be included in the DOUBLE PRECISION statement, or through a COMMON or DIMENSION statement. There is a special complication in using COMMON or EQUIVALENCE statements, because each double precision variable or array member takes twice as much space as a real or integer value. This must be allowed for when using COMMON or EQUIVALENCE.

Constants of double precision are similar to the exponential form of a basic real constant, but you use D for the exponent:

> *real constant* **D** *exponent*   or   *integer constant* **D** *exponent*
> **2.73 D-36** means 2.73×10^{-36} with double precision accuracy.
> **7D0** means 7.0 with double precision accuracy.

Be careful to use the constant 1D0 not 1.0 when you need double precision!

You can give a name to a double precision constant in a PARAMETER statement if the type is declared first:

```
DOUBLE PRECISION PIE
PARAMETER (PIE = 3.14159 26535 89793 23846)
```

This defines PIE to whatever accuracy the machine has available for double precision values. The given value could be truncated, or extra zeros could be added.

An initial value can be assigned to a double precision variable or array member in the DATA statement:

```
DOUBLE PRECISION X
DATA X/1.5DØ/
```

Double precision quantities can be used in FORTRAN wherever real values are allowed, except that operations between complex and double precision values are forbidden. This statement gives a double precision result—try it!

```
PRINT*, 4DØ*ATAN(1DØ)
```

However this does not:

```
DOUBLE PRECISION DPIE
DPIE=4.Ø*ATAN(1DØ)
PRINT*,DPIE
```

The multiplication by 4.0, a real constant, loses the precision. Any real term in an expression throws away the extra precision that you thought you had. Use double precision expertly!

For FORMAT-directed input and output, the D description is used:

```
Dw.d
```

This is similar to the E description for real values. The total field width is w, and d is the number of decimal places expected.

For input, the value given can be in the form of any basic real constant, or any double precision constant. It can also be a simple number, in which case the computer assumes that it is a basic real constant with a decimal point implied before the last d digits. In fact the input data forms for F, E, or D editing are completely interchangeable.

List-directed input/output statements can also be used. For output the computer will print the values in D form, making its own arrangements for the digits and the exponent:

```
PRINT*,4.ØDØ * ATAN(1.ØDØ)
```

In response to a list-directed READ statement, double precision values can be given in D, F, or E form, or as a string of digits, when the value is assumed to have no decimal places.

Example This program calculates and prints the value of π to 30 digits, assuming that the machine has that much precision; it may have a lot less:

```
   DOUBLE PRECISION PIE
   PIE=4.ØDØ*ATAN(1.ØDØ)
   PRINT 2Ø,PIE
2Ø FORMAT(1X,D4Ø.3Ø)
   STOP
   END
```

Exercise Run the above program. Check the result against mathematical tables. This will tell you the extent of double precision on your computer—but not exactly because ATAN will not quite achieve the maximum precision. ATAN provides a double precision result because the argument, 1D0, is a double precision value. Table 19.1 lists the double precision functions.

Table 19.1. Intrinsic functions used with double precision data. All have double precision arguments except for DBLE and DPROD. The type of the result will be the same as the type of the arguments, except with the conversion functions.

Conversion functions:

Name	Meaning
DBLE(*arg*)	Convert *arg* to double precision. For complex argument takes real part.
DPROD(X1,X2)	Double precision product of reals X1 and X2.
INT(D)	Convert D to integer.
AINT(D)	Truncate D to integer part, result is double precision.
NINT(D)	Round D to nearest whole number—result is integer.
ANINT(D)	Round D to nearest whole number—result is double precision.
REAL(D)	Convert D to single precision real.
CMPLX(D)	Convert D complex, imaginary part 0.0.

Other functions:

Name	Meaning
ABS(D)	Absolute value of D.
ACOS(D)	Arccos(D), angle $0 \le \theta \le \pi$ with $\cos(\theta)$=D.
ASIN(D)	Arcsin(D), angle $0 \le \theta \le \pi$ with $\sin(\theta)$=D.
ATAN(D)	Arctan(D), angle $-\pi/2 \le \theta \le \pi/2$ with $\tan(\theta)$=D.
ATAN2(D1,D2)	Arctan(D2/D1), angle $-\pi \le \pi \le \pi$ with $\tan(\theta)$=D2/D1.
COS(D)	Cosine of D, D in radians.
COSH(D)	Hyperbolic cosine, $(e^D + e^{-D})/2.0D0$.
DIM(D1,D2)	Positive difference D1–MIN(D1,D2).
EXP(D)	Exponential function e^D.
LOG(D)	Logarithm to base e, $\log_e$D.
LOG10(D)	Logarithm to base 10, $\log_{10}$D.
MAX(D1,D2,...)	Choose maximum value from D1, D2, ...
MIN(D1,D2,...)	Choose minimum value from D1, D2, ...
MOD(D1,D2)	Remainder D1-AINT(D1/D2)*D2.
SIGN(D1,D2)	Transfer sign of D2 to D1, (sign D2) * ABS(D1).
SIN(D)	Sine of D, D in radians.
SINH(D)	Hyperbolic sine, $(e^D-e^{-D})/2.0D0$.
SQRT(D)	Square root of D.
TAN(D)	Tangent of D, D in radians.
TANH(D)	Hyperbolic tangent, $(e^D-e^{-D})/(e^D+e^{-D})$.

As you would expect, double precision functions can be defined.

Example The following program fragment contains the double precision arithmetic statement function ANGL, which will convert its double precision argument in degrees to a double precision result in radians. Note that the function name, the name of its dummy argument and the names of the variables used with it have all been declared to be double precision.

```
      DOUBLE PRECISION ANGL,X,Y,Z
      ANGLE(Z)=4DØ*ATAN(1DØ)*Z/18ØDØ
        :
```

Example A double precision function DSIN1 is used in the following program to evaluate sin(*x*). The FORMAT specification for printing the result assumes an accuracy of at least 25 decimal places; on some machines it could be much less. Note that the function name and the variables it uses are declared in a DOUBLE PRECISION statement in the main program:

```
      PROGRAM DUBBLY
      DOUBLE PRECISION DSIN1,X,Y
C GET THE ANGLE IN DEGREES
   10 PRINT*,'ENTER THE ANGLE'
      READ*,X
C EVALUATE THE SINE
      Y=DSIN1(X)
C PRINT THE RESULT
      PRINT 2Ø,X
   2Ø FORMAT('THE SINE OF',D2Ø.1Ø,'DEGREES')
      PRINT 3Ø,Y
   3Ø FORMAT('IS',D35.25)
      GO TO 1Ø
      END
```

Exercise Write the double precision function used in this main program. Make it provide the appropriate accuracy for your computer, and compare its results with the SIN fuction used with a double precision angle:

```
      DOUBLE PRECISION FUNCTION DSIN1(D)
C C FUNCTION FINDS SINE OF DOUBLE PRECISION
C ANGLE D TO DOUBLE PRECISION BY USING A
C             POWER SERIES
C       IMPLICIT DOUBLE PRECISION(D)
        :
```

Here is a chance to use implicitly defined double precision names, but be careful. Use the series for sine *x*:

$$\sin(x) = x - x^3/3! + x^5/5! - x^7/7! + \dots$$

4 COMPLEX

Complex values, with real and imaginary parts, arise in many problems of science and engineering. A quantity can be complex because of explicit or implicit typing:

COMPLEX *names*   or   **IMPLICIT COMPLEX** (*letters or range*)

A complex quantity cannot be any other type at the same time. In particular there is no such thing as a 'double precision complex' type.

A complex variable is, in effect, two real numbers, one standing for the real part and the other for the imaginary part of a complex number. Complex variables can be arrays, and so the dimension information can be included in the COMPLEX statement, or perhaps in other ways such as through COMMON or DIMENSION statements. Because a complex variable is a pair of numbers, it occupies twice as much storage as do reals, integers or logicals. Therefore, just as with double precision variables but for different reasons, double space has to be allowed for complex variables when laying out COMMON and when using EQUIVALENCE.

Complex constants are written as a pair of real numbers in parentheses (brackets) with a comma between. The numbers may be signed:

    (-2.0, 1.0) is the engineer's $-2 + j1$, or $-2 + i1$ for purists.

Complex constants can be given symbolic names in PARAMETER statements:

```
COMPLEX FORTY5
PARAMETER (FORTY5=(1.Ø, 1.Ø))
```

Initial values can be assigned to complex variables in DATA statements:

```
IMPLICIT COMPLEX (C)
DATA COHMS/(Ø.Ø, 1.414)/
```

Complex quantities can be included in expressions of FORTRAN intermixed with real, integer and double precision values, except that an operation can never be performed directly between complex and double precision values.

In relational expressions, complex values cannot be compared with double precision values. A complex operand is only permitted when the relational operator is .EQ. or .NE., simply because the other relational operations are meaningless for complex numbers.

Values can be assigned to complex variables or array elements:

   complex variable = arithmetic expression

Here, the complex *variable* has the result of the *expression* assigned to it. For a real, integer, or double precision result, the imaginary part of the new complex value is set to zero.

For formatted input/output of complex values, two real editing descriptions are required for each complex item (either F, E or G descriptions). The one-to-one correspondence between the READ, PRINT, or WRITE list and the FORMAT will be preserved by giving two real fields for every complex member of the list. The output will be two real numbers. Similarly, a complex value occurring in list-directed output will be printed as a pair of real values, with brackets around them and a comma between.

Any of the allowed forms for real input can be used in response to a formatted or list-directed READ—recall that the inputs to F, D and E specifications are interchangeable.

Example The second order differential equation

$$d^2y/dt^2 + 2\ dy/dt + y = x(t)$$

could describe the behaviour of a variety of systems, for example either the mechanical or electrical systems of Fig. 19.1. The complex ratio

$$\frac{Y(\omega)}{X(\omega)} = \frac{1}{-\omega^2 + 2j\omega + 1}$$

is called the frequency response of the system because it describes the relationship between input and output for sinusoidal excitation at a frequency of ω. The following program evaluates the frequency response for a given value of ω and prints it both as a complex number and in polar form (magnitude and phase).

```
      IMPLICIT COMPLEX(R)
      ANGL(R)=ATAN2(AIMAG(R), REAL(R))
C GET THE DESIRED FREQUENCY
      PRINT*,'FREQUENCY RESPONSE USING COMPLEX ARITHMETIC'
   1Ø PRINT*
      PRINT*,'ENTER A FREQUENCY IN RADIANS'
      READ*,W
C FIND RESPONSE AT FREQUENCY W
      RESP=1.Ø/CMPLX(-W*W+1.Ø, 2.Ø*W)
C ALSO GET MAGNITUDE AND PHASE
      XMAG=CABS(RESP)
      XPHA=ANGL(RESP)
C PRINT THE RESULTS
      PRINT 2Ø, W, RESP
   2Ø FORMAT(' AT FREQUENCY',F8.2,' RESPONSE IS',2F8.2)
      PRINT*
      PRINT*,'OR IN POLAR FORM'
      PRINT 3Ø,XMAG,XPHA
   3Ø FORMAT(' MAGNITUDE',F8.2,' AND PHASE',F8.2)
      GO TO 1Ø
      END
```

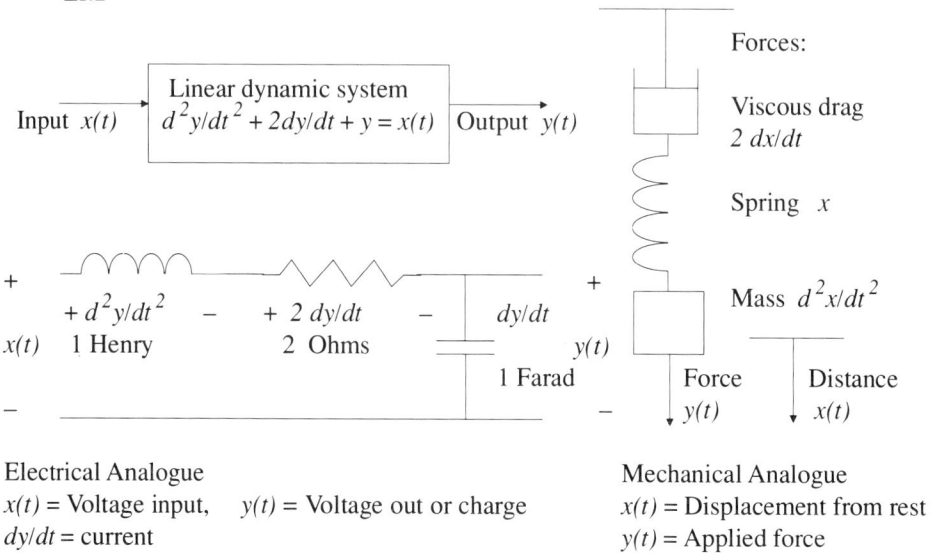

Input $x(t)$ | Linear dynamic system $d^2y/dt^2 + 2dy/dt + y = x(t)$ | Output $y(t)$

Forces:

Viscous drag $2\,dx/dt$

Spring x

Mass d^2x/dt^2

$+$ $+d^2y/dt^2$ $-$ $+2\,dy/dt$ $-$ dy/dt $+$

$x(t)$ 1 Henry 2 Ohms 1 Farad $y(t)$

$-$

Force $y(t)$ | Distance $x(t)$

Electrical Analogue
$x(t)$ = Voltage input, $y(t)$ = Voltage out or charge
dy/dt = current

Mechanical Analogue
$x(t)$ = Displacement from rest
$y(t)$ = Applied force

Fig. 19.1. A linear dynamic system and two physical interpretations of it.

Here, AIMAG, REAL, CMPLX and CABS are intrinsic functions which deal with complex numbers in FORTRAN 77. Table 19.2 lists all the functions with either complex arguments or complex results.

As might be expected, it is possible to define complex function subprograms and complex arithmetic statement functions. The following example has both.

Example A complex function subprogram CARTES is used to convert complex numbers given in polar form into a Cartesian complex number CMPLX.

Main program:

```
      COMPLEX CARTES,CMPLEX
         :
      CMPLEX=CARTES(XMAG,XANG)
         :
      END
```

Function subprogram:

```
      COMPLEX FUNCTION CARTES(X,Y)
C GET RECTANGULAR CARTESIAN CO-ORDINATES OF POLAR NUMBER
C WITH REAL MAGNITUDE X AND REAL ANGLE Y (IN DEGREES)
      COMPLEX RECT
      RECT(P,Q)=CMPLX(P*COS(Q), P*SIN(Q))
      ANGL(Z)=4.*ATAN(1.)*Z/18Ø.
      CARTES=RECT(X,ANGL(Y))
      END
```

Table 19.2. Complex intrinsic functions. A, B are real, integer or double precision arguments.

Conversion functions:

Name	Meaning
CMPLX(A,B)	Complex number (A,B). A and B must be of the same type.
CMPLX(A)	Complex number (A,1.0).
CMPLX(C)	Complex number C, i.e. do nothing.
INT(C)	Truncate real part of C to integer value.
REAL(C)	Truncate real part of C to real value.
DBLE(C)	Take real part of C to double precision, zeros added.
ABS(C)	The modulus SQRT(real part^2 + imaginary part^2), a real value.
AIMAG(C)	The imaginary part of C, a real value.

Complex manipulations:

Name	Meaning
CONJ(C)	The complex conjugate of C, (real part, –imaginary part).
SQRT(C)	The square root of C, $C^{1/2}$.
EXP(C)	The exponential function e^C.
LOG(C)	Natural logarithm, $\log_e C$.
LOG10(C)	Logarithm base 10, $\log_{10} C$.
SIN(C)	Trigonometric sine of C.
COS(C)	Trigonometric cosine of C.

5 LOGICAL

You can make a named quantity be of logical type by explicit or implicit typing:

```
      LOGICAL  names
```
or   `IMPLICIT LOGICAL` (*letters or range*)

You can have arrays of logical values, whose subscript bounds can be given in the LOGICAL statement itself, or in other ways. I have suggested that you should give the bounds in the LOGICAL statement unless the array is in COMMON.

Logical constants have two possible values: .TRUE. or .FALSE. Logical constants can be given names in PARAMETER statements:

```
LOGICAL YES, NO, MAYBE
PARAMETER(YES=.TRUE., NO=.FALSE.)
```

Logical variables can be given initial values in DATA statements:

```
LOGICAL QRAY(4), BEER
DATA QRAY/4*.TRUE./, BEER/.FALSE./
```

Logical variables or constants can be used in logical expressions as described in Chapter 7. These occur only in the relational expressions in IF statements, or in assignment to a logical variable. The hierarchy of all operations in FORTRAN 77 was also described in Chapter 7.

Example A, B and EOR are logical names. These two expresions mean the same thing:

```
EOR=A.AND..NOT.B.OR..NOT.A.AND.B        EOR=A.NEQV.B
```

Logical values can be used in READ, WRITE and PRINT statements. In a list-directed PRINT or WRITE, the computer will print T for .TRUE. and F for .FALSE.:

```
LOGICAL THIS, THAT, OTHER
       :
       :
PRINT*, THIS, THAT.OR.OTHER
```

When a list-directed READ requests input, the first nonblank characters in the value must be T or .T to define a .TRUE. value. Similarly F or .F indicates .FALSE. Note that you do not enclose these in quotes.

With formatted input or output, the editing description which must match a logical item is:

     Lw

where w is the width of the field. A PRINT or WRITE statement produces T or F right justified in the output field. The read statement requires T, .T, F or .F to be the first nonblank characters in the input field.

Example This program prints the exclusive OR of two values:

```
      LOGICAL A,B,C
      PRINT*,'A PROGRAM TO DO THE EXCLUSIVE OR'
      PRINT*,'ENTER TWO LOGICAL VALUES A AND B'
C GET THE INPUT VALUES
      READ 1Ø,A,B
   1Ø FORMAT(2L1Ø)
C ECHO THE INPUT
      PRINT 2Ø,A,B
   2Ø FORMAT(' A =',L2,'  B =',L2)
C FORM THE EXCLUSIVE OR
      C=A.NEQV.B
C AND PRINT THE RESULT
      PRINT 3Ø,C
   3Ø FORMAT(' A.EOR.B =',L2)
      END
```

Exercise Run this and check the truth table for the .EQV. operation, using the input values FRUE and TRALSE.

There are no intrinsic functions in FORTRAN of type logical except for the lexical functions used to compare characters in the ASCII sequence, as described in Chapter 18. You can, however, create statement functions or function subprograms of type logical.

Example NOR is a statement function of two logical dummy arguments:

```
LOGICAL NOR, X, Y
NOR(X,Y)=.NOR.(X.OR.Y)
```

Example NAND is a logical function which computes the NAND (not AND) function:

```
LOGICAL FUNCTION NAND(X,Y)
LOGICAL X,Y
NAND=.NOT.(X.AND.Y)
END
```

Notice that the dummy arguments are declared as logical in the subprogram. The actual arguments also must be of type logical, and any program which uses NAND must declare NAND to be logical also.

Exercise What does this do?

```
LOGICAL NAND,A,B,C
   :
C=NAND( NAND(A, NAND(A,B)), NAND(B, NAND(A,B)) )
```

Apart from relational expressions in IF statements, logical results are infrequently used. When structuring a normal FORTRAN program which does numerical calculations there is no real need for them. Although they can be used quite respectably in forming many of the program structures described in Chapter 9, they are just as likely to obscure the meaning of a program as they are to improve it.

6 Using subprogram names—EXTERNAL and INTRINSIC

The EXTERNAL and INTRINSIC statements are used to inform FORTRAN that a name is the actual name of a function or subroutine, not a variable or a constant. This allows you to pass the name to a subprogram as an argument:

EXTERNAL *names*   or   **INTRINSIC** *names*

These indicate that the names do not stand for values of any type, but are instead the actual names of functions or of subroutines. You use EXTERNAL if the name is one of your own subprograms. You use INTRINSIC if it is the name of a built in (intrinsic) function of FORTRAN, like SQRT for example.

Example Here is a subroutine for finding the area under a curve. To use it you give the name of a function subprogram as the actual value of the dummy argument FNAME.

```
      SUBROUTINE STRAP(BOT,TOP,FNAME,DELTA,ANSWER,NSTRIP)
C SUBROUTINE FOR QUADRATURE BY TRAPEZOIDAL RULE
C INTEGRATES FUNCTION FROM BOT TO TOP, DOUBLING
C NUMBER OF STRIPS UNTIL ERROR IS LESS THAN DELTA
C THE USER SUPPLIES THE EXTERNAL FUNCTION FNAME
```

```
C BOT - INPUT VALUE, THE LOWER LIMIT OF INTEGRATION
C TOP - INPUT VALUE, THE UPPER LIMIT OF INTEGRATION
C FNAME - EXTERNAL VARIABLE GIVING THE NAME OF
C           THE FUNCTION TO BE INTEGRATED
C DELTA - INPUT VALUE, THE DESIRED ERROR BOUND
C ANSWER - OUTPUT VARIABLE, THE CALCULATED INTEGRAND
C NSTRIP - OUTPUT VARIABLE, THE NUMBER OF STRIPS USED
        EXTERNAL FNAME
C SET UP LOCAL VARIABLES FOR EFFICIENCY
        XDELTA=4.Ø*DELTA
        XTOP=TOP
        XBOT=BOT
C INITIALIZE
        NST=1
        H=XTOP-XBOT
        SOLD=(FNAME(XBOT)+FNAME(XTOP))*H/2.Ø
C MAKE THE NEW SUM
   1Ø X=XBOT+H/2.Ø
        NST=NST*2
        SNEW=Ø.Ø
        DO 2Ø K=1,NST,2
          SNEW=SNEW+FNAME(X)
          X=X+H
   2Ø CONTINUE
C FORM NEW INTEGRAND AND ESTIMATE ERROR
        H=H/2.Ø
        SNEW=SNEW*H+SOLD/2.Ø
        CHANGE=ABS(SOLD-SNEW)
        SOLD=SNEW
C DO AGAIN WHILE ERROR.GT.4.Ø*DELTA
        IF(CHANGE.GT.XDELTA)GO TO 1Ø
C FINISHED, RETURN RESULTS
        ANSWER=SOLD
        NSTRIP=NST
        END
```

In the program unit that calls this, you must declare that the actual name is EXTERNAL or IN-TRINSIC. For example:

```
        EXTERNAL ACTUAL
          :
          :
        CALL STRAP(Ø,1,ACTUAL,DELTA,ANS,1ØØ)
```

Subroutine STRAP uses your function ACTUAL to evaluate the curve as a function of X. You could find the area under the LOG function by writing

```
        INTRINSIC LOG
          :
        CALL STRAP(1.Ø, 1Ø.Ø, LOG, Ø.Ø1, ANS, 18)
```

If you wrote

        EXTERNAL LOG

then the FORTRAN LOG function would be unavailable, and you would have to write LOG yourself. Do this if you think you can improve on LOG, but be careful about its type!

The names of intrinsic functions for type conversion, lexical relationships and for choosing the largest or smallest value must not be used as actual arguments—so there is no point in using them in an INTRINSIC statement. A name cannot be both INTRINSIC and EXTERNAL.

7 Statement ordering

Many statements of FORTRAN have rules about their order in a program unit. Here is the last word on statement ordering in a main program:

	Heading: PROGRAM (optional) or FUNCTION or SUBROUTINE or BLOCK DATA		
Comments can go anywhere before END	FORMAT statements can go after heading, before END	PARAMETER Statements	IMPLICIT Statements
			Other Specification
		DATA Statements	Statement functions
			Executable Statements
	END is always the very end		

Note that the PROGRAM statement, mentioned in this table, is a machine dependent statement which may or may not be required by a particular computer. The existence of this statement is allowed by the FORTRAN 77 standard, but its form is not specified.

In Section 2 of this chapter, recommendations (but not rules) were made regarding the order of specification statements as an aid to program clarity.

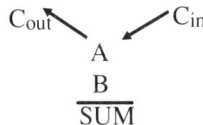

C_{out} ⟍   ⟋ C_{in}
      A
      B
     SUM

8 Problems

Problem 19.1 Fig. 19.2 illustrates a full binary adder with inputs A,B, and C_{in} (a carry input). Write a program to generate and print the sum and carry outputs using a function NOR(X,Y) defined as (.NOT.X.OR.Y) for all operations, i.e. once the NOR function has been defined, the other FORTRAN operations should not be used. Referring to Fig. 19.2,

INPUTS			OUTPUTS	
A	B	Carry	SUM	Carry
F	F	F	F	F
F	F	T	T	F
F	T	F	T	F
F	T	T	F	T
T	F	F	T	F
T	F	T	F	T
T	T	F	F	T
T	T	T	T	T

Fig.19.2. A full binary adder.

$$S = A \oplus B \oplus C_{in}$$

where $A \oplus B$ = exclusive OR of A and B

$$C_{out} = (A \oplus B).C_{in} + A.B$$

Both these equations can be rewritten entirely in terms of the NOR operation.

Problem 19.2 The Newton-Raphson iteration for finding roots of an equation

$$f(x) = 0$$

uses the recurrence

$$x_n = x_{n-1} - f(x_{n-1})/f'(x_{n-1})$$

where x_n is an improvement on the approximate root x_{n-1}. If the function is very flat near the root, then $f(x)$ and $f'(x)$ will be small and there could be some difficulty in evaluating $f(x)$ and $f'(x)$, and in calculating the new x_n using their ratio. Double precision arithmetic can help in such a situation.

By using the Newton-Raphson iteration to solve for $g'(x)=0$, locate the position and value of the minimum of $g(x)$ for

(i) $g(x) = x^4 - 5.2 \, x^3 + 10.14 \, x^2 - 8.788 \, x + 4.5561$

(ii) $g(x) = x^8 - 13.6 \, x^7 + 80.92 \, x^6 - 275.128 \, x^5 + 584.647 \, x^4 - 795.1122 \, x^3 + 675.859132 \, x^2$
$- 328.2709384 \, x + 71.0575441$

Compare the success or otherwise of the solution with and without judicious use of double precision. Because double precision arithmetic is slow, only use it where necessary.

Problem 19.3 The discrete Fourier transform of a series of N real numbers $X_0, X_1, \ldots, X_{N-1}$ is given by

$$Y_n = 1/N \sum_{k=0}^{N-1} X_k \, e^{-j2\pi kn/N}$$

for $n = 0,1,\ldots,N-1$

Y_n is complex. Write a complex function subprogram to compute one value of Y_n for a given real array X of length N and a particular n.

The inverse transform

$$X_k = \sum_{n=0}^{N-1} Y_n \, e^{j2\pi kn/N}$$

for $k = 0,1,\ldots,N-1$

should convert the complex array Y_n containing all the results $Y_0, Y_1, \ldots, Y_{N-1}$ back into one real number X_k. Write a real function subprogram to do this given the complex array Y, length N, and a particular k. It is quite a good test of this to see if an array Y_n computed forward one value at a time can then be put through all the inverses to get the original X_k back again.

Problem 19.4 Find out about Simpson's rule for finding the area under a curve. Implement it in a subroutine which accepts the function name, as SUBROUTINE STRAP did. Compare its accuracy with the trapezoidal rule program given in this chapter for its accuracy as a function of the step size used.

Twenty

Records and files

1 Files, records and statements

This chapter completes our crash course in FORTRAN 77 with a summary of the powerful input and output features of FORTRAN. We begin with some definitions.

Information is always read from or written to a *file*, as ilustrated by Fig. 20.1. Your terminal is a file and so is a printer. Any information that you may wish to write or read using a disk or tape will also be held in files.

Every file is made up of *records*. A printed line is a record. So is a line of input from a keyboard. Whenever a READ, WRITE or PRINT statement occurs, a new record is used. During the transfer of information, however, additional records can begin. For example a new record is created whenever a format directed or list directed PRINT or WRITE statement decides to begin a new line. We described how this might happen in Chapter 6.

There are two kinds of records and two kinds of files. Records can be *formatted* or *unformatted*.

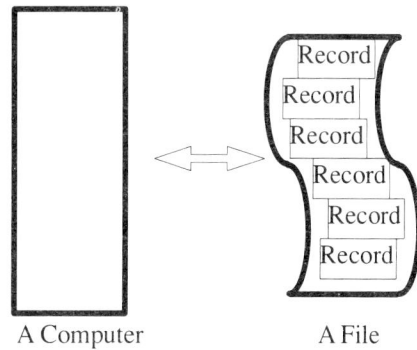

A Computer   A File

Fig. 20.1. Records and files.

Files can be *sequential* or *direct*. So far in this course we have only used sequential files of formatted records. In this chapter we will discover the other combinations.

The input and output statements of FORTRAN 77 are:

READ, WRITE and PRINT for the actual transfer of records to a file.

OPEN, CLOSE and INQUIRE to alter or examine the properties of a file.

BACKSPACE, REWIND and END FILE to manipulate the file.

READ, WRITE and PRINT have more general forms than we have seen before:

READ (*control list*) *data list*	is the general READ statement.
READ *format-identifier*, *data list*	is the special form we have seen before which is for reading formatted records.
WRITE (*control list*) *data list*	is the general WRITE statement.
PRINT *format-identifier*, *data list*	is the special form for writing formatted records on the special output device.

2 Controlling files

Here, the range of control list facilities in the READ and WRITE statements is summarized.

A control list is a number of items separated by commas. There must be one item which is a unit specifier; everything else is optional. The control list items can be any of the following:

UNIT=*unit identifier*   FMT=*format identifier*

REC=*record number*   IOSTAT=*integer variable*

END=*label*   ERR=*label*

(a) The unit specifier UNIT=*unit identifier*

Every control list must contain exactly one unit specifier. If the optional UNIT= is omitted, the unit specifier must be the first item in the control list.

The *unit identifier* can be an integer expression or an asterisk to identify the obvious unit to be used for formatted sequential access, such as your screen and keyboard.

(b) The format specifier FMT=*format identifier*

At most one optional format specifier can be given in a control list. If none is given, then the record to be transferred is of the unformatted type to be described in Section 4 of this chapter. The *format identifier* can be one of these types:

(i) The label of a format statement.

(ii) A character quantity giving the format description.

(iii) An asterisk, specifying list-directed formatting.

If the optional FMT= is omitted, the format specifier must be the second item in the control list, and the first item must have been a unit specifier without the optional UNIT= specifier.

(c) The record number REC=*record number*

This specifier is used for direct access on a file which is connected for direct access. Sequential and direct transfers cannot be mixed without closing and reopening the file.

If a *record number* is given, then the data is transferred to or from the desired record in a direct file. The record number can be any positive integer expression. Direct access input and output are described fully, with examples, in Section 7 of this chapter.

(d) The input/output status IOSTAT=*integer variable*

The computer provides information about the status of the file. The *integer variable* will be assigned a value according to the state of the file as follows:

(i) A zero value if there is no error or end-of-file condition.

(ii) A positive integer value if an error occurs.

(iii) A negative integer value if there is no error but an end-of-file occurs.

(e) The end-of-file condition END=*label*

It is possible that a READ statement could encounter the end of the information in a file. The END= facility allows you to take special action when this occurs.

Example This little program reads the data from unit number 73 until there is no more data, when it prints NO MORE DATA:

```
1Ø READ(73, END=2Ø)
   GO TO 1Ø
2Ø PRINT*,'NO MORE DATA'
```

Exercise In the above example, how would you count the number of records that were present on unit number 73?

In Section 5 of this chapter, you will see that you can mark the end of a file.

(f) The error condition ERR=*label*

   When an error occurs, and there is an ERR= specifier, the input/output transfer is terminated. The position of the file becomes unknown, the IOSTAT variable is set (if there was one), and the program jumps to the given *label* which must be in the same program unit. If an error and an end-of-file occur together, the ERR= specifier will take priority if it is present.

3 Formatted files—made from characters

Formatted files are made from characters. All the input and output that we have used until now has been formatted. Every READ or PRINT statement has contained a format identifier to refer the computer to a specification for the layout of our data. The format identifier ★ is just a special case of this—with it we instruct the computer to use formatted data, but allow it to organize the layout for us. A format identifier can take three forms:

(i) The label of a FORMAT statement which must exist in the same program unit, such as

```
      PRINT 2Ø
   2Ø FORMAT(' FORMAT SPECIFICATION')
```

(ii) A star to specify list directed processing, as in

```
      PRINT*,'HOWDY'
```

(iii) A character expression giving the format specification directly:

```
      READ '(2I1Ø)', KLIP, KLOP
```

or even something wildly clever like this, which uses a predefined line of stars that can be grafted onto any format specification:

```
      CHARACTER STARS*(*)
      PARAMETER STARS=(' (8Ø(''*'')//')
         :
         :
      PRINT STARS//'1X,3I2Ø)',J,K,L
```

In the READ and WRITE statements, if the control list is a unit number, we can use formatted data in much the same way. Traditionally unit 5 was the input device and 6 was the output. In that case these forms are equivalent:

READ (5, *format identifier*) *data list*   is the same as   **READ** *format identifier*, *data list*

WRITE(6, *format identifier*) *data list*   is the same as   **PRINT** *format identifier*, *data list*

The *format identifier*, if it is not a star, refers to a format specification. The format specification is always enclosed in parentheses, and describes fields for the items in the data list by giving a list of specifiers which must match the data list. This means that a suitable format description must exist in the format specification for each data list item, in the correct order. Chapter 6 provided a number of useful descriptions for real and integer numbers, and examples of their use. Later, when we encountered other data types, additional format specifiers were given. Here is a summary of the data types and the format descriptions that might be used with them:

Type of data item	Possible descriptions	Discussed in Chapter
Integer	I only	6
Real	F, E, D or G	6
Double Precision	F, E, D or G	19
Complex	Two fields, F, E, D or G	19
Character	A only	18
Logical	L only	19

Note that real, double precision and complex field descriptions are interchangeable.

Also occurring in format specifications will be character constants enclosed in parentheses, and blanks using the X description. These were also discussed in Chapter 6.

Here are some new descriptions that you may encounter:

(i) Printing of the plus sign—SP, SS, S

Normally the computer is permitted to decide when to print a positive sign. The SP description forces it to print the signs of all values for the remainder of the format specification. The SS description does the opposite—it suppresses the printing of signs for positive values. The S description cancels either of these and allows the computer to decide once more. These descriptions have no effect on input data.

(ii) Interpretation of blanks in input—BN and BZ

Normally any blank in an input number is ignored, except that a completely blank field is zero. The BZ description forces blanks in numbers to be regarded as zeros for the remainder of a format specification. The BN description cancels this. For example, this value with a format specifier of I4 means 3000 if BZ is in force, and 30 if it is not.

    3 0
    . . . .   (The dots show the position of the four characters.)

(iii) Scaling of real values—P

This is a confusing facility because it does completely different things on input and output. In the specifier

k P

k is an integer scale factor which can be negative. At the beginning of any format specification k is zero. When you change it, it persists for the rest of the format.

All real input values without exponents are multiplied by the scale factor 10^k, so that their values are altered. If the input value has an exponent, it is not altered.

On output, the P scaling moves the decimal point in all numbers printed in exponential form. Therefore this applies to all E fields, and to some G fields depending on the size of the data value. Normally the decimal point is placed before the first nonzero digit when a number is printed with an exponent. The P scale moves this *k* digits to the right. (Since *k* could be negative, it might be left!). For example

```
    PRINT 2Ø 1ØØ, 1ØØ, 1ØØ
 2Ø FORMAT(1P, E12.4, ØP, E12.4, -1P, E12.4)
```

will print

```
1.0000E+02   0.1000E+03   0.0100E+04
```

Refer to Chapter 6 for information on how format descriptions are repeated if more data items remain when the end of the description is reached. You will also find in Chapter 6 a list of the ways that a new line of output can occur in the course of one PRINT statement.

4 Files which are unformatted

Formatted files are made of characters. Unformatted files are an image of the memory of the computer, and are very useful to advanced programmers. Often these are called binary files. If a READ or WRITE statement does not include a format specifier, then that statement calls for 'unformatted' data transfers. This should not be confused with list-directed transfers in which the format specifier is *. Unformatted data is transferred in and out in a binary code which uses less space on tape or disk, and is faster than formatted or list-directed operations. For unformatted transfers, you use READ and WRITE statements without a format identifier. In the simplest form, only a unit number is given which identifies the file to be used:

> **READ** (*unit number*) *data list*

> **WRITE** (*unit number*) *data list*

The computer system may have some *unit numbers* set aside for unformatted transfers. There will also be some devices for which unformatted transfers are forbidden, like lineprinters or your terminal. As we will see, you can also create your own files with the OPEN statement.

The records in a file are either formatted or unformatted—they cannot be a mixture of both.

A statement

> **WRITE** (*unit number*) *data list*

transfers the values named in the *data list* to the file identified by the *unit number* in exactly one unformatted record, sometimes called a binary record. It is still true that each new READ or WRITE statement begins a new record. Because there is exactly one record for the entire data list, we do not have the complication of extra records occurring, as happens when new lines begin in a formatted file.

If unformatted data is later to be accessed again by a READ statement, then the READ statement has to be unformatted as well. Exactly the same type should be used in corresponding positions of the data list in the WRITE and READ statements, or you will get some very strange results. Furthermore, although the records that you READ can be shorter than the ones you WRITE, they cannot be longer.

Example Data is prepared by

```
    REAL A(5,8)
      :
    DO 7Ø K=1,5
 7Ø WRITE(11) (A(K,L),L=1,8)
```

It is in five records. The first four columns can be read back by

```
    REWIND(11)
    DO 99
 91 READ(11) (A(K,L),L=1,4)
```

In this example it would be incorrect to try and read the whole array back in one statement, as each record has only 8 values. This READ would fail:

```
    READ(11) A
```

Unformatted transfers can be used with either sequential files, or direct access files. We will find out about direct access files a bit later.

By default, sequential files are connected for formatted transfers. We can overcome this by putting the FORM= specifier in the OPEN statement, as we will see in Section 6 of this chapter. To use a unit that is not preconnected by the computer system for sequential unformatted transfers, use a statement like

```
    OPEN(73, FORM='UNFORMATTED')
```

which connects unit 73 for unformatted sequential access. It is sequential because the ACCESS= specifier is not given.

By default, direct access files are unformatted. Therefore the statement

```
    OPEN(3, ACCESS='DIRECT', RECL=255)
```

connects unit 3 for unformatted direct access transfers. The record length will depend upon the individual computer system—it may well not be 255. Refer to Section 6 of this chapter for more information about OPEN.

5 Sequential files and their manipulation

In a sequential file, records are placed one after another (in sequence) in the file when you WRITE to it. Records can later be read back only in the order that they were written. Usually this reflects the physical organization of the device that the file is on. To write information on a magnetic tape, you would usually start at the beginning and write records on it. You cannot insert a record between two existing ones, because it is physically impossible. Similarly, you can only read the information in the order that it was written. Your terminal and printer or screen are sequential files, which can only be used with WRITE or PRINT. Your keyboard is a sequential file for input only. Direct files, in which information can be placed and retrieved at random, are described later in this chapter.

Three file manipulation statements are available, which can only be used with sequential files: BACKSPACE, REWIND, and END FILE.

At any time during processing a unit can be rewound to start either reading or writing again. If it is already at the beginning it stays there—this is not an error. A file is rewound by:

```
    REWIND  unit number
```

or

```
    REWIND ([UNIT=] unit number [, control list ])
```

for example

```
    REWIND 3    or    REWIND (3)    or    REWIND(UNIT=3)
```

In the control list of REWIND, you can ask for information about the result of the REWIND operation. To do this you can use either (or both) of two specifiers in the control list:

      IOSTAT=*integer variable*   or   **ERR**=*label*

for example

```
REWIND(45, IOSTAT=JOSTAT, ERR=1ØØ)
```

The IOSTAT= specifier sets the given *integer variable* to zero if no error has occurred, or to a positive value if an error does occur. What it means depends on your computer system. For example, a particular value might indicate an attempt to rewind a direct file.

The ERR= specifier allows you to take action in the case of an error. If an error occurs on the file, the program will jump to the statement with the label *label*. A useful example of this is given later in connection with the END FILE statement.

Once you have rewound a file you can reread the information in the file. In a sequential file, the details of the READ must match the WRITE which first created the file. Formatted records are only compatible with formatted records with an equivalent format specification for each field. List-directed statements are compatible with each other, and unformatted records (as described in Section 20.4) can only be read by unformatted READ statements.

Example Data is written according to

```
      DO 66 K=1,6
   66 WRITE(1, 7Ø) I,J,X,Y
   7Ø FORMAT(2I1Ø, 2F1Ø.5)
```

The same program unit could recover it by a compatible READ statement:

```
      REWIND 1
      DO 88 K=1,6
   88 READ(1,7Ø) L,M,W,Z
```

However, because each READ statement begins a new record, partial records can be read. Here the second real value in each record is passed over:

```
      REWIND 1
      DO 91 K=1,6
   91 READ(1,95) L,M,W
```

Example Data is written by

```
      REAL A(5,5)
         :
         :
      WRITE(3,2Ø) A
   2Ø FORMAT(5F5.Ø)
```

and is contained in 5 records because of FORMAT repetition. It can then be reread by

```
      REWIND 3
      READ(3,2Ø) A
```

or by
```
      REWIND 3
      DO 3Ø K=1,5
   3Ø READ(3,2Ø) (A(L,K),L=1,5)
```

Note the order of subscripts. The upper 3 by 3 part could be accessed by

```
      REWIND 3
      DO 5Ø K=1,3
  5Ø  READ(3,2Ø)  (A(K,L),L=1,3)
```

When a unit is rewound to be rewritten, all the old data following the rewrite is lost. Program-mers will sometimes try to get around this but it is not safe. This is best explained in relation to magnetic tape. As shown in Fig. 20.2, a tape is a sequential device. The computer starts from the beginning and writes consecutively before rewinding, when it might read or rewrite. But there is no guarantee on rewriting that the new information takes exactly the same physical space on the tape as the old information, even if the FORMATs are identical. This is because the physical characteristics of the device—start and stop time and the density of information written on the tape—will vary somewhat. So it is not safe to READ after WRITE without a REWIND. Put another way, if a unit is rewound and writing begins on it, all previous informa-tion on the unit is lost. If you don't like that, use a direct file, as described in Section 20.8.

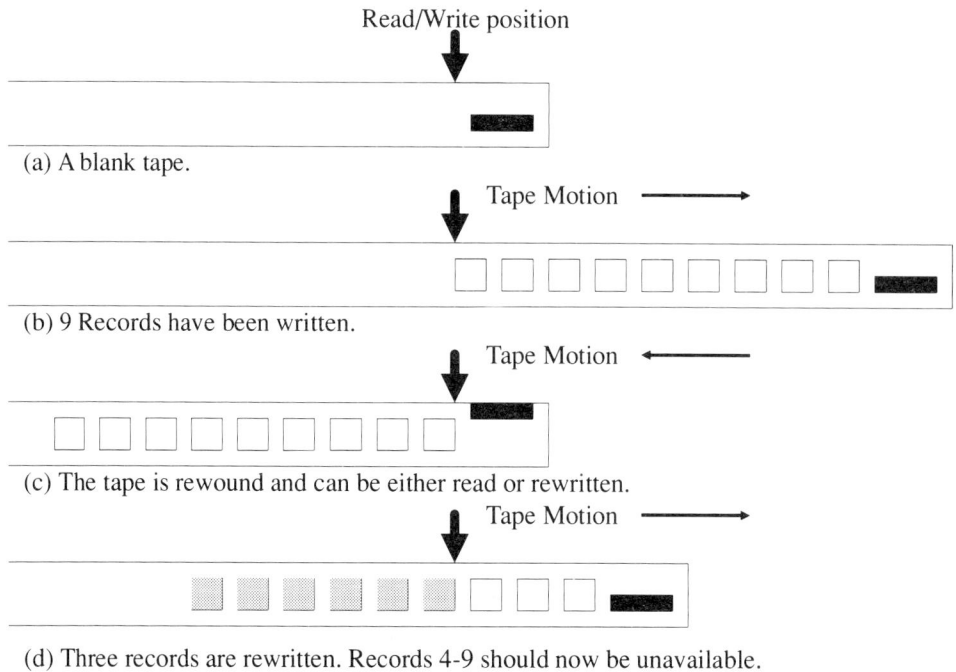

Read/Write position

(a) A blank tape.

Tape Motion ⟶

(b) 9 Records have been written.

Tape Motion ⟵

(c) The tape is rewound and can be either read or rewritten.

Tape Motion ⟶

(d) Three records are rewritten. Records 4-9 should now be unavailable.

Fig. 20.2. On a sequential file, a READ cannot immediately follow a WRITE.

Example You can WRITE, REWIND and READ:

```
      DO 31 K=1,1Ø
  31  WRITE(3,2Ø) K
  2Ø  FORMAT(I1Ø)
      REWIND 3
      DO 32 K=1,1Ø
  32  READ(3,2Ø) K
```

You can also WRITE, REWIND and WRITE, but then everything you wrote before is lost:

```
20 FORMAT(I10)
   DO 31 I=1,10
31 WRITE(3,20) K
   REWIND 3
   DO 32 I=1,2
32 WRITE(3,20) K
```

At this point you would be wrong to write

```
READ(3,20) I
```

You cannot expect to get the value I=3 back this way. To play that kind of game, use a direct access device.

> On a sequential file, never follow WRITE by READ. You must REWIND first.

The BACKSPACE statement

BACKSPACE *unit number*   or **BACKSPACE** (**[UNIT=]** *number]*, *control list*)

causes a sequential file to be stepped back one record on the given unit. The control list items available are the same as for the REWIND statement. It is possible to have the sequence WRITE, BACKSPACE, READ, but then the next operation cannot be READ, for the reason described above. It is not possible to backspace over records written using list-directed formatting.

Example This is a permissible operation on a sequential file. It first writes three records, so that after BACKSPACE the value written as Z is read back into P. This cannot then be followed by another READ:

```
    WRITE(9, 90) X, Y, Z
90 FORMAT(F10.5, F5.2, /, F10.5)
    BACKSPACE 9
    READ(9, 90) P
```

The END FILE statement causes a special end-of-file mark to be written.

END FILE (*unit number*)   or   **END FILE** (**[UNIT=]** *number*, *control list*)

where the *control list* is the same as for the REWIND statement. These special end-of-file marks are sometimes used in data processing to separate groups of records.

Example Here is a useful little subroutine to skip over end-of-file marks on the unit IUNIT:

```
    SUBROUTINE SKIP(N, IUNIT)
C SKIP N FILES ON UNIT IUNIT, WHICH IS ALREADY CONNECTED
    DO 20 K=1,N
10  READ(IUNIT, END=20)
    GO TO 10
20  CONTINUE
    END
```

As a final point, you will need to know that FORTRAN does not automatically position a unit at a particular place at the beginning of a program. It is wise to REWIND tape or disk units before processing. It is unwise, however, to try to REWIND your screen or keyboard!

6 The Properties of a File—INQUIRE, OPEN and CLOSE

The INQUIRE statement can be used to discover all the properties of a file. All files have unit numbers. In addition, a file can have a name which is known to the computer system. The INQUIRE statement can ask about a file by either its name or its unit number:

> `INQUIRE (FILE=`*name,* *enquiry list*`)`

or   `INQUIRE ([UNIT=]` *number,* *enquiry list*`)`

The file name is any character expression in which trailing blanks are ignored, for example

> `INQUIRE (FILE='FRED',` *enquiry list*`)`

In either form of the INQUIRE statement, the enquiry list asks for facts about the file. An enquiry list can contain any of the following specifiers:

IOSTAT= *integer variable*	ACCESS= *character variable*
ERR= *label*	SEQUENTIAL= *logical variable*
EXIST= *logical variable*	DIRECT= *logical variable*
OPENED= *logical variable*	FORM= *character variable*
NUMBER= *integer variable*	FORMATTED= *logical variable*
NAMED= *logical variable*	UNFORMATTED= *logical variable*
NAME= *character variable*	BLANK= *character variable*
RECL= *integer variable*	NEXTREC= *integer variable*

(a) IOSTAT= *integer variable*. An integer value is returned to you. If zero there is no error condition present in the file. A positive value means an error has occurred. If it is negative, there is no error, but the end of the file has been reached.

(b) ERR= *label*. If an error condition has occurred, the program will jump immediately to the statement with the given *label*, which must be in the same program unit.

(c) EXIST= *logical variable*. If the file exists, the *logical variable* gives the value .TRUE.. If the file does not exist the value is .FALSE..

(d) OPENED= *logical variable*. This tells you whether the file is already open or not. At the beginning of a program, some files may already be connected. Other files may have to be connected by an OPEN.

(e) NUMBER= *integer variable*. This is used to discover the unit number of a named file. If there is no such file, the *integer variable* becomes undefined.

(f) NAMED= *logical variable*. This tells you whether the file has a name.

(g) NAME= *character variable*. Use this to find the name of a file which has a unit number.

(h) ACCESS= *character variable*. The *character variable* tells you whether the type of access is SEQUENTIAL or DIRECT. If the file is not connected, it becomes undefined.

(i) SEQUENTIAL= *character variable*. This tells you whether a file can be used for sequential access. The value will be YES, NO, or UNKNOWN. This is not the same as using ACCESS= to find out the current form of access.

(j) DIRECT= *character variable*. In a similar way, this tells you whether direct access is permitted for the file.

(k) FORM= *character variable*. This tells you whether the file is currently connected for use with formatted data or unformatted data, by giving FORMATTED or UNFORMATTED. If the file is not connected, then the *character variable* is undefined.

(l) FORMATTED= *character variable*. This tells whether a particular type of data is permitted for the file. The result is YES, NO, or UNKNOWN. This is not the same as using FORM= to find out the current form of access.

(m) UNFORMATTED= *character variable*. In a similar way, this tells you if unformatted data is allowed with this file.

(n) RECL= *integer variable*. This asks for the maximum permitted record length of a direct access file. If the file is connected for sequential access, or if it is not connected at all, the *integer variable* becomes undefined.

(o) NEXTREC= *integer variable*. This tells you the number of the next record in a direct access file. When a direct file is first connected, the next record is number 1. After a READ or WRITE which the last record used is record number n, the next record is $n+1$.

(p) BLANK= *character variable*. This tells you whether blanks are NULL or ZERO if the file is connected for formatted input/output. If it is connected for direct access, or not at all, the result is undefined. Normally if a file is connected for formatted transfers, blanks are interpreted as nulls, i.e. they have no meaning in numerical fields. However we have seen that a BN or BZ editing specification could override this in an individual format. In the OPEN statement, which is described next, it is possible to change the normal interpretation of blanks.

The OPEN statement

> **OPEN([UNIT=]** *number,* *specification list***)**

will connect the file and define its characteristics using the file specification list.

The following are the available specifiers for the OPEN statement:

IOSTAT= *integer variable*	ACCESS= *character value*
ERR= *label*	FORM= *character value*
FILE= *name*	RECL= *integer value*
STATUS= *character value*	BLANK= *character value*

(a) IOSTAT= *integer variable*. This is the only specifier in the OPEN statement which returns a value to you. Its meaning is the same as in all the other input/output statements.

(b) ERR= *label*. If an error condition has occurred, the program will jump immediately to the statement with the given *label*, which must be in the same program unit. This could happen, for example, if a program tries to open a file for direct access but direct access is not permitted for that file.

(c) FILE= *name*. This is the name of the file in your computer's filing system that you wish to open. If you do not give a name, the computer will open a suitable file for you. The *name* is a character value in which trailing blanks are ignored.

(d) STATUS= *character value*. This allows you to tell the computer what to do about finding (and later disposing of) this file. If there is no STATUS= specifier, the value UNKNOWN is assumed.

The *character value* can be:

OLD	The file must already exist in the computer system.
NEW	The file must not exist already. The computer creates a new one.
SCRATCH	Must not be specified for a named file. A scratch file is discarded when closed by a CLOSE statement or when the program terminates.
UNKNOWN	The computer decides what kind of file it is.

(e) ACCESS= *character value*. The value must be SEQUENTIAL or DIRECT. The default is SEQUENTIAL. If you ask for DIRECT and it is not allowed, an error condition occurs.

(f) FORM= *character value*. The value must be FORMATTED or UNFORMATTED. If not given, a sequential file is formatted, whereas a direct access file is unformatted.

(g) RECL= *integer value*. This is the record length, which must be given for a direct access file. For formatted records, this is the maximum permitted number of characters. For unformatted records the required length will vary between computer systems. A record length must not be given for a sequential access file.

(h) BLANK= *character value*. This specifier can only be given for a formatted file. It determines the interpretation of blanks in numeric fields, as discussed earlier in this chapter. It can be either NULL or ZERO depending on whether blanks are to be ignored or treated as zeros. (An all blank field is always zero.) If no BLANK= specifier is given, NULL is assumed.

When using an OPEN statement, it is important to know whether the file is already connected. If it is, then the file remains in the same position and only the BLANK= specifier can be changed. To make some significant change, the file should first be closed by a CLOSE statement and then reopened.

A file can only be connected to one unit number and a unit number can only be connected to one file. If a program tries to connect the same unit number to an additional file, then the first file is automatically closed. If a program tries to connect the same file to an additional unit number, an error occurs.

The CLOSE statement disconnects a file:

> **CLOSE([UNIT=]** *number, specifiers***)**

The possible specifiers are:

> IOSTAT= *integer variable*   ERR= *label*   STATUS= *character value*

(a) IOSTAT= *integer variable*. This has the same meaning as has already been described for other input/output statements.

(b) ERR= *label*. If an error occurs, the specifier causes the program to jump to the statement with the given *label*, which must exist in the same program unit.

(c) STATUS= *character value*. This tells the computer what to do with the file. The value could be either KEEP or DELETE. KEEP means that the file continues to exist and could be reconnected. However, you cannot KEEP a file opened as a SCRATCH file—they are always deleted. If you give DELETE the file ceases to exist. If no STATUS= specifier is given, all files are kept except those which were designated as SCRATCH files when they were opened.

7 A text processing example

The program given here shows you how to open a file whose name the user enters when the program is run—now that is useful! Each record is scanned backwards to find the first non-blank character—remember that the character variable LINE will be filled with blanks if the value which is read is too short. This example reads an entire record and the length of LINE is 132. You could increase this if necessary. Then, we count the occurrence of symbols in the file over a range of codes from LFIRST to LLAST. These are the machine dependent codes. Finally the results are presented both numerically and as a graph:

```
      PARAMETER (LFIRST=33, LLAST=127)
      INTEGER LETTRS(LFIRST:LLAST)
      CHARACTER NAME*16, LINE*132
      DO 10 L=LFIRST, LLAST
         LETTRS(L)=0
   10 CONTINUE
C GET THE NAME OF THE TEXT FILE
      PRINT*, 'COUNT THE NUMBER OF OCCURRENCES OF SYMBOLS'
      PRINT*,'FROM NO ',LFIRST,' TO NO ',LLAST,' IN A FILE'
      PRINT*
      PRINT*, 'ENTER THE NAME OF THE TEXT FILE'
      READ (*, '(A)') NAME
      OPEN(1, STATUS='OLD', FILE=NAME)
   20 READ(1, '(A)', END=60) LINE
C FIND THE LAST NONBLANK CHARACTER
      DO 30 L=132, 1, -1
         LAST=L
         IF(LINE(L:L).NE.' ') GO TO 40
   30 CONTINUE
C COUNT THE FREQUENCY OF EACH SYMBOL IN RANGE LFIRST TO LLAST
   40 DO 50 L=1, LAST
         INDEX=ICHAR(LINE(L:L))
         IF(INDEX.GE.LFIRST .AND. INDEX.LE.LLAST) THEN
            LETTRS(INDEX)=LETTRS(INDEX)+1
         END IF
   50 CONTINUE
      GO TO 20
C PRINT THE RESULT - COMPLETE WITH A GRAPH
   60 DO 70 L=LFIRST, LLAST
         PRINT 80,L,CHAR(L),LETTRS(L),('*', LL=0, LETTRS(L)/4)
   70 CONTINUE
   80 FORMAT(' CHAR ',I3,' SYMBOL ',A1,' FREQ ',I3,' [',40A1)
      END
```

By default a file is sequential and formatted. The OPEN statement in the example is like:

`OPEN(UNIT=1,FORM='FORMATTED',STATUS='OLD',ACCESS='SEQUENTIAL',FILE=NAME)`

Exercise Write a program which will convert all alphabetic characters in a file from lower case to upper case. This could be useful if you have entered a FORTRAN program in lower case and your computer does not like it.

8 Direct access files

A direct access file is one in which a computer program can read or write any desired record from the file. For example, magnetic disk storage is usually organized so that the computer can seek out any desired record at any time. Not all input/output devices can be used as direct access files. Each computer installation will have a number of devices available as direct and/or sequential files.

To achieve direct access, FORTRAN 77 uses the REC= specifier as described in the previous section. The first record in a file is record number 1, and data can be written to or read from any desired part of the file by specifying the record number.

A file cannot be available for direct access and sequential access at the same time. An OPEN statement can connect it for direct access provided that this is allowed for the particular device. Once connected, an error condition arises if the wrong form of access is used. However, a file can be closed and reopened for a different kind of access.

In a direct access file, the physical records on the device used for the file are all of the same length. This 'block' length is the maximum number of characters that can be written or read by a formatted transfer, and to a certain extent this can be controlled by the OPEN statement. Every record has a record number, and in the file the records occur in order. Therefore if a file created by direct access is later read by sequential access, the records will be found in order of their number, starting with record number 1.

Formatted and unformatted records cannot be mixed in any kind of file. In a direct access file, you must not use list-directed formatting. Therefore if a file created by sequential access is later read by direct access, the records must all be the same length and not written by list-directed statements.

Example You wish to read some data from a sequential file whose name is IN.TEXT, and divide the even and odd numbered records into the top and bottom halves of a new file, OUT.TEXT. This reordering is illustrated by Fig. 20.3.

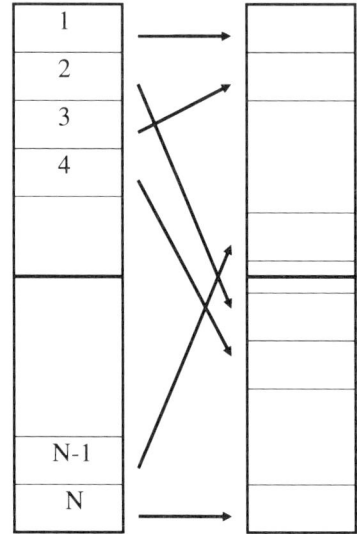

Fig. 20.3. Even-odd reordering of a sequential file is easy as a direct file.

Here is the program to reorder 16 records:

```
C SEQUENTIAL AND DIRECT ACCESS IN ONE PROGRAM
      CHARACTER DATA*72, INFIL*8, OUTFIL*8
      PARAMETER(NUMBER=16,INFIL=' IN.TEXT',OUTFIL=' OUT.TEXT')
C OPEN THE FILES
      OPEN(6, FILE=INFIL, STATUS='OLD', ACCESS='SEQUENTIAL')
      OPEN(7, FILE=OUTFIL, STATUS='NEW' ,ACCESS='DIRECT',
     + FORM='FORMATTED', RECL=132)
C DO THE REARRANGEMENT
      DO 10 KREC=1,NUMBER
        READ(6, '(A)') DATA
        LEREC=1 + KREC/2 + (NUMBER/2-1)*MOD(KREC+1,2)
        WRITE(7, '(A)',REC=LEREC) DATA
        PRINT*,'COPYING INPUT ' ,KREC, ' TO OUTPUT ', LEREC
   10 CONTINUE
```

The key to the reordering is the calculation of the new record number, LEREC, from the original order in the sequential file. You could now read them back and print their new order:

```
C PRINT REARRANGED RECORDS IN ORDER
      DO 2Ø MREC=1,NUMBER
         READ(7, '(A)', REC=MREC) DATA
         PRINT*, DATA
  2Ø CONTINUE
      END
```

Because character data has been used, any formatted file could have been rearranged in this way. This same file could be reopened as a sequential file, and the data read back.

If a formatted transfer needs several records then several records of the direct access file are used. In this example records 7, 9, and 11 are written on the direct access file on unit 10. Records 8 and 10 have been skipped over because of the / in the FORMAT specification:

```
      INTEGER IRAY(3, 3)
                :
                :
      WRITE(1Ø, 2Ø, REC=7) IRAY
  2Ø FORMAT(3I1Ø/)
```

If you ask for a record which is larger than the maximum permitted for the particular file, then an error has occurred (which could be detected by an IOSTAT= specifier). However, a transfer in either direction can use only part of a record as in several of the above examples.

Finally, common sense will tell you that you can only read back what has actually been written. A program cannot expect to read values from a record that have not been written, or more values than were written in a record. In this program DUMB would become undefined after the READ statement:

```
      SMART=1.Ø
      DUMB=2.Ø
      WRITE(16, REC=11) SMART
      READ (16, REC=11) SMART, DUMB
```

9 Problems

Problem 20.1 A file skipping subroutine was given as an example at the end of Section 5 of this chapter. It could fail for all kinds of reasons. You can only have end-of-file marks in sequential files, for example. The file may not exist, and it may not be open. Perhaps an error occurs while it is trying to do its job, for example if you run off the physical end of the file. Try to use the filing facilities of FORTRAN 77 to make the subroutine as secure as you can.

Problem 20.2 Write a FORTRAN program to process a Pascal program so that all the keywords of Pascal are capitalized, and all other items are lower case. Do not capitalize a keyword if it appears in a comment or in a character string. Why process a Pascal program? Because it is easier to find the keywords than it would be in scanning a FORTRAN program.

Problem 20.3 Write a program to prepare an alphabetical list of all the words that occur in a file of text, together with the number of times they have occurred. You may agree that it is a bit tricky to define a word of English, but try. If you can get some examples of writing then investigate the vocabularies of the authors. Do you think you could tell one author from another just by the frequency of common words?

Problem 20.4 Investigate the distribution of word and sentence lengths in some files of text. Is this a more subtle test of identity?

Problem 20.5 Investigate the frequency of occurrence of the letters of the alphabet in some files of text—expressed as a percentage of the total number of letters in the file. Sort the results into order from most to least common. Can you see any logic in the arrangement of letters on your keyboard? What about the old hot metal typesetting machines—the top row of keys was e t a o i n s h r d l u? A statistical question—have you enough text to be sure of the order?

Problem 20.6 Now look at the frequency of occurrence of pairs of letters in files of text. What is the best way of expressing this, and of presenting it? Are there pairs that always occur? Never? What fun.

Appendix

A summary of FORTRAN 77

This appendix summarizes the useful and enduring features of FORTRAN 77, with cross-references to their descriptions in the main body of the text.

1 FORTRAN Standards

Early versions of FORTRAN were not standardized. The first standard, generally known as FORTRAN IV, was produced by the American National Standards Association (ANSI) as ANSI No. X3.9-1966. FORTRAN 77 is ANSI X3.9–1978, and was also accredited by the International Standards Organization (ISO) as ISO 1539–1980. Many implementations have extensions which are not standard.

2 FORTRAN 8X

A new standard to replace FORTRAN 77 is in an advanced stage of development, called FORTRAN 8X. It is stated that all standard FORTRAN 77 programs will be accepted by a FORTRAN 8X compiler. However, there are a number of ways in which what you think is a correct FORTRAN 77 program may not actually be standard, even though it works. An example is the omission of the SAVE statement from subprograms whose variables you expect to persist between calls (see Chapters 10 and 13).

Certain FORTRAN 77 features are *deprecated* in FORTRAN 8X—meaning that they are singled out for deletion from a future version. I have indicated what some of these are in the main body of this text, and also in Section 17 of this Appendix. Of particular interest in FORTRAN 8X will be:

(i) Relaxing the constraints on layout and spelling.

(ii) Introducing MODULE subprograms, which can be imported by a single USE statement. Eventually this will replace COMMON.

(iii) Introducing whole array operations. As well as shortening and clarifying the coding of loops, these open up a rich vein of possibilities in parallel processing.

(iv) Allowing you to create data types and objects, for which operations can be defined. This assists in using abstract data types, which have been stressed as a programming methodology in this test.

(v) Explicit recursion will be permitted, making the simulations of Chapter 14 unnecessary, except in the pursuit of efficiency.

3 The form of FORTRAN programs

A FORTRAN program consists of one or more *program units*. A *program unit* might be a *main program* or a *subprogram*. Every program unit must end with an END statement. A main program may begin with the optional PROGRAM statement (Chapter 2). A subprogram unit must begin with a FUNCTION (Chapter 10), SUBROUTINE (Chapter 11) or BLOCK DATA (Chapter 17) statement.

A program which contains a main program can be executed. A program which contains only subprograms must be linked in some way with a main program before it can be executed.

4 FORTRAN statements

A FORTRAN program unit consists of *statements* or *comments*, written in lines from columns 1 to 72 of each line. Each statement or comment begins on a new line. A statement may continue on additional lines.

> *Comments* contain **C** in column 1 and any text in the rest of the line.

> *Statements* begin in column 7 of their first line, except that columns 1 to 5 may contain a numeric *label*.

> A statement continues on further lines if a character is in column 6 of the continuation lines.

See Chapter 2 for further details.

5 Characters and names

FORTRAN 77 allows only capital letters and a limited range of other symbols (Chapter 2).

A FORTRAN *name* begins with a letter, and can have up to five further characters which are either letters or numbers (Chapter 2).

A *name* might represent

> (i) A variable or array or dummy argument (all of these have a type).

> (ii) A constant defined by a PARAMETER statement (which has a type).

> (iii) A function, either user-defined or built-in (which has a type).

> (iv) A subroutine (no type).

> (v) A named COMMON block (no type).

It is poor style to use the same name for more than one of the above items, even though some combinations are allowed.

6 FORTRAN data types—constants and variables

FORTRAN variables, arrays, dummy arguments and constants all represent data items which have a *type* and a *value*. Character items also have a *length*.

Initially, the values of variables are undefined unless given by a DATA statement or assigned to named COMMON in a BLOCK DATA subprogram (also with a DATA statement). Later they may become defined through assignment or input, either directly or through use as an actual argument of a subprogram which defines them. The effect of association through COMMON or EQUIVALENCE must also be taken into account.

By default, FORTRAN applies *implicit typing* to names. Normally names beginning with I, J, K, L, M or N are integer, all others are real. This can be confirmed or altered to other types by the IMPLICIT statement. The types of built-in functions cannot be altered (Chapter 19).

Types other than real or integer require either explicit typing through a *type* statement, or an implicit scheme using IMPLICIT.

The names of the FORTRAN Types are:

INTEGER—values which are exact integers, over some machine-dependent range (Chapters 4, 5).

A *basic integer constant* is a number written without a decimal place, for example 123

REAL—values with decimal places, over some range and to some limit of precision depending on the machine (Chapters 3, 5).

A *basic real constant* is written with a decimal place, for example 1.23, or in *exponential* form, as 123E–2.

COMPLEX— a pair of reals (Chapter 19).

A complex constant is written as a bracketed pair of real constants, separated by commas, for example (1.23, 4.56).

DOUBLE PRECISION—like a real value, but with extra decimal places (Chapter 19).

A double precision constant is written like the real exponential form, but with D, as in 123D–2.

LOGICAL—takes the values .TRUE. or .FALSE. (Chapter 19).

A logical constant is written as .TRUE. or .FALSE. .

CHARACTER— represents symbols (Chapter 18). A character value has a *length* attribute.

A character constant is written between single quotes, e.g. 'HI'. Embedded quotes are represented doubled, as 'DOESN''T'. In a FORMAT specifier, you may encounter embedded embedded quotes, for example in

```
PRINT'(''DOESN''''T'')'
```

7 Arrays and subscripts (Chapters 12, 13, 16)

An array is an ordered collection of variables of one type, addressed by up to seven subscripts. An array is declared by the DIMENSION, COMMON or *type* statements, in which it is given *subscript bounds*, for example

DIMENSION *name* (*bound1*, *bound2*, ...)

The *subscript bounds* are *integer constant expressions* giving the maximum and minimum values of the particular subscript:

minimum **:** *maximum*

Maximum must always be given. If *minimum* is omitted, it is assumed to be 1, in which case the colon must also be omitted.

The size of the array along a particular subscript's dimension is *maximum–minimum*+1. The total size is the product of all the subscript sizes.

If an array is passed as an actual argument to a subprogram, some alternatives exist for expressing the subscript bounds in the subprogram. Remember, however, that the array must originate at the highest level program unit that uses it, where it must have actual, truthful constant subscript bounds.

The alternatives are;

(i) A bound can be an integer expression involving only variables which are dummy arguments of the subprogram—these are called *adjustable* or *variable* subscript bounds.

(ii)The final subscript bound can be *—called an *assumed size.*

In using an array, an actual subscript expression is used to select a member of the array:

name (subscript1, subscript2, . . .)

A subscript must be an integer expression—there is no conversion permitted from another type. The correct number of subscripts must be given. However, array names may be given without brackets or subscripts in some situations where the whole array is intended, for example in input/output statements, DATA statements, as dummy arguments and in declarations of type, COMMON or EQUIVALENCE.

The actual subscript should lie within the subscript bounds. However a subscript value is not checked. This allows some tricky forms of cheating, and is also a common source of error. The layout of arrays in memory and some of these possibilities are discussed in Chapter 16.

8 FORTRAN expressions

Expressions combine *values* (variables or constants) through *operations* to give a *result* which has a *type*. During the evaluation of an expression, intermediate results can arise of different types, and can only be operated on as allowed.

The operations available in FORTRAN, and their *priority* are:

( )	Expressions in brackets	Highest
**		
* or /	Arithmetic Operators	
+ or–		
//	Character concatenation	
.GT., .GE., .EQ., .LE., .NE.	Relational operators	
.NOT.		
.AND.	Logical operators	
.OR.		
.EQV. or .NEQV.		Lowest

Operations of equal priority are evaluated from left to right. Operations of higher priority are done before those of lower priority. Exceptionally, a series of exponentiations is evaluated right to left—2**3**4 is 2**(3**4).

The character operation of // or *concatenation* is available between character values only. The rules governing the lengths of the operands and results are described in Chapter 18.

(a) An *arithmetic expression* which involves addition, subtraction, multiplication, division, and exponentiation can contain mixtures of real, integer, complex, and double precision values. All combinations are allowed except those between complex and double precision values.

(b) The *type* of an arithmetic expression depends on the order of the operations. The priority of arithmetic operations was described above and in Chapter 3. To determine the type of value that occurs in each stage of the evaluation of an arithmetic expression, first determine the order of the operations, then follow the evaluation through in the correct order. Refer to Table A.1 to get the result of each operation.

Table A.1. The result of arithmetic operations between values of various types.

One value ↓	Integer	Real	Double Precision	Complex
Integer	Integer	Real	Double Precision	Complex
Real	Real	Real	Double Precision	Complex
Double Precision	Double Precision	Double Precision	Double Precision	
Complex	Complex	Complex		Complex

The other value

(c) *Relational operations* compare arithmetic values to give a *logical result* (Chapter 7).

Integer, real, double precision and complex values can be compared in relational expressions in all combinations except that:

Only .EQ. and .NE. can be used with the complex type.

Complex values and double precision values can never be compared.

(d) *Logical expressions* are formed in the manner described fully in Chapter 7. There are no operations mixing logical values with values of any other type.

Logical values cannot be compared in a relational expression—but of course the *logical operators* themselves cover all the necessary cases.

(e) *Character expressions* have been described in Chapter 18. Character entities can only be compared with character entities. There are no operations which mix character entities with values of any other type.

9 The statements of FORTRAN 77

FORTRAN 77 statements are classified as follows:

(i) Specification statements:

DIMENSION	IMPLICIT
EQUIVALENCE	PARAMETER
COMMON	EXTERNAL
Type statements	INTRINSIC
SAVE	

(ii) *Type statements* are a special category within the specification statements:

INTEGER	COMPLEX
REAL	LOGICAL
DOUBLE PRECISION	CHARACTER

(iii) Executable statements:

Assignment statements	DO
ASSIGN (Do not use)	READ
GO TO	WRITE
Assigned GO TO (Do not use)	PRINT
Computed GO TO (Do not use)	REWIND
Arithmetic IF (Seldom used)	BACKSPACE
Logical IF	ENDFILE
Block IF	OPEN
ELSE IF	CLOSE
ELSE	INQUIRE
END IF	
CALL	CONTINUE
RETURN	STOP
END	PAUSE

All statements not appearing in the list of executable statements are called nonexecutable statements. They are:

All *specification statements*	ENTRY
Statement function definitions	BLOCK DATA
PROGRAM	DATA
FUNCTION	FORMAT
SUBROUTINE	

The order of statements in a FORTRAN program is specified. Usually this follows the common sense rule that an item must be defined before it is used, although typing and dimensioning can be done in several different ways:

	Heading: PROGRAM (optional) or FUNCTION or SUBROUTINE or BLOCK DATA		
Comments can go anywhere before END	FORMAT statements can go after heading, before END	PARAMETER Statements	IMPLICIT Statements
			Other Specification
		DATA Statements	Statement functions
			Executable Statements
	END is always the very end		

10 The assignment statement

> *variable* = *expression*

(a) An *arithmetic* assignment assigns an *expression* of integer, real, double precision, or complex type, as described above, to a *variable* or array element of any of these types.

(b) A logical *expression* may only be assigned to a logical *variable* or array element.

(c) A character *expression* may only be assigned to a *variable* or array element or substring of type character.

11 Non-executable statements

Items in square brackets are optional.

(a) Specification statements

DIMENSION *name* (*bounds*) [, *name* (*bounds*) . . .] (Chapters 12,13,16)

> declares arrays and their *subscript bounds*.

Type *names* [(*bounds*) , *name* (*bounds*) . . .] (Chapter 19)

> declares *names* to be of the specified type, also can declare subscript bounds. *Type* is INTEGER, REAL, COMPLEX, DOUBLE PRECISION, LOGICAL or COMPLEX. CHARACTER type also has a *length* attribute as described in Chapter 9.

COMMON *name* [(*bounds*)] [, *name* [(*bounds*)], . . .] (Chapter 17)

> declares variables to be in blank COMMON, also can declare *subscript bounds*.

COMMON [/ *name* /] *name* [(*bounds*)] [, . . .] (Chapter 17)

> declares variables to be in named COMMON, also can declare *subscript bounds*.

IMPLICIT *type* (*letter or range* [, *letter or range*]) [, type . . .] (Chapter 19)

> where *range* is *letter--letter*, *Type* is INTEGER, REAL, COMPLEX, DOUBLE PRECISION, LOGICAL or COMPLEX. CHARACTER type also has a *length* attribute as described in Chapter 9.

> Specifies a spelling convention for implicit typing of names by their initial letters. The default for a program unit is identical to

> ```
>        IMPLICIT REAL(A-H, O-Z),  INTEGER(I-N)
> ```

> which can be confirmed or altered by the IMPLICIT statement.

PARAMETER (*name* = *constant* [, *name* = *constant* . . .]) [, (. . .)] (Chapter 10)

> Gives names to constants. Converts from the type of the given *constant* to the type of *name* if necessary—the type of the constant does **not** specify the type of the name.

EXTERNAL *name* [, *name* . . .] (Chapter 19)

> The *names* are the names of separate program units. Used to specify that a name is not an intrinsic one, i.e. to allow you to write your own SQRT function. Also allows you to pass the *name* as an argument to a subprogram.

INTRINSIC *name* [, *name* . . .] (Chapter 19)

> The *names* are the names of intrinsic program units. Allows you to pass the name of an intrinsic function like SQRT as an argument to a subprogram.

SAVE [*names*] (Chapters 10, 17)

In a subprogram, the named variables are to have their values preserved for a future entry to the subprogram. Widely ignored but potentially important.

(b) Other non-executable statements

Statement function definitions:

name (*dummy arguments*) = *expression* (Chapter 10)

Defines a function available only in the same program unit, using *dummy arguments* and local values to define the result, with conversion to the type of *name* if necessary.

BLOCK DATA (Chapter 17)

Heading for a subprogram containing only specification statements. Used to assign initial values to a named COMMON.

DATA *variable list* / *constants* / [, *variable list* / *constants* / . . .] (Chapter 10)

The given *constants* are assigned in one-to-one correspondence to the list of *variables*. The *variables* might be array names, and implied DO-loops can be used for subscripts. (See under DO statement and also Chapter 12).

FORMAT (*Specification*) (Chapters 6, 20)

Give the layout of formatted input/output information. This statement is always labelled. See also section on FORMAT.

FUNCTION *name* [(*dummy arguments*)] (Chapter 10)

also **type FUNCTION** *name* [(*dummy arguments*)] (Chapters 18, 19)

Heading for a FUNCTION subprogram. The function name has a type. *Type* is INTEGER, REAL, COMPLEX, DOUBLE PRECISION, LOGICAL or COMPLEX. CHARACTER type also has a *length* attribute as described in Chapter 9. See also section on subprograms and arguments.

PROGRAM *name* [(*options*)] (Chapter 2)

Optional heading for a main program. *Options* are machine dependent.

SUBROUTINE *name* (*dummy arguments*) (Chapter 11)

Heading for a subroutine subprogram. The subroutine *name* does not have a type. See also section on subprograms and arguments.

12 Executable statements

Items in square brackets are optional.

(a) Control and similar statements

CALL *name* [(*actual arguments*)] (Chapter 11)

Associates the *actual arguments* with the *dummy arguments* of subroutine *name*, then invokes subroutine *name*. See also Section 14 of this Appendix.

CONTINUE (Chapters 8, 9)

No action is taken, and the program continues to the next executable statement. When labelled, it is useful as the final statement of a DO loop.

DO *label variable = start, finish* [, *step*] Chapters 8, 9

This is the principal facility for looping (repetition, recurrence) in FORTRAN 77. A statement with the given *label* must exist later in the program. All the statements from the DO up to and including the label are repeated with the *variable* taking the successive values *start, start+step*, . . . until it reaches or passes *finish*. If *step* is omitted, it is 1. A number of rules apply, as detailed in Chapter 8. A fundamental rule is that the number of repetitions is predetermined, so that altering **any** of the DO parameters (*variable, start, step,* or *finish*) **does not** affect the number of times the loop is repeated. DO-loops and IF blocks can be nested within each other.

An implied DO-loop is available in the list of an input/output statement, or the variable list of a DATA statement, both explained in Chapter 12. You can nest implied DO-loops:

(*list, variable = start, finish* [, *step*])

END (Chapter 2)

This must be the last statement in each and every program unit. At the end of a main program, it terminates execution (like STOP). At the end of a subprogram it returns control to the calling program (like RETURN).

GO TO *label* (Chapters 4, 7, 9)

Jumps to the statement with the given *label*. A much reviled statement, the GO TO is the accessory after the fact in the creation of spaghetti programs. Respectable programmers use it only to simulate respectable control structures. See Chapter 9.

IF (*logical expression*) *statement* (Chapters 4, 7, 9)

If the *logical expression* is true, the given *statement* is executed, otherwise it is not.

the block **IF** (Chapters 4, 7, 9)

IF (*logical expression*) **THEN**

true statements

[**ELSE IF** (*logical expression*) **THEN**

true statements]

[**ELSE**

false statements]

END IF

In its basic form, the *true statements* between IF and END IF are executed if the *logical expression* is true. Before END IF, as many ELSE IF clauses as required can be used, with finally at most one ELSE statement.

Block IF structures can be nested within block IF structures or DO loops (Chapter 8).

RETURN (Chapter 11)

In a function or subroutine subprogram, returns control to the calling program unit. END has the same effect, but RETURN can be put anywhere.

STOP (Chapter 7)

In any program unit, terminates execution of a program. END as the final statement in a main program has the same effect, but STOP can be put anywhere.

(b) Input/output statements (Many Chapters, details in Chapter 20)

Input/output devices are controlled or manipulated by the statements BACKSPACE, CLOSE, END FILE, INQUIRE, OPEN and REWIND (Chapter 20). All these have the form:

   action   control list

Input/output *values* are transferred by various forms of READ, WRITE and PRINT (Chapters 2, 3, 4, 6, 20) of the form

   action   control list [*values*]

Input/output is **formatted** if the *control list* includes a *format specification*, as detailed in the next section and in Chapter 6. Special forms of READ and WRITE, and all PRINT statements are also formatted, as described below and in Chapter 20.

Input/output is **unformatted** if the control list does not contain a *format specifier* as detailed below and in Chapter 20.

Input/output can be **sequential** or **direct**. Most users will be familiar with *sequential* transfers. Every sequential transfer starts a new *record* (line) of input or output. Additional lines can occur during processing (See Chapters 6 and 20). Direct transfers permit records to be read from or written to chosen parts of a file at random, if the nature of the physical device permits this. See Chapter 20 for details.

Refer to Chapter 20 for the *available control list* items for each input/output statement:

   BACKSPACE *control list* (Chapter 20)

   CLOSE *control list* (Chapter 20)

   END FILE *control list* (Chapter 20)

   INQUIRE *control list* (Chapter 20)

   OPEN *control list* (Chapter 20)

   PRINT *format* [, *values*] (Chapters 2, 3, 6, 20)

   READ (*control list*) [*variables*] (Chapter 20)

   READ *format* [, *variables*] (Chapters 4, 6, 20)

   REWIND *control list* (Chapter 20)

   WRITE (*control list*) [*values*] (Chapter 20)

13 FORMAT specifiers

Chapter 6 was devoted to the FORMAT facility. The layout of data in formatted data transfers is controlled by a *format specification*. This can be:

(i) * to indicate *list-directed* processing. This is only available for sequential devices, and permits the computer system to decide the layout of output (Chapter 6)

Example

```
    PRINT*,'HELLO'
```

(ii) The label of a FORMAT statement. Notice the space to avoid carriage control:

```
    PRINT 21
 21 FORMAT(' HELLO')
```

(ii) The *format specification* given directly, within quotation marks. Note that the brackets are part of the format specification:

```
PRINT '(1X,''HELLO'')'
```

A *format specification* is made up from *editing descriptions*, which must be separated by commas unless one is the slash, /, or colon, :. These specify either *layout* instructions for data items, or *actions* to be taken between data items.

(a) Actions

n	number of similar items
*k***P**	scale factor
/	begin new line (No comma is required before or after this description)

n (repeated group)

*n***X**	insert *n* blanks here
TR*n*	Jump to the right by *n* spaces, inserting blanks. This has the same effect as *n***X**.
TL*n*	Jump to the left by *n* spaces and begin replacing previous output. Cannot jump beyond the beginning of a line. It does not overstrike output, but replaces it.
T*n*	Jump to column *n*.
BN	Blanks in numeric fields which follow are ignored, except that an all blank field is zero. This is the default for formatted files, but can be changed by the OPEN statement. Each formatted transfer begins with the default for that file.
BZ	Blanks which follow are interpreted as zero.

In printing signs, the computer system can decide whether plus signs are to be printed by default. You can dictate what happens by using the **SS** or **SP** descriptions. The **S** description returns sign printing to the default state, whatever that was. Each formatted transfer begins with the default for that file.

SS	Print only minus signs on following numeric data.
SP	Print all signs on following numeric data.
S	Return to the default sign printing convention.
:	Cease format processing if there are no more items to be transferred.
' character constant'	Insert these characters in the output
*n***H** *characters*	Insert the next *n* characters in output. This is an obsolete version of a character constant. It is tedious to have to count the characcters in a constant, and errors will occur if the count is not exact. A character constant in quotes is now almost always used.

When an input/output transfer reaches the end of a format specification and more items remain to be transferred, a new record of output begins, meaning a new line, and the format specification is repeated from the first embedded left bracket if there is one, or from the beginning of the format specification if there is no embedded group.

When an input/output operation has transferred all its data items and the end of the format specification has not been reached, the remaining actions are processed until a data description is reached, or a colon stops it.

(b) Layout descriptions for data

Notation used: *w* field width   *n* number of similar items
                           d number of digits   *e* number of digits in exponent

(i) Integers

    [*n*] **I***w* [.*d*]   Integer

n integer fields of width *w* are processed, with at least *d* digits printed (the presence of the *d* will provide leading zeros).

(ii) Reals

Data types compatible with real format descriptions are real, double precision, and complex, which is a pair of reals. On output, any list item can be used with any real description. On input any list item can be used with any real description, and furthermore the actual data given can conform to any description. For example data given to an **F** description can be in **E** or **F** form, and so on. However double precision input data should be passed through the **D** description if the number of digits of precision to be given in input data exceeds the single precision of the machine—otherwise digits will be lost.

    [*n*] **F***w.d*   Real, no exponent

n real fields of with *w* having *d* decimal places are processed.

    [*n*] **E***w.d* [**E***e*]   Real with exponent

n real fields of width *w* and *d* decimal places are processed in exponential form, with *d* significant digits shown. If **E***e* is given the exponent has *e* digits.

    [*n*] **D***w.d*   Real, no exponent.

On output, same as **F**. On input, transfers data in double precision.

    [*n*] **G***w.d* [**E***e*]   Real with exponent if necessary.

Transfers data in **F** form, unless an output value would exceed *w* digits, when it uses the **E** form.

(iii) Other fields

    [*n*] **L***w*   Logical (Chapter 19)

Transfers *n* logical values of width *w*. On output, prints **T** or **F**. On input, accepts character string beginning with T or F. Note that in list-directed input, this must be in quotes.

    [*n*] **A** [*w*]   Character (Chapter 18)

Transfers *n* character strings of width *w*. Strings may be padded with blanks or truncated to match the width *w* to the length of a character item being transferred, see Chapter 18.

14 Subprograms and arguments (Chapters 10, 11, 13)

A *function subprogram* is a program unit beginning with the FUNCTION statement, and ending with END. Within the function, a value must be assigned to the function's name, which is returned as its value (Chapter 10).

[type] **FUNCTION** *name* [(*dummy arguments*)]

[statements of FORTRAN]

name = expression

[more statements of FORTRAN]

END

A function has a type implied by its *name*, or given explicitly by the optional *type*. The types of the *dummy arguments* are determined by their spelling, or by IMPLICIT or type statements in the subprogram. A function is used by another program unit in an expression with a term:

name ([*actual arguments*])

Note that if no *actual arguments* are given, the empty brackets are required.

A *subroutine subprogram* is similar to a function, except that its *name* does not have a type associated with it, and it does not return a value (Chapter 11).

SUBROUTINE *name* [(*dummy arguments*)]

[statements of FORTRAN]

END

A subroutine is referred to by the CALL statement:

CALL *name* [(*actual arguments*)]

When a subprogram is executed, the *actual arguments* are the names of variables, arrays or constants, or they are expressions which are evaluated and placed in temporary storage. The *actual arguments* then become associated with the *dummy arguments* of the function. The *actual arguments* should correspond by order and type with the *dummy arguments*. The subprogram is executed using the *actual arguments* as the *dummy arguments*. Care is required that a subprogram does not replace the value of an argument which is a constant. To be safe, a constant can be placed in brackets to make it an expression.

When arrays are used as arguments, it is necessary to give information about the subscript bounds (Chapter 13). This can be done in one of three ways:

(i) Give a constant (truthful) bound, which is inflexible.

(ii) Pass the bounding information as an argument and then give the bounds as integer expressions involving constants and dummy arguments of the subprogram.

(iii) Give the final bound (only) as *, an assumed size.

The scope of variables used in a subprogram is confined to the subprogram unless:

(i) They are *dummy arguments*, in which case they are associated with the *actual arguments* of the subprogram.

(ii) They are variables in blank COMMON or named COMMON, where they are shared by all program units which declare associated variables in COMMON.

15 Storage allocation—COMMON (Chapter 17)

All variables, constants and arrays used by a program are given space in the computer's memory. Normally this is transparent to the programmer. In discussing the use of arrays as subprogram arguments, the need to ensure that each array originates with constant *truthful* array bounds has been emphasized.

Blank COMMON is a mechanism for specifying the arrangement of variables and arrays in a part of memory which different program units can share:

   COMMON *variables*

The *variables* are given space in the order specified. Each program unit can have its own COMMON declarations and name different *variables* to occupy that space. They are then said to be *associated*. Care is required in laying out COMMON if it is to be used for different purposes at different times.

Variables in blank COMMON cannot be given initial values in a DATA statement. However a named COMMON can be created to make shared memory exclusive to a group of program units:

   COMMON / *name* / *variables*

Variables in named COMMON can be given initial values in a BLOCK DATA subprogram.

16 Storage association—EQUIVALENCE (Chapter 17)

Storage *association* occurs when a named variable shares space with another. There are two ways of associating variables which are in *different* program units:

   (i) In using a FUNCTION or SUBROUTINE subprogram, the *actual arguments* from the calling program are associated with the *dummy arguments* of the subprogram. If you alter a dummy argument within the subprogram, you change the value of the actual argument. This can be embarassing back in the calling program if you thought the actual argument was a constant!

   (ii) Through blank or labelled COMMON, variables become associated directly through their position in memory.

Variables within the *same* program unit can become associated using the EQUIVALENCE statement:

   EQUIVALENCE (*variable names*)

This forces the named *variables* (which may be of different types) to occupy the same space. This means they cannot have different values at the same time. Using EQUIVALENCE is now considered to be bad form. It was important as a means of saving space in computers when space in memory was more restricted than it is now.

Using EQUIVALENCE:

   (i) Character entities can be associated only with other character entities.

   (ii) Variables or arrays of all other types can be associated in any combinations. Every integer, or real, or logical value will take one unit of storage. Every complex or double precision value will take two units of storage.

17 Some obsolete features

A number of features of FORTRAN are included in FORTRAN 77 for historical reasons. As far as possible, old FORTRAN programs are supposed to work in new versions of FORTRAN. This means that some obsolete features are maintained. In general they have been superceded by more modern features, and it is poor style to use them. They may be removed from future versions of FORTRAN.

In the author's opinion, the following FORTRAN 77 features should not be used:

the *arithmetic* IF statement

> **IF** (*expression*) *label1*, *label2*, *label3*
>
> If the integer part of the *expression* is negative, the program jumps to the statement with *label1*, if 0 to *label2*, and if positive to *label3*. The block IF is a better structure in near-ly all circumstances.

the *computed* GO TO

> **GO TO** (*expression*) *label1*, *label2*, . . .
>
> If the integer part of the *expression* is 1, jump to *label1*, if 2 to *label2* and so on. A *block* IF is much better. This truly horrible and dangerous statement should never be used.

the *assigned* GO TO

> **GO TO** *integer name*
>
> This is awful. The program jumps to a label which must have been assigned to the *integer name* previously by an ASSIGN statement:
>
> **ASSIGN** *label* TO *integer name*
>
> Always use a *block* IF instead.

Alternate entries to subprograms:

> **ENTRY** *name* (*dummy arguments*)
>
> This statement can occur anywhere in a subprogram and provides an alternative entry point. The rules concerning *dummy arguments* and the scope of variables in the subprogram are made more complex by this statement. It is never necessary. Everything it offers can be done by using COMMON. Do not use it.

Alternate returns from subprograms

> A subprogram can be made to return to an arbitrary label in the program unit that called it. In the dummy argument list of a subprogram, you can put * to indicate an *alternate return*. The RETURN statement can then be used in the subprogram in the form
>
> **RETURN** *integer expression*
>
> If the value given by the *integer expression* is 1, the first *alternate return* is used. If 2 the second, and so on.
>
> The actual targets of the alternate returns are given as actual arguments when the subprogram is called. The actual argument is written as a starred label number, for example
>
> ```
> CALL STUPID(X, Y, *10, *20)
> ```
>
> The first *alternate return* from this is the statement with label 10. The second is 20.

It is **really *awful*** to have control pop up at an arbitrary label, as if there were a secret GO TO. Don't use it.

EQUIVALENCE is frowned upon.

Finally, you may be interested to know that COMMON will be replaced in FORTRAN 8X by a more useful MODULE subprogram. A disadvantage of COMMON is that every program unit that uses it must declare it independently, which makes it tedious to set up, horrible to alter and prone to error. A MODULE is declared only once, and everything in it can be picked up by a USES statement. Roll on, FORTRAN 8X!

Index